UNHOLY MESSENGER

The Life and Crimes
of the BTK Serial Killer

STEPHEN SINGULAR

A LISA DREW BOOK
Scribner
NEW YORK   LONDON   TORONTO   SYDNEY

SCRIBNER
1230 Avenue of the Americas
New York, NY 10020

Copyright © 2006 by Stephen Singular

SCRIBNER and design are trademarks of
Macmillan Library Reference USA, Inc., used under license
by Simon & Schuster, the publisher of this work.

For information about special discounts for bulk purchases,
please contact Simon & Schuster Special Sales:
1-800-456-6798 or business@simonandschuster.com

Designed by Kyoko Watanabe
Text set in Sabon

Manufactured in the United States of America

1   3   5   7   9   10   8   6   4   2

Library of Congress Cataloging-in-Publication Data is available.

ISBN-13: 978-0-7432-9124-8
ISBN-10: 0-7432-9124-7

UNHOLY
MESSENGER

All said and done, my friends, it will be an ill day for us if what most humans mean by "religion" ever vanishes from the earth. The fine flower of un-holiness can grow only in the close neighborhood of the Holy. Nowhere do we tempt so successfully as on the very steps of the altar.

—The devil speaking in
The Screwtape Letters by C. S. Lewis

PROLOGUE

Pastor Michael Clark had just finished writing his Sunday sermon and was satisfied with it. He'd been a minister for more than two decades, and it was always difficult finding new ways to talk about sin and salvation, about God and evil or the darkness clashing against the light. On this Friday he felt good about his message and choice of words. He'd composed them in his office at Christ Lutheran Church in Park City, Kansas, which held knickknacks he'd collected over the years. Stuffed toy frogs perched on bookshelves and a plastic armadillo sat on a table, along with some props he used when performing as a clown. Pastor Clark looked something like the actor Karl Malden, with a paunch and a small bump on his round, prominent forehead. He was a born ham, and when he put on his outlandish polka-dot uniform, with a big red nose and a yellow mop on his head, he turned into "Rufus," who enjoyed both entertaining and assisting people struggling with grief. Pastor Clark knew a lot about grief and personal tragedy. Laughter was one of his major weapons against sadness, and he used it every chance he got. Once or twice he'd conducted church affairs in his clown outfit, which challenged his small-town, rural congregation. The few hundred members of Christ Lutheran were low-key, practical people, not given to wild outbursts of irreverence or humor. Their spiritual expectations didn't include many frills.

"I want my minister," says a worshipper, "to give me just one thing to hang on to each Sunday, when bad things happen during the coming week. I don't want him trying to solve the world's problems from the pulpit. That's somebody else's job. I want him to help *me* when I need help with something real—after the trouble hits—as it always does. That's what we're payin' him for."

Christ Lutheran was set out in the countryside a few miles north of Wichita and had a sloping metal roof and a modest steeple. Half-circled by a stand of pines and surrounded by wheat fields, a horse farm, and long, flat stretches of land, it evoked a large, ranch-style home. The air was so quiet and peaceful you could hear the pine-needle whispers and the soft creaking of the swing set behind the church. It was the kind of friendly, open place where people waved at you from their cars, even if they'd never seen you before. When Pastor Clark had arrived at Christ Lutheran half a decade earlier, some folks hadn't known quite what to make of him. He liked to go up to strangers, especially women, and ask if they wanted to see one of his stool samples. If they didn't turn their back on him or walk away, he'd pull a small, black container from his pocket, labeled STOOL SAMPLE, and take off the lid. Inside was a tiny, carved three-legged stool.

"I learned a long time ago," he says, "that certain people won't like you if you joke around and have too much fun. I can deal with that, but don't try to make me miserable. That's not gonna work."

With his sermon finished and the clock approaching 12:30 p.m., he was hungry and ready to eat. He left his desk, slipped into his winter coat, and started down a short hallway toward the front door. On his left was the church's large, spare sanctuary, and facing him at the hall's end was a dining area where the congregation had coffee and cookies between the two Sunday-morning services. Everyone at Christ Lutheran knew everyone else—knew their children, jobs, extended families, and religious habits. They enjoyed gathering in the dining room to have a cup and trade local gossip or talk about church business. Right above this area, on the second floor, were the new Bible-study classrooms, completed last fall. The church's top lay official, Dennis Rader, had pushed hard for the construction of these rooms and overseen much of the building during the second half of 2004.

Eight weeks ago, on January 1, 2005, he'd been elected president by the congregation and now chaired the monthly council meetings and set the agenda for the upcoming year. Pastor Clark referred to him as Christ Lutheran's "spiritual leader" and Rader was at the church about as much as the minister was, tireless in his dedication to details—washing the windows, painting the stripes on the asphalt parking lot, and cleaning up after events. Pastor Clark had become so used to having Rader nearby that on Sunday mornings he didn't look around before calling over his shoulder, "Dennis, could you please light the candles on the altar?" Or, "Dennis, have you checked the sound system?" Or, "Dennis, are the programs ready to be handed out?" Rader and his wife, Paula, who sang in the church choir, were the backbone of the congregation. After thirty years of service at Christ Lutheran, and decades of building goodwill, loyalty, and trust, Dennis was the natural choice for president.

Buttoning up his coat, Pastor Clark glanced through the two sets of glass doors that led out to the parking lot. He saw a man in a black leather coat with three other men lined up behind him. The pastor thought they were salesmen, which struck him as odd and annoying. Why would four men come to a church to try to make a sale? They didn't have an appointment and he didn't have any time for them. He didn't care what they were peddling; he was getting hungrier by the moment. All he wanted to do was jump into his red-and-white pickup—the one with the RUFUS license plate—and go eat. He'd be polite with these guys, the way he was with everyone, but get rid of them fast.

As he charged through the first set of doors, the man in the dark leather coat opened it slightly and revealed a shiny police badge.

The minister stopped cold.

"Uh-oh," he muttered to himself. "This can't be good."

The three other men now revealed their badges in what could only be called a show of force.

Pastor Clark approached them, unlocking the second set of doors. The lead officer stepped inside and introduced himself as Lieutenant T. K. Bridges with the Wichita Police Department. The trio of backup followed him in, also identifying themselves as officers, and although the minister looked for humor in almost every situation and had thought of making a joke about their presence in his church, he could tell they were in a serious mood and held his tongue. At the same time, he couldn't help wondering how long this was going to take and when he might get lunch.

Lieutenant Bridges pulled out two pages of typewritten material and showed them to the preacher.

"I have a search warrant for your church," Bridges said.

"What's going on?" the minister asked, trying to maintain calm. "What's this about?"

"Can we talk in private?"

"Sure," the pastor said, turning and leading them down the hall toward his office, only ten or fifteen yards away.

"You cannot believe," he would say later, "how many bad things can go through your mind in the time it takes to walk that far."

Nothing that passed through his mind during the next thirty seconds was anywhere near what Lieutenant Bridges had to say. The officer didn't wait to be asked to sit down but lowered himself into Pastor Clark's chair, which he'd just been sitting in to write the sermon. Covered with golden cloth, it had a soft cushion and an afghan draped over one corner. Pastor's Clark took the visitor's chair. Glancing at the stuffed frogs, the plastic armadillo, and the clown props scattered throughout the office, Lieutenant Bridges explained that the church was now part of a criminal investigation and then slowly read the search warrant line by line, adding that the other officers were preparing to search the premises this afternoon. While they did, the pastor would not be allowed to go anywhere by himself, including the restroom.

The minister didn't argue with any of this, but again asked what they doing in his church.

Speaking clearly and evenly, Lieutenant Bridges said that Dennis Rader had just been arrested, fifteen minutes earlier, as a suspect in the BTK serial murder case.

The pastor grasped for something to say. Then he asked him what he meant and the officer repeated what he'd just said. Then the minister asked him again, unable to fathom what he was being told. He'd only lived in Wichita for a little more than four years and was not very familiar with this BTK case, but everyone had been talking about it lately, and the local media would not leave it alone. It was impossible to have been in the city since last March and not have picked up some information about the gruesome string of murders back in the 1970s. The minister wasn't drawn to these kinds of stories, and all he really knew was that something horrific had happened in Wichita and no one had ever been arrested for it.

Trying again to comprehend, Pastor Clark posed another question: Had the president of his congregation really been taken into custody in connection with the BTK case or was there a mistake?

No mistake, the officer said. The head of this church had just been arrested for the murder of at least eight people.

"Dennis Rader," the pastor said, "has been arrested for the BTK serial killings?"

"Yes."

"Are you saying that Dennis Rader used this church as part of his crimes?"

"That's what we're looking into."

"How did he do that?"

The lieutenant couldn't answer that question and returned his focus to the search warrant, sending the other men off to look for various items in the church. Lieutenant Bridges informed Pastor Clark that Rader had already requested the minister come to see him at once, but when the preacher asked if he could do that this afternoon, Bridges wasn't sure. As the officers dispersed through the church, leaving one in Pastor Clark's office to watch him, he grabbed the phone and began making calls.

He reached his wife, Jan, then a church official, and then the Central States Lutheran Synod in Chicago, with its special department for handling crises, explaining that one had just erupted. His congregation was about to face not just an overwhelming shock, but the scrutiny of local, national, and international media. The pastor's phone had already begun ringing with requests for interviews, and TV trucks were heading toward Park City. The synod put him in touch with its crisis consultant, Bishop Gerald Mansholt, who was on his way to Wichita to steer them through the coming ordeal. The church was planning a counseling session for worshippers the next afternoon so people could talk openly about Rader's arrest, the first of several where the congregation would gather and pray and vent.

An hour or so later, Pastor Clark was finally able to leave and get something to eat. He then drove into downtown Wichita and turned onto Main Street, with its row of buildings including the Epic Center (housing the FBI), City Hall (holding the Wichita Police Department), the Eighteenth Judicial District Court House (home to the district attorney's office), and the Sedgwick County Detention Facility (where inmates were confined during their legal proceedings). Arriving at City Hall, Pastor Clark was told that he couldn't speak to Rader this afternoon, because the man was under interrogation and because the minister didn't have with him the papers showing he'd been ordained. He could, after all, have been an impostor. He drove back to the church and continued trying to manage the chaos unleashed by the arrest.

By late afternoon, the press had located Christ Lutheran's Web site and gotten hold of church officials' names. Those who received calls from reporters were saying little or nothing at all, but their first instinct—that this was a terrible joke—had passed. The trouble was real, being broadcast everywhere in Wichita, and becoming national news. Their second instinct was that their president was innocent or should at least be presumed innocent until proven guilty. As a group they may have tended to believe that people taken into police custody were usually guilty of something, but these were hardly normal circumstances. This wasn't a story about a common criminal busted for a run-of-the-mill offense. Folks at Christ Lutheran and throughout the metropolitan area had lived with the BTK saga for decades. He wasn't just another felon, but a monstrosity, a demonic creature, the worst person in the region's history—so devious and clever that he could avoid detection during the biggest and longest investigation ever conducted by the Wichita Police Department. He hadn't just fooled the police but humiliated them by sending the media and the WPD communications mocking their efforts to catch him.

Pastor Clark liked to use the word *process*—as in, "The congregation is having some difficulty processing this event"—and he knew that the process his church was entering would go on for months, if not years.

A first step occurred the following night at 11 p.m., when the minister finally had time to sit down and reread the pages of the sermon he'd completed on Friday just after noon. Thirty-six hours ago, his sermon had appeared in good shape, but now he ripped up these pages, took out a new sheet of paper, and started over. Everything had changed. The world was no longer the same, and neither was he. The blank page reflected the hole just blown into his theology. Until yesterday at 12:30 p.m., he'd thought he understood human nature and the nature of evil fairly well, but this was no longer true. His belief in God wasn't shaken—he'd been through too much for that—but his perceptions were. Things weren't at all what they seemed to be, and people must have been far more complex, and far more deceptive, than he'd grasped—if this was human behavior he was confronting and not something much stranger than that.

Normally it took him several days to come up with a sermon, but not tonight. He started writing with an intensity he rarely had and kept it up until he finished, just after 1:30 a.m. As Saturday gave way to Sunday morning (the first church service was only seven hours away), he was commencing on a spiritual journey as unpredictable as the rest of his life had been. It would take him over thousands of miles of paved road and down other highways that don't have road signs or speed limits or pavement of any kind. If Dennis Rader was who the police said he was, there had to be more to reality than the pastor had yet discovered.

In his first sixty years, the minister had seen his faith profoundly tested at least twice, and in both instances he'd met that challenge with his convictions intact. He knew what he believed because he'd lived it, both before and after his own life had been shattered by personal loss. The most important thing to him was not having a "broken relationship with God," and that relationship was about to be stretched in ways he could never have imagined. The third great test of his faith had arrived, and he was preparing to rethink some of the most basic questions he'd wrestled with in seminary and since taking

to the pulpit. The spiritual and the criminal, the sacred and the pro-
fane, had landed right on his church's door step.

In the months ahead, he'd think back to that particular Friday
afternoon—February 25, 2005—and say, "I really believe we need a
new paradigm of evil. The old way of looking at evil, using the psychological model, just isn't enough anymore. In that model, if somebody dropped Susie on her head as a little girl and she went on to do
bad things as an adult, we could explain all this away because of her
childhood. Her head injury was the start of her problems and caused
her later behavior. What I'm dealing with now, since the arrest, can't
be explained by that model. If Dennis is really BTK, something more
must be going on, and I've got to know what it is. Question is, Does
God want me to know more? If He does, I'll be moved in the right
direction.

"I never thought about demons or devils or anything like that
before February twenty-fifth, 2005. Never crossed my mind, but now
I can't stop thinking about it. We've got to be open to new ideas if
we're going to get some real answers. I don't think we understand
what evil is or how it operates. I don't think we're close to that, and
I think a lot of people don't want to ask these questions because of
where that might lead us. Bottom line is, we need a new definition of
evil."

A SERIAL KILLER IS BORN

And what rough beast, its hour come round at last,
Slouches towards Bethlehem to be born?

— W. B. YEATS, "THE SECOND COMING"

I

O N SUNDAY MORNING, January 17, 2004, Dennis Rader walked outside and picked up the *Wichita Eagle,* the local newspaper he read closely, especially on weekends. Sometimes, he cut articles or ads featuring girls or women out of the paper and kept them in one of his private collections. He had thousands of pictures of females stashed around the house and at work, which he looked at whenever he felt restless or in need of a sexual rush. As he opened the paper, the main headline stunned him: "BTK Case Unsolved, 30 Years Later." A reporter named Hurst Laviana had written a story about Wichita's greatest mystery, recapping the terror that had infiltrated the city in the 1970s, after the WPD had announced that a serial killer was in their midst. The article described the crimes, the victims, the maddeningly unsuccessful one-hundred-thousand-hour investigation, and the bizarre behavior of BTK himself, evoking the most perplexing issues all over again. How was it possible that a city renowned for its police work could not find this predator? Why hadn't the FBI and other national resources brought into the case been able to help? Would the WPD and Wichita's 340,000 citizens ever know the truth? The story suggested that by 2004 all these questions had likely become moot, because BTK was probably dead.

Rader read the article slowly and read parts of it again, stopping to nod or smile. The words brought on a flood of exciting and powerful memories of his heyday, back in his thirties and forties. He'd been unstoppable then, uncatchable, invincible. No one had had a clue who he was or where he lived or worked, and they still didn't. He'd done it all, never made a major mistake, and felt lucky to have held on to his freedom. Now that he was about to turn fifty-nine, he'd more or less put BTK into retirement, but this article was stirring something within. Over the next few years, he'd planned to take all of BTK's drawings, pictures, and writings, transfer them onto CDs, and place everything in a safe-deposit box for others to find after his funeral. On the CDs, he'd have laid it all out just like the credits at the beginning and end of a movie, listing the names of the people who'd played a part in the criminal drama, describing their roles, thanking some of them, and calling the whole thing BTK Productions. Wouldn't that be a kick—not just to his wife and children and the people at Christ Lutheran, who thought they knew their husband and father and fellow worshipper, but to the entire city of Wichita and its incompetent police department! The bogeyman had been living right next to them all along, going to his job each day, coming home and watching BTK reports on the evening news with his wife, and praying at one of their churches. They'd only get the satisfaction of solving their grand mystery after he was gone—and he'd get the satisfaction of never having spent a day in prison.

One section of Laviana's article struck him the hardest, the part about a local lawyer named Robert Beattie, who taught a criminal justice course at Friends University. For years Beattie had been researching the BTK murders and was putting together a book about the case. While the police generally felt that BTK was either in prison or had left Wichita or died, Beattie held out the hope that somebody might one day read his book and, as he'd told the *Eagle,* "come forward with some information—a driver's license, a watch, some car keys. . . . I'm sure we will be contacted by both crackpots and well-meaning people who have little to contribute. But I do not think we'll be contacted by BTK."

Beattie's words angered and stimulated Rader because for years he'd been trying to write his own book. The attorney had thrown down the gauntlet. How could some lawyer who'd never met him presume to know who BTK was or what he'd accomplished during the height of his criminal career? Or why he'd done all those things? How could anybody have any understanding of the case unless that person knew what had gone through BTK's head or the feelings that had raced through his body before and after a kill, and how he'd picked out his victims, and what had taken place in the rest of his life, when he wasn't stalking a woman? Who the hell did this Beattie think he was—trying to answer such questions without knowing anything about the subject?

Rader laid aside the paper and calmed down, considering his options. Maybe BTK had gone away too soon. Maybe he could bring him out of retirement for just one more fling with the media and the Wichita Police Department. Not much else was going on in his life right now. His job as a Park City compliance officer, issuing tickets to people whose dogs ran loose or who violated other local ordinances, had become a mindless routine. His kids were grown and out of the house, and he and Paula had drifted into a place in middle age where nothing seemed capable of being new. Only his church work really called to him because he was fond of Pastor Clark and serious about being a good Christian. He'd read a lot of Scriptures and didn't wait till Sunday morning to pray to God. For three decades, Jesus Christ had been his personal savior, and he renewed that commitment every week in the sanctuary. He'd do anything for his minister and congregation.

He was bored, really, once he stopped to think about it—doing little more than waiting to leave his job in a few more years and start drawing Social Security. He was isolated too, in that part of himself he'd never been able to share with others, yet still wanted to. Dennis Rader wasn't lonely, but BTK was.

"It might be fun to stir the hornet's nest," he muttered to himself, smiling again.

He'd always itched to do something creative, so why not bring back BTK and see what happened? It wasn't as if he'd ever really put all that to rest. He still had "hiding holes" around the house, where he tucked away pictures, drawings, and slick ads taken from fashion magazines. He had swimsuit ads, bra ads, pictures of brides, and images of celebrities, Halle Berry and Meg Ryan, all taped to three-by-five index cards. He had ads of young boys, young girls, and women of all ages, plus Barbie-doll knockoffs. One hiding hole was a box he kept right below his work uniforms in the bedroom. Another was a drawer with a secret bottom in a linen closet. A third was a green plastic tub filled with mementos. His wife had never looked in any of these places or suspected a thing, even though they'd lived in the same nine-hundred-foot-square house for the past thirty years. It wasn't her way to pry into his affairs, and if she ever tried to do that, he knew how to brush her off with a glib comment or two. Didn't take much to steer Paula in another direction. Outside in the driveway was his camper, where he kept more memorabilia. A few blocks away, in his office at City Hall, was the Mother Lode of information sitting right by his desk, a locked metal file cabinet holding computer floppy disks, newspaper clippings, maps, Polaroid pictures, puzzle books, and neatly marked file folders with transparent covers. No matter what he was doing, Rader was extremely well organized and stayed on top of the details.

He was also absolutely sure of one thing: nobody could tell his story but himself. He was a man no one knew—no one on earth—and it had been that way since early childhood, because he was certain that nobody could understand or accept who he really was, not even God. For years, he'd been trying to tell people who he was without revealing anything about himself—just one of his contradictions. He'd wanted to remain unknown but craved media attention and getting credit for his crimes. He could be utterly normal and grotesquely abnormal. He'd seemed to want help with his compulsions but resisted the notion that anybody could help him. He'd toyed with the police and given them hints about his identity, but didn't want to get caught. For years he'd admired law enforcement but treated them with contempt. He wrote in a tiny handwriting so that his words were nearly indecipherable, using language not to reveal but to distort and cover up. He'd pull back the mask of anonymity just enough to entice before sliding it back over his life. He could be genuinely kind and unspeakably vicious. And he'd always been amazed at how easily the police and the public could be misled, by just a few misdirecting clues. People weren't nearly as smart as they thought they were.

He looked at some other headlines, needing to think about all this and weigh the risks and potential benefits before making a decision. Age had slowed him down and he wasn't as quick mentally as he used to be; he couldn't afford a single mistake. Almost two months passed before he took action.

II

THE LETTER WAS POSTMARKED March 17, 2004, and arrived at
the *Eagle* offices two days later. A clerk opened the envelope,
glanced at the contents, and casually dropped the whole thing into a
plastic bin. The paper received hundreds of pieces of mail each day,
and at least a couple were usually weird or provocative, so this one
didn't immediately stand out. Glenda Elliott, whose job included
reading the incoming mail, found the letter, read it, and was intrigued
enough to pass it along to Tim Rogers, the assistant managing editor.
Rogers gave it to Hurst Laviana, who'd written the BTK article last
January, telling him to photocopy it and take the original over to the
Wichita Police Department. Laviana handed the letter off to Captain
Darrell Haynes, who was so unmoved by what the reporter had given
him that it sat on his desk for the next three days. When Laviana followed up and asked Haynes about the contents of the envelope, the
captain realized he'd never looked at them.

Every police department has a stack of cold cases on file, but by
March 2004 the BTK case was just about frozen solid, a ghost buried
along with the 1970s and '80s. It had long since entered the realm of
legend or urban myth, an unsolved set of murders perfect for terrifying a new generation of Wichita kids. For decades local youngsters
had grown up hearing about the killings and turning them into a
slumber-party game. Boys and girls liked staying up late at a friend's
house, flipping off the lights, snuggling under the covers, and scaring
the hell out of each other with tales of what had once taken place
just a few miles, or a few blocks, away. A bloodthirsty madman had
roamed these streets, a nameless beast had sneaked into strangers'

homes, cut their phone lines, and hid in their closets, waiting to attack. He liked to Bind women in particular with cords—tying elaborate knots around their ankles, wrists, and throats; he liked to Torture them slowly, bringing them up to the point of death and then letting them breathe; he liked to Kill them finally, with relish. Bind, Torture, Kill: BTK. He wasn't merely interested in taking lives, but enjoyed watching people suffer and defiling them after they were dead. And he hadn't just terrorized his victims, but an entire population of one-third of a million people.

All that had long since faded into Wichita's past. The murders lived on mostly in the ongoing pain of the victims' relatives and the haunted memories of those who'd worked the homicides and studied the evidence.

"The thing about this case is that it never left you," says Tony Ruark, a Wichita psychologist who in the late 1970s had responded to a police department request for mental health experts to assist the investigation. After countless hours of legwork, detectives hadn't been able to make any progress and thought psychologists might uncover something they hadn't. Ruark volunteered for the job, and during the next eighteen months he looked at the crime-scene photos, drawings, and writings by BTK, offering his expertise. The case remained impenetrable, but left an indelible mark on the psychologist.

"If he'd ever been caught," Ruark says, "I always wanted to sit down and explore BTK's childhood with him. Learn everything I could about it. Did he have childhood sexual experiences? Did he have homosexual experiences? Did he practice bondage with a girlfriend or wife or others? He'd masturbated at some of the crime scenes, and sexual fantasy was clearly a driving motivation for him.

"I studied the crime-scene photos, and once you've seen them, that never goes away. Ever. These were women and children. The detectives from that era felt the same way I do. Every few years, I'd pick up the phone and talk about the case with some of them, because none of us could let it go. I'd pull out my case files and look at the evidence once more because I was fascinated with it and wondered if he was still out there. One of my goals was to live long enough to know who he was. To be able to do everything that BTK did—and do it without a conscience—was the most extreme thing I'd ever seen."

After getting around to reading the letter, Captain Haynes took it upstairs to the homicide division, where on March 22 it made its way to Detective Dana Gouge. Inside the envelope was one sheet of paper holding a photocopy of a driver's license and three photocopied Polaroid pictures of a dead woman lying on a floor in three different poses. In each image, her clothes had been arranged a little differently, so the photographer could get just the effect he wanted. The right-hand corner had a symbol similar to one that had been used by BTK. Detectives Gouge and Kelly Otis showed the license and pictures to Lieutenant Ken Landwehr, who handled WPD murder investigations and had worked on the BTK case off and on for the past two decades, including three years of intense concentration in the 1980s.

Back then the WPD had put together a task force called Ghostbusters (after the popular Bill Murray movie of that time), in one last major push to solve the homicides. Ghostbusters was unsuccessful, but for Lieutenant Landwehr, as for virtually everyone else who'd hunted for BTK since the mid-1970s, the investigation had crept into the mind and the psyche and lodged there. Even if you tried to stop thinking about it, you couldn't. The suffering BTK had created was too deep and widespread and didn't lessen over time. Any police officer who'd spoken to the victims' relatives couldn't give up trying to solve the case. Nobody could do the things BTK had done and get away with them forever, could he? This wasn't supposed to happen in Wichita, Kansas, which in 1945 had been given the Grand Award from the National Safety Council for being the safest city in America. It had won the same award in 1958, 1959, and 1960 and was not the sort of place to get befuddled or terrorized by a mass murderer— let alone for more than thirty years.

Once the homicide division had examined the license and photos inside the envelope, surprise and then shock filtered through the WPD. Nearly eighteen years earlier, on September 16, 1986, Vicki Wegerle, a young mother of two kids, had been strangled to death in her home at 2404 West Thirteenth Street. Only one thing had been stolen from her house that day: her driver's license. Police crime-scene pictures had not been taken of the body, because she'd been removed from the residence by Emergency Medical Services and driven to a hospital before law enforcement arrived. Until now, BTK had never given any indication that Vicki Wegerle had been one of his victims, but the return address on the envelope was Bill Thomas Killman, 1684 S. Oldmanor, Wichita, KS 67202. The initials spelled out BTK but no one in the city was named Bill Thomas Killman, and there was no street named Oldmanor.

After twenty-five years of silence, BTK appeared to be back, and law enforcement had to come up with a measured response. It also needed a leader to carry the case forward, someone who could inspire confidence that these murders would one day be solved. Lieutenant Landwehr was the obvious choice.

He'd built a stellar reputation both within and beyond his department. His superiors had great faith in him, and younger homicide detectives looked for any opportunity to spend time with him because they felt he could mentor them. Landwehr had taught a police course at Wichita State University, and in 2004 it was going to take all of his education and experience to confront the largest challenge of his career. In the late 1970s, the BTK murders had caused panic in Wichita. The WPD didn't want that to happen again, but the license looked real and the photos of Vicki could only have been taken by someone in the house when she was dying. The police needed information and leads from the public—now—because if BTK was back, he was probably ready to kill again.

After talking over strategy, the WPD sent Detective Otis into the *Eagle* offices, where he asked the editors not to publish a story about this new development immediately, and the paper agreed to hold off. Within days, the police department was ready to make its first major pronouncement on the case in nearly a quarter of a century.

At 10 a.m. on March 25, Lieutenant Landwehr addressed a jammed press conference at City Hall, announcing that the dormant BTK investigation was now officially reopened. The Sedgwick County Forensic Center was processing the new letter for DNA samples and fingerprints, while foreign DNA found under Vicki's fingernails was being tested with technology that hadn't existed eighteen years earlier. Other DNA evidence, from semen left behind at 1974 and 1977 crime scenes, had been in storage for nearly thirty years but could also be examined with modern methods and equipment. The police had a national fingerprint and DNA database to work with, and DNA samples from the Wegerle murder were being sent to the FBI's Combined DNA Indexing System, or CODIS. It held more than 1.5 million offender profiles, taken mostly from inmates as they were being incarcerated.

The Federal Bureau of Investigation, the Kansas Bureau of Investigation, and the Sedgwick County Sheriff's Department had all been called into the case. The WPD was preparing to assemble a new BTK task force, with homicide detectives looking into other unsolved murders and checking to see if any potential suspects had just been released from prison.

On March 25, Lieutenant Landwehr used the press conference to remind his audience of a few details of the 1986 murder and why the WPD was going to all this expense and effort to kick-start a new investigation.

"Vicki Wegerle was the mother of two children," he told the media. "Her two-year-old child was at home with her at the time of her death. Her husband was at work. Her other child was at elementary school. . . . The photographs appear to be authentic. I'm one hundred percent sure it's BTK."

The police were setting up hotlines for the public to send in tips anonymously, either through the phone, mail, or e-mail.

"This is the most challenging case I've ever worked on," Landwehr said, with characteristic understatement. From the beginning, he was trying to strike exactly the right tone because the authorities believed that BTK was watching Lieutenant Landwehr. Secretly, they hoped to start a dialogue with him.

Shifting his tone and appearing to address his remarks directly to the killer, he added, "The individual would be very interesting to talk to."

III

WITHIN DAYS OF THE press conference, thirty-two phone and e-mail leads had come into the hotlines, as both dread and paranoia seeped back into Wichita. All around town, people who'd been suspicious of others for years were calling in with BTK tips. Neighbors were turning in neighbors, and enemies were evening up old scores: just dial the tip-line, wait for the police to arrive at your target's doorstep, and watch him squirm. No one was safe from this process. Ex-cops were going to come under scrutiny along with media figures, former city officials, and convicts. By the spring of 2004, the national press, which had been much smaller and less aggressive when the BTK case had first broken in the late 1970s, was always looking for the next spectacular crime story, especially one surrounded by mystery. Lawyers, journalists, and assorted commentators were more than eager to get on television and speculate about any murder. The BTK case was perfect for that, and CNN, Fox News, CBS, and MSNBC were soon reporting on the return of Wichita's notorious serial killer. *Inside Edition, Dateline NBC,* and *Good Morning America* weren't far behind. Retired criminal profilers were talking about who BTK might be, and the Internet was ablaze with theories about the murderer and nasty criticism of the WPD for failing to solve the case (police chiefs and entire WPD administrations had come and gone since the department had started looking for BTK).

Some profilers felt that the killer was a lone wolf who lived and worked by himself in Wichita proper because he knew the city extremely well. He had to be single. Anybody who could perform such antisocial acts, particularly against women, would stand out if he were active in the community or married and would have been identified long ago. But other profilers weren't so sure: perhaps BTK had honed cunning skills at fitting into society and was a master at disguise. Maybe he looked and lived almost exactly as everyone else did, except when he was killing. Maybe his cover was his "normality." And he obviously had to be quite intelligent to have escaped detection for so long. A Web site named CatchBTK.com was soon up and running, averaging fifty thousand hits a day. One of the hottest online theories was that BTK had a terminal illness and wanted to offer up a confession before he died.

Across Wichita more doors were being locked and porch lights were burning throughout the night. People had started carefully checking their closets and peeking behind shower curtains. A new generation of local young women (half of the killer's victims had been females in their twenties) were learning what the letters *BTK* stood for. Gun shop owners, locksmiths, pepper-spray salesmen, dead-bolt retailers, and security-system installers were flooded with requests for more self-protection devices. Marksmanship classes saw an immediate spike in enrollment. The people calling these businesses weren't talking in general terms about finding more ways to feel safe from urban crime, but asking for help in combating BTK. Since he'd often cut the telephone line of a victim's residence before entering her home, Wichitans wanted to know if a landline had been snipped, could they install a backup cellular system that would still function? The first week the WPD tip-line was in place, it received 365 BTK leads. That number quickly tripled.

While the local populace began arming and protecting themselves, the *Eagle* printed a blunt editorial that spoke for the whole city:

"We had thought we had put this behind us. But after more than two decades of silence, the BTK strangler has returned like a recurrent nightmare. It's unclear what he wants—more publicity for his crimes? He might get more than he bargained for. He might get justice."

To bulk up the new investigation, law enforcement was pulling in not just more homicide detectives but police from all over the department. The WPD had beefed up significantly with federal dollars given to it in the 1990s by the Clinton administration; it now had 692 officers and detectives scattered among four bureaus—North, South, East, and West—and each bureau had a SCAT made up of eight officers. The Special Community Action Team didn't answer 911 calls (a low rung on the police ladder), but conducted street-level law enforcement and handled shootings or other violence. The SCATs included the gang units responsible for investigating drug sales and turf wars between the Bloods and the Crips, commonplace even in small metropolitan areas like Wichita. Each SCAT now prepared to donate a member to the BTK investigation, and these officers, under the direction of Lieutenant Landwehr, began meeting on the sixth floor at City Hall to get their assignments.

One huge job was answering the tips that constantly poured in via the phone: from local citizens, from people across Kansas, and from others throughout the United States, including a number of psychics who'd just become familiar with the case. The latter insisted on telling the authorities who BTK was, where to find him, and how many people he'd actually killed over the years. Several claimed that he was the same person known as the Zodiac killer, who'd once terrorized San Francisco. One psychic was absolutely convinced that BTK was hiding in a barn in Iowa. She had the barn picked out and couldn't understand why the WPD didn't get up there and arrest him right now. Another said that all the BTK crimes were part of a mob operation. Some of the tipsters were so overbearing and outrageous that the police stopped taking their calls, but if anyone came up with a specific name as a potential suspect, investigators felt compelled to pursue the lead. The WPD handled all the in-state names but passed along the out-of-state ones to the FBI. This was one massive and time-consuming job, but another was going through lists of inmates who'd just left prison.

Other officers were assigned to gather information on suspects, locate them, and collect DNA swabs from their mouths. DNA left behind decades earlier at three crime scenes established that BTK was a white male, probably in his fifties or sixties, so the police went forth and knocked on doors throughout Wichita—startling middle-aged Caucasian men everywhere and swabbing everyone from reporters to psychologists. Sometimes, detectives forgot whom they'd swabbed and came back for a second sample. Most of those asked to give DNA were good-natured about it, but forty or fifty people saw the whole process as a bad joke, a desperate attempt to catch someone who would never be caught—or an entirely futile search for a dead man. In the end, most everyone cooperated.

"Nobody," says a task force member whose job was swabbing, "slammed the door in my face."

The DNA collection would continue for months, with all the samples being sent to a lab and examined for a match with the evidence. The search was comprehensive and exhaustive, but just as frustrating as the earlier efforts had been. The police swabbed five hundred, then a thousand, and ultimately sixteen hundred potential suspects across Wichita, but none of their DNA matched what was on file.

The problem was that they weren't looking a few miles to the north, in Park City.

IV

I N 1541, Francisco Vásquez de Coronado, in his search for the
mythical "golden cities of Quivira," ventured into what would
become south-central Kansas. He didn't find any gold but met up with
the Wichita Indian tribe, who'd been living there for centuries in grass
houses. The Arkansas River ran through this flat, fertile landscape,
pulling in Native Americans who'd hunted the game and used this
water long before the region had any written history. Coronado
moved on, but three hundred years later the first white settlers arrived,
trapping and trading goods with the Wichita. One early pioneer was
Jesse Chisholm, who lent his name to the famous trail that saw 6 million cattle herded north from Texas to Kansas from the 1860s to the
1880s. Following the Civil War, the Wichita were "removed" to
Indian Territory, and the white settlers took hold along the banks of
the Arkansas. One site became known as Wichita and evolved into a
commercial outpost that expanded with the coming of the railroad
in 1872. The town became a distribution point for cattle from Texas,
as carloads of beef were shipped a thousand miles to the east so people living on the seaboard could enjoy a well-cooked steak.

By 1871, Wichita was an incorporated city, and the looming war-
fare of the twentieth century would be excellent for the local econ-
omy. In 1917, the first private commercial plane, the Cessna Comet,
was built in Wichita, which was soon calling itself "the air capital
of the world." Cessna, Learjet, Beechcraft, and Boeing were all
founded locally, and during World War II, Boeing was converted
from a private business into a governmental manufacturing base for
U.S. military bombers. A significant part of the domestic war effort

in the 1940s was centered in Wichita, and its airplane factories were open twenty-four hours a day. Any functional adult could walk into one of these businesses and get a decent-paying job. Money was flowing and the city was jumping. Movie theaters, dance halls, and restaurants never closed so that people getting off work in the middle of the night had someplace to unwind. Oil was discovered and fortunes were being made, as Wichita built a reputation as a bastion of free enterprise. The city fostered a number of start-up businesses named Pizza Hut, White Castle, Coleman, and Koch (oil and gas) Industries. Like other urban environments, Wichita grew outward in every direction, creeping to the edge of small towns that had once been out in the countryside. By 2004, the metropolitan area had made its way up to Highway 96, the east-west highway that borders Wichita on the north. The sprawl was approaching Park City but hadn't yet enveloped it.

Located at the intersection of I-135 and Sixty-first Street North, Dennis Rader's hometown is encircled by cornfields, wheat fields, horse farms, and open pasture that could be used for grazing cattle or turned into hay. A bulbous, blue water tower rises above the village, which looks like a truck stop crowded with churches. Small brick or frame houses line the narrow, winding streets, and everything about the town shouts out modesty, junk food, and piety. As you drive in from the east on 61, you pass the Park City Baptist Church, the Park City Christian Church, the Church of the Nazarene, and the Calvary Temple Assembly of God, all within a few hundred yards. The churches are a curious reminder not just of how faith-based tiny Midwestern towns are, but of how much conflict spirituality has generated over the centuries. Since Martin Luther was excommunicated from the Roman Catholic Church in 1521, countless Protestant denominations have sprung up over minor disagreements in biblical interpretation or theology. It's astounding that a town the size of Park City, only a handful of blocks from one end to the other, can support all this organized religion.

Past the four churches are a liquor store and a Curves franchise where women work out with weights, do aerobics, and get in shape. Then come Taco Bell, Wendy's, Subway, Applebee's, and a Kentucky

Fried Chicken all thrown together at Park City's hub. Christianity and fast food mingle here, right in the middle of the nation and of the cultural war that has been shaping American life since the 1960s. During the summer of 1991, when the antiabortion group Operation Rescue picked a city in which to take its strongest public stance ever, it chose Wichita. For a week, protesters shut down abortion clinics, picketed doctors, chained themselves to fences, lay down in the street, and filled the jails with their civil disobedience. Some saw this as a political turning point in both regional and national history. Wichita had long been a Democratic-leaning town, because of its strong union membership in the local manufacturing industries, but now the city began a gradual shift to the right. The use of a cultural "wedge" issue, such as a woman's right to choose whether to have a child, had successfully been employed in south-central Kansas, and a lot of other places, to tilt votes toward the Republican Party.

Today, on AM and FM radio in the Wichita listening area, station after station broadcasts a round-the-clock stream of evangelical Christianity, railing against the sins of homosexuality, divorce, stem cell research, sex outside of marriage, the theory of evolution, and abortion—along with the need to confess your guilt and be saved by Jesus. The sending forth of this religious doctrine into this setting is not new, but the saturation and intensity of this process is. In recent years, the Christian right has made sexuality the center of its battleground in the fight of good versus evil, and nowhere is human difference, diversity, and complexity more under attack than on these constant broadcasts. God is the giver of an absolute set of rules and regulations—anyone violating them, particularly in the realm of Eros, is in sin and subject to the whip and sting of shame. A few hours' drive to the north of Wichita is the state capital of Topeka, where a fanatical preacher named Fred Phelps has gained a national reputation as the most outspoken despiser of gay people in the United States. His mantra—"God hates fags"—has brought embarrassment to the entire region. The state's education system, meanwhile, is a leader in the debate to add the teaching of "intelligent design" to science classes. Regardless of the merits of this argument, it makes Kansas an easy target for late-night comedians.

Yet nothing here, as in any other place, is simple. Combined with this never-ending rant against the evils of desire is the business of selling entertainment through the power of sex. Along with preaching, country music pervades local radio. Fifty years ago, Hank Williams sang with real feeling about being hurt by a woman's "cheatin' heart," while today country superstar Toby Keith croons about the prospect of fooling around with two eager young females at the same time: nothing like a threesome among willing strangers. The contradictions are everywhere and have only deepened during the past few decades. Sex and the vast fear of sex mingle uneasily in the American mainstream and come to a heated clash in these competing radio programs. It's perfectly okay to use raunchy lyrics to sell CDs and make millions for the singer and music executives, but if you venture off the beaten sexual path, you're going to feel like hell afterward. And what about someone who senses from an early age that he or she might not be normal to start with? What does God have to say about that? Who would speak to these people about the conflict inside?

Evangelizing and country and western aren't the only things heard on the radio in this part of the country. Jazz and classical music are also broadcast on publicly funded Radio Kansas, and there's something magical about driving across the prairie at night with the windows down and a soft wind blowing through the car and Miles Davis playing his lonely trumpet into the darkness. There's something hopeful about rolling over the ocean of open green land in the lovely Flint Hills north of Wichita and listening to Beethoven hammer out his insistent feeling that mankind was made to push against the grain and should always defy the odds in reaching for greatness. Anyone living out here who sees himself or herself as different from others can understand some of the sorrow and loneliness that Miles put into his horn or some of the rage against convention that Beethoven always felt compelled to express. Rebellion in such a place always put you out further onto the margins.

If you exit Park City at sunset and drive south on I-135 toward downtown Wichita, a skyline juts up before you, hanging in the air just a few miles away. By the standards of most metropolitan areas, the office buildings are small and not very contemporary-looking, but compared to Park City, Wichita is the shining palace on the hill, with its Starbucks and Barnes & Nobles, its high-end outlet malls, and its expensive, well-kept neighborhoods. In terms of money and sophistication, it's far more than just a few miles away from the village to the north. Small towns are known for their simplicity and cities for their complexity, and most people feel more comfortable living in one place or the other, but sometimes nothing is that clear-cut.

Not everyone born into a small town has simple tastes and desires. Not everyone can be just like his father, no matter how hard he tries to be.

V

Rader was born March 9, 1945, in Pittsburg, Kansas, and baptized in the local Lutheran church, before his family moved to Park City. His father, William, who'd had a military career, found employment at a Wichita power plant, while his mother, Dorothea, was a grocery store bookkeeper. His parents were the sort of folks who fit the pattern of countless other Midwestern mothers and fathers. They were strict but decent and taught their four boys to be honest, thrifty, humble, and not to call a lot of attention to themselves. Work hard, respect authority, support the armed forces, don't get far into debt, vote Republican, pray to God for help when you need it, and ask for salvation when you die. Don't show anger in public or get too upset over anything. Sex was a necessity but bounded by fear. For generations throughout the heartland, people had been raising their children with these basic and unswerving ideas and values, with most youngsters adapting to them well enough. Kansas was a true red state long before anyone had ever heard of such a thing.

Rader's early years had seemed normal, with fishing or canoeing trips on the Arkansas River, bike rides with his pals around Park City, and playing games with his younger brothers. He liked to tussle with his siblings and sometimes dominated them physically, but a lot of big brothers were guilty of that. How many older brothers had sat on younger ones or tickled them until they screamed for help or wet their pants? Wasn't that all just part of a rough-and-tumble boyhood in the Midwest in the 1950s?

Dennis was a good-looking young kid, with sensitive and intelligent eyes. These parts of his face—the sensitivity, the intelligence,

29

and a sensuality that came into his features as he got older—became pronounced during his adolescence, right up until he reached adulthood. At one point, he had long sideburns and looked a bit like Elvis Presley or evoked the aw-shucks handsomeness of singer Glen Campbell. His good looks would not last. As he aged and his experience darkened, the handsomeness gradually went away. He gained weight, his hairline began to recede, he wore glasses, his eyes grew duller, as if something not there when he was young had slowly emerged and taken over his face.

Decades later, childhood friends and high school classmates would be interviewed about Rader, and all had trouble recalling anything odd or disturbing about his family or about the nice-looking young fellow who'd passed through their own childhood and teenage years in the small town. In this environment, where everyone knew everyone else reasonably well, nobody noticed his secret life, just as much later nobody around him would notice that he'd turned into a monster.

When he was quite small, he visited his grandparents' farm and developed a fascination with watching chickens get slaughtered. It stimulated him. One day he killed a cat, perhaps by accident. At first the death startled him, but he liked the feeling this had given him, one of power and control and of having a real effect on something that he could see. He almost never felt that way. His father didn't seem powerful, but distant and remote. His mother was the more potent of his parents and handed out the discipline. Sometimes she spanked him, and this filled him with an odd rush of excitement, even arousal of a sort that he didn't understand. He was pretty sure he shouldn't have felt that way when he was being punished, but he did. Something must have been wrong with him.

He wished there were someone to talk to about all this, but there wasn't. The people at church or school wouldn't like the things that went through his mind or the impulses that had begun racing through his body. His parents couldn't grasp anything he was going through, and besides, he didn't want to upset them. It was important that they saw him as a good boy who didn't cause trouble, the white sheep of the family, the oldest and most responsible son. One of his younger brothers was the black sheep—a term Dennis never wanted applied to himself. He thought about talking with his brothers, but they weren't old enough to understand, and his friends would be frightened off if he told them the truth.

He couldn't stop thinking of the dead animal or what it had felt like to knock the life out of another creature. It was exhilarating, much more exciting and interesting than his day-to-day routine in Park City. He daydreamed about it, fantasized about doing it again, which helped him escape and feel good for a while. Maybe he would kill something else. Maybe he would do it to a dog. That had to be a bigger thrill than taking down a cat. He wondered if anyone else had these kinds of thoughts but knew he shouldn't ask. People around him never talked about these things, but about other subjects: making money or playing sports or getting along with folks in town or whatever had happened at school that day or what to do on the weekend. Nobody asked him about his fantasies or desires because everyone was too busy or distracted. Words weren't very important to others, even though he liked them and wished he were a lot better at using them. He was a lousy speller and at times had difficulty putting together full sentences when he spoke or wrote. People said he wasn't any good with language but that didn't really matter. This wasn't a practical skill he would need when he got older.

At eight or nine, he saw pictures in a detective magazine. How they fell into his hands was a mystery, but he couldn't stop staring at them. They showed adult females tied up in bondage positions. The photos were staged, depicting women frightened and in pain. They were being tortured, and mock terror was in their eyes. Some of the images were captioned with the women begging to be let go from the belts or ropes that bound them—or begging for their lives. Rader enjoyed the pictures, which produced in him a complicated response.

He didn't identify just with the person who'd done the tying up but also with the women. That was how he felt a lot of the time: tied up or tied down, as if something was always holding him back or keeping him from feeling what he wanted to feel or doing what he wanted to do, but he didn't know what it was. Why did he think of himself as being so powerless and out of control? His parents hadn't molested him or beaten him or denied him anything that he needed to live and be fairly comfortable. He didn't know how to talk about all this or give it a name, but when he looked at the pictures, something changed. The images gave him a focal point for his own experience and made him feel good. He went back to them again and again and had a secret desire to create his own little pictures or works of art, but nobody around him thought he had any talent for that, and they weren't shy about pointing that out. Actually, his drawings were pretty good, better than his writing, but others disparaged them. Artistic talent was something girls pursued, and he didn't want to be called a sissy, or something worse. He wanted to create things, pretty things, but that felt wrong.

The bondage pictures produced feelings of pleasure and of fear, both of which seemed to get stronger each time he looked at them. Back in the mid-1950s, even if he'd been talking about all this with sophisticated adults, it's unlikely they would have understood much about the chemical responses moving through his brain and body. The mapping of brain chemistry was a distant idea, particularly when it came to connecting it to potentially aberrant behavior. It wasn't yet understood that the release of endorphins caused a good feeling, and the release of adrenaline caused a conflicting sensation of fear. In young Rader, the two things were being mixed together every time he did something he thought he shouldn't be doing but that felt good. Many kids may have been getting endorphin releases from athletics or dancing or other physical activities, but before age ten Rader was being wired differently and no one had a clue.

Until recently, he'd been just one boy who didn't have things to hide from the world, but that had also begun to change. He had divided into two kids—one of them a brother, a good friend, and an obedient son, while the other was much more complex and unpredictable. He wanted to do things nobody else did, simply because they were fun, but nobody was allowed to see this complexity or strangeness because that could only lead to trouble and might hurt his parents. Sometimes people around him talked about phases— "Johnny is just going through a phase"—and he wondered if that was what was happening to him. Maybe all this would go away as he got older; he'd outgrow it and become normal. Maybe other boys went through these kinds of things but never talked about it either.

Even if you had weird feelings or crazy impulses, you were supposed to keep them inside and control them, manage them yourself and not be a burden to others. That meant you were good and strong. A cardinal virtue in Park City was that you shouldn't stand out or be too different or complain. God never made a problem too big to handle; you were supposed to figure things out on your own and take action because that's what boys and men do.

In grade school, he made sketches of tied-up girls and had a fascination with pictures of mummies, because they were bound up in cloth. He cut out photos of females in magazine ads and drew dark lines on them, as if they were imaginary cords or ropes. By high school, he'd developed an attraction to Annette Funicello, the Mouseketeer on the popular kids' TV show. In one of his favorite and most elaborate fantasies, he wanted to kidnap her and do sexual things to her in California, even though he knew this could land him in prison. The whole time he was growing up, he believed that somebody—a parent or a teacher or a friend or *anybody*—would eventually catch him doing something bad and stop him, but no one did.

As his childhood ended, he'd already normalized the destruction of numerous small animals and experienced the amazing power that came with this. First a cat went down, then a dog, then a bird, and then some other deaths, each one becoming part of an elaborate ritual. His favorite place to kill was in a barn, where he could be alone with a critter, tie it up with barbed wire, and strangle it to death. Watching things die conjured up the memory of those pictures of women in pain, except this was so much more thrilling and real. Cats and dogs couldn't beg for mercy but made incredible sounds when being choked, and their eyes were filled with terror. When he was holding life and death in his hands, nobody could deny that he was having an effect on the world around him. Even he could see that effect and feel powerful for a little while, until the feeling went away and he was empty again.

He didn't kill animals because he didn't like them. As a boy he had a dog that he loved deeply, a pattern that continued when he became an adult. He always enjoyed having a dog around for walks, just the two of them out getting some exercise and taking in the neighborhood. Animals were wonderful companions, once you got to know them, but if they remained strangers they were worthless and didn't matter. After finding stray cats or dogs in Park City, he'd lure them to a barn and tie them up and snuff out their lives.

He wanted to share his secrets with others but was left alone with this other boy growing inside him. It would let him be for a while but always came back with newer and bigger demands, which he kept giving in to. Afterward, he couldn't feel the things the other boy had done in the barn because that wasn't really him doing it. And it didn't really make any difference what the other boy did because nobody noticed him anyway. Observation and communication were not valued or stressed.

Rader's childhood friends would describe his father, an ex-marine, as God-fearing and stern. As a young man, Dennis was also serious-minded, and people remembered him as having little sense of humor. He rarely laughed or cracked jokes. To his boyhood pals, he often appeared to have drifted off somewhere else, someplace they couldn't go or weren't welcome. Unlike so many other Kansas schoolboys, he didn't participate in sports or fiddle with cars or join clubs or play a musical instrument or dance, didn't collect baseball cards, build model airplanes, or read books. He liked slipping off by himself and dwelling on the things he couldn't get out of his head. Before reaching puberty, he'd done things his classmates could never have imagined doing and knew the secret thrill of killing. Beyond that, he'd learned that killing had produced no consequences. God hadn't reached down from heaven and stopped him from strangling a cat. His life hadn't suddenly gotten worse because he'd run over a dog. No one had a hint about his private universe or saw him for just how powerful a person he could be.

One time when he was fifteen, he went on a canoe trip on the Arkansas River after a huge rainstorm. The water was several feet higher than usual, and he and the younger boy in his canoe got separated from the others in their group, hitting a dangerous patch of white water that cascaded around their small craft and threatened to tip them over. If they fell in, they were sure to drown. The other boy was too small and too weak to paddle against the current, but Rader found the strength to keep the canoe afloat and moved it toward the shore. After struggling for what seemed like hours, he got both of them to safety and was a hero in the eyes of everyone who'd seen what he'd done. For a few moments, he was the good boy he desperately wanted to be, but such moments never lasted.

With the coming of the 1960s, psychotherapy had taken hold not just on both coasts but throughout much of the country. One of the finest psychiatric facilities in the nation was the Menninger Clinic in Topeka, and while many Kansans may have dismissed the notion that they could have benefited from counseling, they were proud of the institution and felt that it did a lot of good for others. Getting treatment for your inner life was no longer a foreign idea. There were now boys growing up in Kansas towns the size of Park City who were quickly identified as violent kids who did terrible things to animals and were clearly headed for trouble. Their parents took action, getting them to Menninger's or other psychiatric facilities and trying to understand this behavior and alter it. They made an effort to break a link in this process or slow it or divert it in other things. They demanded that their sons, or daughters, put words to their feelings and examine their urges with a professional.

But nobody realized what young Rader was going through, and he was afraid to speak about it. And did he really want to? What else had he ever found that he was good at or that made him feel so alive and in control and powerful?

He'd already become perfect at hiding his real life, his shameful life, the one he couldn't mention out loud. If he just shoved it away or pushed it down, it would eventually leave him alone.

VI

IN 1963, Rader graduated from Heights High School just outside Park City. This was a few years before the upheaval and cultural revolt of the 1960s that swept through the country and reached into nearly every corner of America, including rural Kansas. By decade's end, all across the Midwestern plains you could find teenage males and females protesting the Vietnam War; supporting the civil rights movement and the advance of minority, gay, and women's causes; experimenting with interracial dating; forming rock bands and breaking the law by smoking marijuana or taking stronger drugs; bitterly criticizing the government and starting to question every aspect of parental and social authority. The sons and daughters of the baby boom generation were symbolically slaying fathers and mothers from coast to coast; the old ways of doing things were surely dying, and a New Age of peace and freedom was at hand. Parts of this rebellion were shallow, but some of it cut deeper, and no one who lived through that time as an adolescent was completely untouched by it. It cracked open the door to alternative ways of thinking about almost everything, and for one brief moment being "different" was almost a virtue, instead of something to be denied or feared.

Rader missed all of that because he was just a little too old. After high school, he decided to follow in his father's footsteps and joined the air force in Kansas City in June 1966. He wasn't really that drawn to military life, but it was a family tradition and he was determined to maintain it. Following a month of basic training at San Antonio's Lackland Air Force Base, he was assigned to a technical school at Sheppard Air Force Base near Wichita Falls, Texas. In 1967–68, he was stationed at Mobile, Alabama's Brookley Air Force Base, where he was a maintenance specialist and part of the air force's Ground Electronics Engineering Installation Agency. When signing up for active duty, he'd hoped that his time in the military would alter some of his habits. Maybe the discipline and camaraderie of the other men in his outfit would have a positive effect on him and he wouldn't have all those feelings and desires anymore. Perhaps being a member of the greatest fighting force on earth would give him the sense of power he so much enjoyed. Wearing a uniform might allow him to feel something good consistently, and the other stuff would simply go away. If he could just keep everything tidy and orderly, the way the military liked it, his other problems would disappear.

He spent six months at Kadena Air Base in Okinawa and two more years at Tachikawa Air Base near Tokyo, learning in these rather exotic locales what he later called his "knowledge of sex." During four years in the military, he was a fine soldier and earned a number of awards, including the National Defense Service Medal, the Small Arms Expert Marksmanship Ribbon, and the Air Force Good Conduct Medal. After achieving the rank of sergeant, he was honorably discharged in August 1970 and left without anyone suspecting him of engaging in anything other than excellent behavior. His hidden actions in the military had been every bit as discreet as they'd been before he'd put on the uniform.

In the air force, he'd no longer just looked at pictures of females in bondage, but began making his own detailed drawings of women tied up and helpless and in pain, staring up at the viewer with beseeching eyes, begging to be set free. He wrote captions on some of them with fearful words or cries coming from the victims' mouths, but he was no more comfortable showing these images to anyone in his unit or sharing his intimate thoughts with his fellow soldiers than he'd been as a boy or a teenager in Park City. Who could possibly understand what he was doing or how it made him feel? The pictures weren't really his work anyway; they came from that other young man who'd joined the air force with him.

Rader was meticulous about his appearance. His uniform had to be perfectly clean and pressed, his shoes had to shine, and his hair was never allowed to be disorderly, but that other person inside his skin, who didn't yet have a name, was sloppy and reckless. He made a huge mess of things, and if his clothes got disheveled in the middle of a fantasy or his hair got mussed, that was all right. You couldn't be perfect all the time—you just couldn't show your imperfections to others. They'd judge you harshly for that or punish you, and you'd have let them down. As soon as the fantasy ended and the drawings had been put away, he'd straighten himself up, comb his hair, and look the way he was supposed to. Each time he departed one military post for another, he'd destroy all the pictures so that nobody could find them during the move or uncover the evidence of his obsessions. After he'd settled into a new base, he'd start making new drawings, and things went on this way until his discharge in Denver.

Back in Park City, he was getting tired of drawing and looking at images in "girly books," which offered nothing more than lifeless images on a two-dimensional page. As a teenager, he'd taken a couple of larger chances and gone window peeping, even breaking into a house in the middle of the day to steal a woman's underclothes. That had temporarily relieved the tension inside him, but it always came back, fed by a shapeless, invisible source. He'd toyed with the thought of seeking professional help, which was abundant in both military and civilian life, but that might have looked bad on a future air force or employment record. He could have done what a lot of other men did and found prostitutes to act out his fantasies with, but that was too risky and complicated. It would mean revealing buried pieces of himself to another human being—something he'd never done before.

By the early 1970s, Rader had taken a job with the Coleman camping-supply factory in Wichita, the same place a lot of young people went when they weren't certain about their career path or didn't feel they could get work elsewhere. He'd become attached to a young woman, and the couple were talking about getting married and starting a family. Paula Dietz, a local girl who'd also attended Heights High, came from a modest background like his own, and they naturally gravitated toward each other. The wedding was set for May 22, 1971, when the groom was twenty-six and the bride twenty-three. The military hadn't changed anything about Rader's secret life, but marriage probably would. You entered into marriage to "settle down"—to put the wilder feelings and desires of youth behind you and move on to more responsible things. Many guys did bizarre stuff and had strange fantasies before they got married—he'd heard some stories in the air force—but matrimony was supposed to take care of all that. It was what his father had done, wasn't it, and hadn't things turned out all right for him? It was what most people did. Once he and Paula were living together and he was working forty hours a week, there wouldn't be much time to think about those other things. Marriage was definitely the answer. A lot of people got married to feel more normal.

Then he joined Christ Lutheran Church, because those urges would go away if he became a regular worshipper with his wife and later with his children. God and Jesus would help him cope with these disturbing issues, and his faith would ease the anxiety that kept returning in stronger and stronger ways. And if he did give in and do something bad, his religion would offer him forgiveness and even salvation. That's what he'd been taught from childhood on: the way to eternal life was through a profound surrender to and belief in the sacrifice of Christ on the cross. He'd died for everyone's sins, and if you accepted him as your personal savior, you too were saved, no matter what you'd done. Faith was what counted, not deeds. Yet he wondered why, after taking a wife and attending church every Sunday morning, he was still tormented by these feelings and conflicts. They would have gone away with age and maturity. He was, after all, a law-and-order Republican who didn't believe in doing illegal things.

The first years of marriage were tolerable. He liked being with a woman who paid him a great deal of attention and saw him as important and filled with promise. He cared for Paula and wanted this to work. Staying busy was good and he stayed plenty busy at his job, but there was always free time to be alone and explore his other life. Lately, he'd been reading about murder and serial killers, including Jack the Ripper, who'd killed prostitutes in the East End of London in 1888. He'd named himself, after mutilating some of his victims and removing their body parts. Following one of his early crimes, he wrote a letter to London's Central News Agency that read, "I am down on whores and I shant quit ripping them till I do get buckled." Signed, "Jack the Ripper." Despite flaunting himself and his murders, he was never caught.

Rader found it incredible that a serial killer could avoid arrest and keep his identity concealed forever. Jack must have been extremely intelligent and cunning to do what he did undetected and then carry on with the rest of his life. He must have been able to shift gears from one part of his personality to another "as easily as an eighteen-wheeler," as Rader phrased it to himself. Rader was kind of like that too. Maybe he and Jack had other things in common.

VII

ANOTHER SET OF MURDERS had recently become prominent much closer to home. If most everyone growing up in Kansas in the 1950s and '60s held some awareness of the Menninger Clinic, they'd also heard of the Clutter killings out west in the fall of 1959. On November 14, Dick Hickock and Perry Smith, who'd met as inmates in a Kansas prison earlier that year, drove south from suburban Kansas City and stopped in the small city of Emporia to buy some rope at Haynes Hardware. After picking up yards of it, they headed west and rode all afternoon and night across the state, arriving at Herb Clutter's farmhouse at 11 p.m. They believed that Clutter, asleep inside with his wife and two teenage children, kept at least $10,000 locked in a safe. After making this quick, easy score, they planned to take off for Mexico to pursue an even greater fortune down there. As they pulled into Clutter's driveway, Hickock reminded his partner once again that they couldn't leave behind any witnesses. When they awoke Mr. Clutter, neither he nor his terrified wife or children had much cash on hand—about $50 total—and that was all the money in the house.

Perry Smith stole a radio from one of the teenagers' bedrooms and carried it out to the car. He thought about bolting, getting away from Dick and the Clutters and forgetting about the failed robbery, but he felt as if he were an actor in a movie and the movie wasn't finished and he needed to go back inside to find out how it ended. As a boy, he'd been separated from his family by the actions of an alcoholic mother and a nomadic father, spending time in a foster home where he was beaten by nuns. Years of abuse and personal failure had filled him with an explosive rage, but he seemed calm on this chilly November night until he got back in the house. The movie suddenly lurched forward and the rage detonated—Smith tying up the stunned family and killing all four of them with a shotgun. Before slitting Mr. Clutter's throat, he laid him out on a mattress box in the basement to make him more comfortable. He liked the man, Perry always said, right up to the moment he sliced his throat.

Two months later, Smith and Hickock were arrested in Las Vegas and bought back to western Kansas for their trial. They were convicted in the spring of 1960 and spent nearly half a decade on death row. During those years, Truman Capote visited them many times while writing his classic true-crime book, *In Cold Blood,* published soon after the men were put to death by hanging in 1965. The murders and Capote's account of them laid a chilling hand over the state of Kansas and far beyond. If the assassination of President Kennedy ended the collective innocence of American society in November 1963, Kansans had experienced something like that four years earlier, when the Clutters were slaughtered by two small-time thieves who hadn't found the money they were looking for.

For many readers of Capote's book, the utterly soulless killing of the Clutter family signaled that life was no longer as simple or as safe as it had once been, not even out there in quiet, wholesome farm country. Citizens everywhere started locking their doors at night. Drivers along back roads and interstates stopped picking up hitchhikers, and more lights were installed around homes to illuminate larger patches of darkness. People didn't keep as much money at the house, so nobody would get the idea that they were rich or easy targets.

Rader had followed the Clutter case and was aware that neither Smith nor Hickock alone was a killer, but together they'd made a lethal combination: a third person who became a mass murderer. Rader didn't have to meet anyone else to start taking larger criminal risks. The person inside him had been thrashing around in more and more disturbing ways, jacking up the tension and taking over his mind until something felt ready to crack. The military hadn't driven this force away, and neither had getting married or finding a job or attending church and praying in the sanctuary every Sunday morning or taking Communion with the rest of the congregation. The symbolic blood and body of Christ that passed from the hand of the minister to the lips of the worshippers may have brought relief to others and peace throughout the rest of the week, but not to him. Instead of going away, the things he'd felt as a youngster had only grown larger and stronger.

He'd gotten to know this other person so well that he'd given it a name and a face—Factor X, or sometimes Rex—and imagined it as a demon that resembled a small, nasty-looking, demented frog. He drew pictures of the creature who kept coming round and fueling his fantasy of having a live, pretty, helpless woman at his command. Rader didn't have to look at pictures in magazines anymore—just thinking about a bound woman was enough to arouse him. For a while, masturbation satisfied his urges, but then it wasn't enough. On the outskirts of Wichita, he found an all-night convenience store run by a woman working alone. He'd wait until there were no customers inside, enter the store and at gunpoint force her into a car, tie her up and take her into the countryside, fulfill his fantasy, and dump her body in a hidden location. After casing the store, he decided not to follow through, struggling against his impulses and holding out the hope that they would still go away. He wasn't giving in to Rex without a battle.

At Wichita's Twin Lakes Mall, he found a woman and stalked her outside, but she turned on him and scared him away. He went back to his fantasies, eventually finding another woman and going so far as to dig her a grave in the countryside. He broke into her house and stole her driver's license and Social Security card as he lay in wait, but she didn't come home and it was getting late and he had to get back to Paula before she became suspicious. Whatever else he was, he was determined to be an excellent husband.

He could fight all this off alone, the way men were supposed to, before anything really bad happened. He was better and stronger than Hickock and Smith, who couldn't hold down jobs or build the kind of love he had with his wife or attend church every Sunday and pray with the congregation. Those two were born criminals, but he admired law enforcement and always had, thinking from time to time about being a cop himself. He just had a couple of nasty habits, which he could learn to control and overcome. He wasn't a criminal but an upstanding citizen, just as his father had been. His dad was his role model, and it had apparently never occurred to Rader that it could be any other way—or that following in his father's footsteps hadn't solved any problems, but only deepened them.

The men of William Rader's generation had gone abroad and fought wars in Europe and Japan, but the younger Rader had entered a new world and faced a very different kind of battle. Men of every stripe and background had been affected by the enormous social and political changes that had followed the 1950s, and had begun rethinking their relationship with work, money, sex, women, therapy, religion, race, homosexuality, emotions, aggression, and violence, confronting issues of all sorts and discovering that their fathers' challenges and their fathers' answers were not always their own. They were taking a thousand or a million interior journeys to learn more about themselves, how they functioned, and what they could do to cause less pain to themselves and others. This new war, even for men who joined the military and served in Vietnam, was far more with themselves than with any exterior enemy. Self-acceptance was the heart of this new battlefield.

Some found salvation in embracing born-again Christianity, which pulled them back from the brink of self-destruction and many forms of abuse, while others looked for spiritual paths beyond the mainstream. Still others threw themselves into extreme physical activity or careers or devotion to family and children, but at the bottom of all this searching was the knowledge that ragged emotional issues (call them demons) had to be confronted and managed or they could destroy marriages, families, relationships of every kind, and oneself. Something fundamental was changing in the culture and men found themselves either working with this change or pushing against it. How a man defined himself in relation to women was becoming central to his identity. Fearing, hating, or needing to control or hurt the opposite sex was often the result of words unspoken and feelings unexplored, tears never shed and secrets never shared, breakdowns never experienced and breakthroughs never achieved—an entire process denied or retarded. If ignored long enough, demons tended to get bigger, crueler, and much more demanding.

Rader had aped his father in every important decision of his life: joining the military, getting married and settling down in Park City, becoming an active Lutheran, and voting the Republican ticket. The psychological transitions that many people went through by separating from their parents or their parents' values was something he'd never done or attempted doing. He wasn't a born criminal or one who'd been pushed in that direction because of abuse. He thought he could will himself into being normal and conventional—and then his problems would go away. He was more different from his father than he could have ever dreamed, but as a young man he hadn't rebelled in any minor ways against his background, so his rebellion later on was against everyone and everything imaginable—against the notion of society itself.

VIII

His family and church would have disapproved. He was supposed to love only his wife and stay faithful to her, but he couldn't stop looking at other women, all kinds of women. Their faces, shapes, voices, clothes, scents, eyes, and laughter—all of it filled him with desire and conflict and anger, because women had always tried to control him and tell him what to do. First his mother, then Paula. Young women, older women, dark-haired women and blondes, it didn't matter. Men were like props in a stage play or stick figures of little interest, but women were alive and vibrant—even the pictures of them that he kept in his wallet or at his job conveyed that. Sometimes, before going to work at Cessna or after ending his shift, he would drive around town to see who was outside in the front yard or walking down the street. Lately, he'd been watching a Hispanic woman and her preteen daughter, unable to shake their images from his mind. He'd first noticed the woman at the Coleman plant, where they'd both been employed, and now decided to cruise by her house at 803 North Edgemoor in northeast Wichita.

One day he lost his job at Cessna and felt more powerless and ineffectual than he had in years. Paula was working at a Veterans Administration hospital, but was barely making enough to cover their bills. He wasn't bringing home a paycheck or going to work forty hours a week and had a lot of time to dwell on the pretty woman and the pretty young girl he'd seen beside her. Of course, he hadn't told his wife about any of this and wouldn't dare mention that he was attracted to Hispanic-looking people with their darker skin and features. He didn't want to hurt Paula's feelings. She was sweet and nice and kind, but with her short hair and Midwestern features and paler skin, she didn't look like *that*. He and Paula had a good sex life, but there were limitations. He could perform with her but wanted to have experimentation and bondage in the relationship, because that gave him a much greater sense of power and control. With Paula, he'd had to put aside many of his desires because he knew she wouldn't understand them. It wasn't that he didn't love her; he just wanted something more.

After that first drive-by, he kept going past the house on North Edgemoor, scouting the location to see how much traffic moved along this street and who lived in the neighborhood. He'd given this activity an official name, trolling, which meant following women without being seen and watching their routines to learn when they came home at night or went to work in the morning. He shouldn't be so drawn to people of another race—there was something wrong with that. Spanish women were a little different from the ones he'd grown up around, and he liked the differences more than he should have, but it wasn't possible for someone like him to be with someone like that.

The location of the North Edgemoor house was ideal: it was on a corner lot, so there were neighbors on only one side; an open, detached garage set next to it; and the back door looked easy to break into. He'd followed the mother enough to know when she dropped off her kids at school in the morning and came back home. He had her schedule down to the minute. By now, his trolling had evolved into what he called stalking, and he'd given the entire process a name. It was called a project, but the project itself needed a label, something he could use as shorthand when thinking over and refining the details of the overall scheme. Because of the pretty girl he'd seen walking next to her mother, he'd chosen the name Little Mex. After trolling and stalking, he "locked in," selecting a time frame for execution of the plan.

The final step was what he called a ruse, which would allow him to hide in the garage and get him inside their home without causing panic. Because he still had problems with language, he didn't pronounce the word *rooz,* but rhymed it with *cuss.*

*   *   *

On the morning of January 15, 1974, he drove into the city and parked his car at a Dillon's grocery store. Leaving Dillon's on foot and wrapping his air force parka tightly around him to ward off the cold, he walked across frozen patches of snow toward 803 North Edgemoor, his pockets stuffed with rolls of black tape, rope, wire cutters, gloves, a knife, a .22 handgun with hollow-point bullets, and other supplies. It was 8:30 a.m. and school had started by now. The pretty woman lived there with her husband and several children, but the man and older kids would be out of the house, leaving only the mother and daughter. When he reached the address, he jumped the fence and went to the back door, jimmying the knob, but it was locked—he was so nervous he dropped his knife and forgot to pick it up. Pulling out the wire cutter, he snipped the telephone line at the rear of the house, placed a nylon mask on his face, felt for his gun inside the parka, and waited. He should leave now, just get out of here before someone saw him, but the fantasy wasn't complete.

He walked into the detached garage, rubbing his gloved hands together to get warm. Looking around at the random collection of family belongings, he saw a dog's paw prints in the dirt on the garage floor. They looked fresh. The animal must have been inside the home, and that wasn't part of the plan. Detail and organization were critically important so that everything could unfold in a controlled, orderly, efficient way and there wouldn't be a big mess. Messes were upsetting and he didn't want to fight with a dog. This was a bad idea. If he left now, he'd be okay, but what about all the things he'd imagined doing once he was alone inside the house with the females? He'd been dreaming about this moment for years—all those rehearsals played out in his mind were just like watching a movie, and the movie needed a big ending.

It was twenty minutes till nine and getting colder by the minute, but his hands weren't cold at all. He was so nervous they were sweating profusely and filling his gloves with water. Somebody was going to spot him in the garage and chaos would break loose or the dog would sniff him and start to bark. Rex did not want to deal with an animal.

For years Rader had tried to hold Rex at bay, acting out every fan-

tasy he could think of and even going over to his parents' basement
in Park City, stripping naked, and dressing up in women's clothes.
He'd looped a cord around his neck and tied it to a sewer pipe and
staged hanging himself, but this didn't solve the problem or take away
the anxieties or desires, and he couldn't think of any other way to get
rid of them. Maybe if he gave in to his impulses just this once, it would
satisfy the urge and he'd be all right. He could go back home to Paula
and calm down and be the Christian husband he ought to be. All this
would finally be done and he could ask God for forgiveness.

His hands were shaking and he couldn't wait much longer. He
could still change his mind and leave, just go. Traffic was picking up
on the street and he heard a noise and—

The back door opened and a nine-year-old boy emerged, letting
his dog out into the yard. The youngster had a full head of dark hair
and a wonderfully open smile. His chin came to a point at the bottom of his face, making him quite handsome. At the moment his teeth
were chattering and he looked eager to get back inside the warmth
of his home.

The boy and the dog alarmed Rader—only females were supposed
to be in the house. A male child wasn't part of the plan, and neither
was that animal.

Rader stared at the boy and his face hardened, his eyes going
blank—a mean, flat look settling into his features. His body coiled,
ready for the inner spring to be released and the struggle to be over
at long last.

He charged from the garage and toward the terrified boy, whose
name was Joey Otero.

BTK withdrew his gun and shoved the child into the house. The
dog stayed out.

IX

THE BOY'S FATHER, Joseph Otero I, loved cars, airplanes, and playing the bongos. He liked to flirt and make jokes but could also be quite demanding, expecting straight A's from his five kids, and when they got excellent grades, he didn't hesitate to tout their accomplishments in front of others. Otero had worked hard to build a life in a foreign country and was rightfully proud of his achievements and his family. Born in Puerto Rico, he'd come to America as child and grown up in New York City's Spanish Harlem. The streets of Manhattan taught him a toughness he used to become a local boxing champion. His passions ran toward fighting and for a young woman named Julie, who'd also come from Puerto Rico as a child, sailing to the United States on a banana boat. Joseph pursued her as diligently as he went after his opponents in the ring. They were married in a big church wedding, and their firstborn, Charlie, arrived almost nine months later to the day. Hanging up his boxing gloves, Joseph joined the air force and was stationed in the Panama Canal Zone for seven years, retiring from the military as a master sergeant and moving his family to Wichita in the autumn of 1973. He had a commercial pilot's license and wanted to live in the small Midwestern city because of its reputation as the Air Capital of America. By January 1974, after finding work as a mechanic and flight instructor at Rose Hill Airport, the thirty-eight-year-old was just beginning to explore life in Wichita and its aircraft industry.

His wife weighed only a hundred pounds, but Julie Otero quickly taught people not to take her lightly. During her husband's air force career, she decided to enroll herself and her children in judo courses being offered at one of the bases. It was a good way to spend time with her kids, and you never knew when you might need self-defense skills. Turning judo into more than a hobby, she earned her brown belt, entered tournaments, and won one trophy after another. The small woman threw around opponents nearly twice her size. After coming to Wichita, the thirty-four-year-old found work at the Coleman plant, one of the city's main employers, but was let go in a companywide labor reduction. Like Joseph, she was fiercely protective of her family and proud of her cultural heritage and efforts to establish a new life in the United States. She wanted to succeed in America and assimilate, but not disregard her roots. As her children grew up, she paid them a penny for every word of Spanish they learned and spoke to their mother.

In September 1973, eleven-year-old Josephine Otero was the fresh face in the sixth grade at Adams Elementary. Her new friends welcomed her by calling her Josie, and by January 1974 the shy and soft-spoken girl was starting to feel comfortable at the school. The TV cartoon *Josie and the Pussycats* was popular at the time, and the other sixth graders liked to sing its catchy theme song to their attractive new classmate with the long, dark hair. She laughed and sang along, a happy girl who enjoyed Barbie dolls and painting and poetry, but as determined to succeed and as tough as her mother, with outstanding grades and a yellow belt in judo. Of all five children, she probably had more ambition and drive than anyone else; her parents must have sensed that when naming her Josephine Estrella: "Josie Star."

Joseph Otero II, age nine and called Joey, was usually the center of attention in the family—not just as the adored youngest child but because his brothers and sisters liked to use him for judo practice. He may have been easier to handle than his older siblings, but he was still no pushover. He fought back as best he could, but rarely lost his temper because he knew he was safe and the other Otero kids—Charlie, fifteen; Danny, fourteen; Carmen, thirteen; and Josephine—loved him. Even though he'd started the 1973 school year late, Joey was an immediate hit with the girls at Adams Elementary because of his good looks, while the boys envied him because of his judo skills and his ability to ride Charlie's minibike in front of them. Children weren't the only ones who liked him. On his fifth birthday, Joey received a dog, Lucky, a shepherd mix who could be mean to strangers but was close to the young boy. The two like to roll around on the floor and tussle, but when things got a little too rough, Lucky knew to stop and protect the smallest Otero child. When he bared his teeth or growled, it was a fiercesome sight.

By afternoon on January 15, the winter sun had turned the snow on the ground into slush. At twenty minutes to four, Charlie Otero was walking home from school, as Danny and Carmen ran along ahead of him. They entered the small, one-story, wood-frame house before he did, and moments later when he stepped through the front door, he heard wailing and crying in his parents' bedroom. Charlie ran toward the terrifying sounds and stepped inside the room. His brother was bent down and cradling the body of his father on the floor, his sister holding his mother, who lay diagonally across the bed. Neither parent was breathing and both had been tied at the ankles and wrists. Charlie smelled fear and death in the room, and when he realized his parents had been killed, something died inside him as well; in that instant he lost his religion and later said that if there was a God, he hated Him from now on. He picked up a yardstick and snapped it in two.

Acting on instinct, Danny ran into the kitchen and grabbed a knife, cutting loose his mother and father and shaking them in the hope they might still move, but they didn't. He picked up a phone to call an ambulance but there was no dial tone.

He ran outside, sprinting up and down the street until he found a neighbor, Dell Johnson, telling him to come fast because his father was dead.

Johnson went into the Otero house and glanced at the bodies, immediately heading home to call the police. When the WPD arrived, they did a cursory examination of the parents before expanding their search of the residence. A priest would be brought in to assist the police in informing the Otero kids about what else they found that afternoon.

Even veteran homicide detectives with years of experience viewing crime scenes were not prepared for what they saw in the house
and would spend decades trying to get the images out of their heads.
Four members of the Otero family had been bound and strangled
with the kind of cord used on venetian blinds. Three victims—Joseph,
Julie, and Joey—were in first-floor bedrooms with bags or pieces of
clothing tied around their heads. A coat had been placed under
Joseph because his ribs had recently been injured and were hurting,
an apparent gesture by the killer to make him more comfortable
before he died, just as Perry Smith had done with Herb Clutter fifteen years earlier in western Kansas, before slitting his throat.
Josephine wasn't on the main floor and seemed to be missing. Lucky,
the shepherd mix, was unharmed and locked up in the fenced-in
backyard.

After the discovery of the first three bodies, Detective Gary Caldwell decided to look for Josie in the basement, slowly descending the
stairs with a flashlight burning in front of him. While reaching around
in the semidarkness for a light switch, his hand bumped into something and he moved the beam of light in that direction—then leaned
back in horror. Josie, wearing only socks and a sweater, was standing up and hanging from a sewer pipe. Her panties had been pulled
down, and her dark hair tumbled forward over her face, her limp
body held in place by a cord. Everything inside the Otero home was
overwhelming, but the sight of the dead, partially nude child, her
dangling feet barely touching the basement floor, would give Caldwell
nightmares for years to come. Josie's posture invoked a profound
sense of shame, an endless capacity to haunt. The savagery of the
murders suggested they might have been driven by revenge, but
revenge for what? An unholy message had been sent, but what did it
mean?

None of the victims had been sexually assaulted, but semen was
found in the basement and on Josie's inner thigh. An initial examination of the fluid indicated that it was associated with type O blood,
but that didn't mean much, as all semen reverts to type O within
twenty-four hours after it's been discharged. No other clues had been
left behind, but a neighbor did report seeing a dark-complexioned

man wearing a rumpled hat drive away in the Oteros' car, a 1966 beige Oldsmobile Vista Cruiser, at about 10:30 a.m. That evening, the Cruiser was found in the Dillon's parking lot at Oliver and Central. The keys weren't in the car and all the fingerprints inside the vehicle belonged to Joseph or Julie Otero. The killer had also stolen a radio, just as Perry Smith had done at the Clutter home. No prints retrieved from the bags tied around the victims' heads were from a stranger. Lab investigators spent twelve hours processing the crime scene and discovered only one print, on the back of chair, most likely deposited by the strangler. He'd also left DNA in the semen in the basement, which could be preserved indefinitely.

After everyone else had left the crime scene and all the evidence had been removed, police detectives Bernie Drowatzky and Gary Caldwell stayed in the Otero home that first night, along with a psychic, watching endless streams of cars pass by the residence that had just become Wichita's most notorious address. They spent the whole night inside the house, thinking the killer might come back, but he didn't. It was astounding to the police how one man had been able to subdue a family of four, all of whom had been trained in self-defense, then tie them up, torture them, and kill them one by one. And why hadn't the dog put up a fight or at least begun barking?

Following the attack, Rader had run into the Oteros' garage and stolen their car, driving it to Dillon's and picking up his own vehicle. When he realized he'd forgotten the knife he'd dropped two hours earlier, he returned to the crime scene in his own car and parked in the garage, frantically hunting for the weapon and finding it by the back door. His temples were pounding with a crushing headache— as if Rex were beating against the interior walls of his head with a hammer—so after going home he swallowed a couple of Tylenol to relieve the pain. Collecting all his bondage sketches from the house, and putting them together with the evidence of the crime, he drove into the woods and burned everything, racing back to Park City before Paula got home from work at the VA. By the time she arrived, his headache was gone and Rex had vanished and they spent a pleasant evening together.

As the Oteros were flown to Puerto Rico for burial, seventy-five officers were assigned to the case. Fanning out across Wichita and working eighteen-hour days, they contacted more than a thousand people the first week, setting up roadblocks to stop drivers for questioning and sending out bulletins to five hundred other law enforcement agencies. The *Wichita Eagle* joined the investigation and created a "secret witness program," encouraging citizens to phone in anonymous tips. They poured in and eight hundred people were quickly interrogated, but none of this activity established a credible lead. The WPD was starting to wonder if the roots of the crime weren't based in Wichita. Within a month of the slayings, Police Chief Floyd Hannon and a military adviser, Major William Cornwell, flew to Puerto Rico to speak to Otero relatives, traveling on to the Panama Canal Zone, where Joseph Otero had served for more than half a decade. The chief thought the murders might have been caused by a financial dispute between the head of the Otero family and others in Central America, but no linkages were made between this suspicion and the evidence in the case.

The trail was growing cold, but not the level of fear in Wichita. Gun sales, the installation of new security systems, and enrollment in self-defense classes were booming. Women locked every door they could, and children didn't play outside without adult supervision. Fathers were sleeping by their front or back door with firearms nearby, when they slept at all.

X

JULIE OTERO HAD WORKED at the Coleman plant where Rader had been employed. Twenty-one-year-old Kathryn Bright, who'd grown up in Valley Center, north of the city, also worked at Coleman. After graduating from high school in 1971, she'd briefly attended the University of Kansas in Lawrence before coming back to Wichita and taking the factory job. On April 4, 1974, less than three months after the Oteros were found murdered, she returned home when she usually did, but this time something was different. She didn't arrive alone but with her nineteen-year-old brother, Kevin, visiting her from Valley Center. Kevin was a slight, mop-haired young man with a friendly manner, who loved his sister and always looked forward to coming into the city and spending time with her.

Killing the Oteros hadn't solved the problem either. The same tension and fantasies had come back, so Rader decided to plan another project. He'd seen Kathryn one day when driving past her home on his way to have lunch with Paula. During the meal, he'd tried to focus on what his wife was saying but was distracted and edgy, unable to get Kathryn off his mind. Since then he'd been trolling and stalking her for weeks, sitting in front of her house in his car and making notes. Her looks and style had captivated him—the long blond hair, denim clothing, and antique beaded purse. She fit the profile he wanted: she lived alone and didn't have a boyfriend. There was no "present male" around to interfere with the plan, as there had been at the Oteros'. He'd learned a lot from that experience. For one thing, it had taken far more pressure to strangle a human being, especially an adult, than it had a cat or a dog, and that had surprised him. He had a medium build, at five foot ten and about 180 pounds, and was reasonably strong but was going to need more strength for these projects. His hands could go numb in the two to three minutes it took to choke the life out of someone, so they'd better be in shape. At work or sitting at home and watching TV with Paula, he'd lately been squeezing a reddish rubber ball—with LIFE IS GOOD written on it—to build up endurance in his fingers. If he couldn't stop, he wanted to become more organized and efficient doing this kind of work.

After trolling and stalking Kathryn, he locked in on her, working through the final details of the project, which he'd named Lights Out. Tonight, he hadn't cut her phone line because he didn't want the police to connect this crime with what had happened at the Oteros'. He'd brought along rope but not venetian-blind cord and had a .357 Magnum pistol in a shoulder holster, in addition to the .22 handgun he'd used before. Changing your mode of operation was important, he'd read, because patterns and repetition tipped off the cops. For Lights Out, he'd come to Kathryn's home carrying some books so he could pose as a college student, but nobody had answered his knock on the front door. He walked around the house and punched out the glass in the back door, sweeping it up into a neat pile so Kathryn wouldn't notice the mess if she entered that way.

Once inside the house, he carefully inspected the layout before sitting down in her closet on a chair made from her clothes and waiting. While fiddling with the .22, he accidentally hit the trigger, and with the safety off, the gun fired. He worried that Kathryn would smell gunpowder when she got home and was getting antsy because Paula would be expecting him soon and he didn't want to upset her or make her ask uncomfortable questions. She hadn't noticed anything different after the Otero murders, a huge relief. Paula was a critical part of all his thinking and planning, especially when they went out socially or attended church, because no one married to such a decent and caring person could be suspected of murder.

When the Brights walked through the front door, he heard noises but thought she was alone. Slowly, Rader came out of the bedroom and then pointed the .22-caliber Colt Woodsman automatic pistol at Kevin and Kathryn, explaining that he was in trouble in California, there were wanted posters of him in that state, and all he needed was food and a car. If they'd give him $100 in cash and Kathryn's car keys, he'd let them be, but she refused to hand over the keys. He hesitated, angry and confused because his well-crafted plans were starting to go haywire again. He told Kevin to tie up his sister in one of the bedrooms, and the young man, being held at gunpoint, did as he was told. Steering Kevin into the other bedroom, he bound him with a knotted-up stocking and turned up the stereo loud—a trick he'd learned from reading detective magazines—so that Kathryn wouldn't be able to hear what he intended to do to her brother.

Going back and forth between bedrooms, he spoke to Kathryn and then Kevin, laying him down on the floor and placing a pillow under his head. Grabbing the stocking, he began to strangle him, tightening the fabric around his neck, but the material wasn't as strong as venetian-blind cord and he couldn't get a proper grip. Kevin was only five foot six and weighed 115 pounds, but he knew this was a death struggle and fought back with all his strength. Breaking free, he grabbed the man's .357, aimed the barrel at the intruder's stomach, and fired twice, but the gun jammed. Rader wrestled the gun away, brought out his .22, and pulled the trigger—the bullet hitting Kevin in the forehead. As he lay on the floor unconscious, the shooter went back into Kathryn's room.

When Kevin came to, he heard his sister and the man arguing, then the horrific sound of a woman being strangled. He ran into her bedroom, saw Kathryn tied up on the bed, and jumped on her assailant, tearing the .357 away from him again and firing it, but once more it failed. They fought and Rader shot the .22 into Kevin's face, hitting him right below the nose, ripping open his lip and taking out two teeth. Kevin crumbled to the floor but remained conscious, and as the man went back into Kathryn's room, it gave her badly wounded brother a chance to escape. He ran outside shouting and looking for help. A driver spotted him and took the bleeding teenager to Wesley Medical Center, roughly a mile away.

With her brother gone, the young woman was no match for her attacker, but she fought back ferociously. Unable to get her under control, he took out a knife and stabbed her seven times in the back and four in the abdomen, then fled the house. When the police arrived, she'd crawled out of her bedroom and was lying in a pool of blood on the living room floor, her hand clutching the phone. She was also rushed to Wesley Medical Center but died five hours later. Kevin spent the next two weeks at Wesley before being released, with damage to his face and brain. Because of his injuries, Kevin's eyewitness accounts about what the killer had looked like and how he'd behaved during the assault were never given the seriousness they might otherwise have had. The police couldn't be certain if they were looking for a white man, about twenty-five to thirty years old, five feet ten, and 180 pounds, or searching for a Hispanic male with a darker complexion. Initially, the Bright case seemed to have no connection to the murder of the Oteros. While recovering, Kevin told investigators about the killer's claim that he was wanted in California, and the police took this as a truthful and important piece of information. They began looking for a fugitive from out of state instead of a man who lived in the metropolitan area.

Before leaving the crime scene, Rader had taken Kathryn's keys, as he'd done at the Oteros', but when he tried to steal her car, it wouldn't start. Panicking, he ran all the way back to the Wichita State campus, where he'd parked his vehicle, gasping for breath and afraid the police were right behind him. He drove home fast and cleaned up, destroying his bloody clothes and hiding the gun and other things he'd taken with him to Kathryn's in his Hit Kit. While scrubbing his knife, it struck him how slick human blood was and how different it felt from all other liquids. That wasn't something he'd learned by reading about murder or studying the exploits of Jack the Ripper. After washing up, he went over to his parents' residence and slipped the gun into a box belonging to his father, putting sawdust on top of it. He hadn't been able to get the blood off his suede shoes and stashed them in a chicken coop at his parents', but then feared his dad or mom might stumble across them. So he burned them. No one noticed a thing, just as they never noticed him killing a dog or a cat. He needed to do something to give his crimes more meaning.

After cutting an article out of the paper about the death of Kathryn Bright, he filed it in his growing collection of written material, pictures, and drawings. He looked at the article to relive the murder, disappointed with the outcome, because nothing had gone as he'd expected. No matter how many plans he'd made or how much thought had gone into a project, events hadn't turned out as he'd hoped, and that was frustrating. The wrong people kept showing up and things slipped out of his control, and he hadn't had enough time alone with the females to do all he wanted to do. It had been messy and bloody and noisy, what with those children screaming at the Oteros' and shooting Kevin Bright. And it was maddening that after doing all this, no one knew he was the killer because the police were so clueless. He'd already begun thinking of them as the Keystone Kops. Maybe he should offer them an assist.

For years Rader had held secret ambitions to become a writer, but like many people he hadn't known what to write about. He'd wanted to pursue drawing too, but hadn't had any original subject matter, until now. As a child no one had encouraged him to pursue his artistic outlets, but as an adult there was nobody to stop him. In childhood he'd wanted to create pretty things, but those impulses had been stifled, so he'd create ugly ones now.

XI

By October 1974, six months after the Bright murder, 780 individuals had been interrogated by the WPD regarding the Otero slayings and a number had been connected to sex crimes. The police were not only looking for a sex criminal but, at the start of the investigation, for a bizarre individual likely to stand out in the community. His appearance and behavior were probably indicative of his deviant intentions. Who else but an obvious madman was capable of such horrors? Anyone who could break into a busy household on a weekday morning, while the kids were preparing sandwiches for school, and tie up and strangle four people simply could not be that normal. Anybody who could kill Josie Otero in the way she'd died and then leave semen on her body couldn't be someone who looked or acted like the rest of us. Or could he? When the Oteros were murdered in early 1974, criminal profiling was a new field. The FBI's Behavioral Science Unit at Quantico, Virginia, which assisted law enforcement around the country in pursuing serial killers, was in its infancy. The feds were starting to create proactive strategies, interrogation techniques, and other programs designed to help local police look for mass murderers, but it was hardly a science. And the WPD was not yet convinced it was pursuing a serial killer.

None of the 780 leads moved the detectives any closer to a serious suspect, although there had been one peculiar development. In October 1974, a young man was apprehended by the police while attempting to have sex with a duck and then confessed to killing the Oteros, implicating two other men. All three were arrested, and it was soon apparent, all suffered from mental problems. Their arrests for the Otero murders were reported in the *Eagle* on October 18, 1974, and four days later a man telephoned Don Granger, the paper's director of community affairs. Granger was in charge of the Secret Witness hotline, which had been receiving tips on the Otero case since last January.

"Listen and listen good," the man told Granger, "because I'm not going to repeat it."

He stated, calmly and firmly, that the Oteros' killer had placed a letter in a mechanical-engineering textbook at the main downtown branch of the Wichita Public Library, near the WPD. Then he hung up.

After Granger passed this information along to the police, Detective Bernie Drowatzky went to the library and, while searching on the second-floor mezzanine, found the letter in a stack of books. Addressed to the Secret Witness program, it was an original copy of a typed document and contained many spelling mistakes, which may or may not have been deliberate. Echoing the writings of Jack the Ripper, the letter insisted that its author and nobody else was responsible for the Oteros' deaths. The letter showed both an extraordinary attention to detail and a cold-blooded need to state the facts of the murders. It presented a near-scientific examination of the event and a childlike fascination with what actually happened to people when they'd been tortured and strangled to death.

It began:

Otero Case

I wrote this letter to you for the sake of the tax payer as well as your time. Those three dude you have in custody are just talking to get publicity for the Otero murders. They know nothing at all. I did it by myself and no ones help. There has been no talk either. Let's put it straight. . . .

Joe:
Position: Southwest bedroom, feet tie to the bed. Head pointed in a southerly direction.
Bondage: Window blind cord.

Garotte: Blind cord, brown belt.

Death: The old bag trick, and strangulation with clothes line rope.

Clothed: White sweat shirt, green pants.

Comments: He threw up at one time. Had rib injury from wreck
   few weeks before. Laying on coat.

Julie:

Position: Laying on her back crosswise on the bed pointed ina
   southwestern direction. Face cover with a pillow.

Bondage: Blind cord.

Garotte: Clothes line cord tie in a clove-hitch.

Death: Strangulation twice.

Clothes: Blue housecoat, black slack, white sock.

Comments: Blood on face from too much pressure on the neck,
   bed unmade.

Josephine:

Position: Haning by the neck in the northwest part o the
   basement. Dryer or freezer north of her body.

Bondage: Hand tie with bind cord. Feet and lower knees, upper
   knees and waist with clothes line cord. All one length.

Garotte: Rough hemp rope ¼ dia., noose with four or five turns.
   New.

Clothes: Dark, bra cut in the middle, sock.

Death: Strangulation once, hung.

Comments: Rest of her clothes t the bottom of the stairs, green
   pants, and panties. Her glasses in the southwest bedroom.

Joseph:

Position: In the east bedroom laying on his back pointed in
   eastern direction.

Bondage: Blind cord.

Garotte: Three hoods, white T-shirt, white plastic bag, another
   T-shirt. Clothes-line cord with clove-hitch.

Death: Suffocation once, strangulation-suffocation with the old
   bag trick.

Clothes: Brown pants, yellow-brown stripe T-shirt.
Comments: His radio is missing.

All victims had their hand a tie behind their backs. Gags of
pillow case material. Slip knotts on Joe and Joseph neck to hold
bag down or was at one time. Purse contents south of the table.
Spilled drink in that area also, kids making lunches. Door shade
in red chair in the living room. Otero's watch missing. I needed
one so I took it. Runsgood. Thermostat turn down. Car was
dirty inside, out of gas.

The author now switched his voice, moving back and forth
between the first person and third. He referred to one part of himself
as "my friend" and the tone was no longer so cold or inhuman:

I'm sorry this happen to society. They are the ones who suffer
the most. It's hard for me to control myself. You probably call
me "psychotic with sexual perversion hang-up." When this
monster enter my brain, I will never know. How does one cure
himself? If you ask for help, that you have killed four people
they will laugh or hit the panic button and call the cops.

I can't stop it so the monster goes on, and hurt me as well as
society. Society can be thankful that there are ways for people
like me to relieve myself at time by day dreams of some victims
being torture and being mine. It is a big complicated game my
friend of the monster play putting victims number down, follow
them, checking up on them waiting in the dark, waiting,
waiting . . . the pressure is great and sometimes he run the game
to his liking. Maybe you can stop him. I can't. He has already
chosen his next victims or victims. I don't who they are yet. The
next day after I read the paper, I will know, but it to late. Good
luck hunting.

YOURS TRULY GUILTILY

P.S. Since sex criminals do not change their M.O., or by nature
cannot do so, I will not change mine. The code words for me

will be . . . Bind them, toture them, kill them, B.T.K., you see he at it again. They will be on the next victim.

The WPD, after much discussion and debate with others who specialized in mass murder, felt it best not to publicize this letter. If the authorities refused to give BTK the attention he was seeking, it was more likely he wouldn't kill again. Law enforcement believed that in the fall of 1974, but did reach out to the author in a quiet way. For three days at the end of October, the *Eagle*, with input from the WPD, ran the following ad:

B.T.K. Help is available. Call 684-6321 before 10 p.m.

Nobody responded to this message and Rader didn't seek help from anyone. His fantasies didn't go away and neither did his cravings. He continued sketching pictures of women in bondage, as he'd been doing since adolescence, and had made a lengthy narrative account of the murder of Kathryn Bright, just as he had of the Oteros and would of other crimes in the future. It wasn't enough to kill people, he'd discovered, he needed to make images of the events and document them with words. The physical stimulation of killing, the chemical charge in his brain and the adrenaline rush coursing through his body, faded quickly and so did the notion that he'd actually had an effect on those around him.

Since he couldn't feel what his victims felt as they'd struggled for their lives in front of him, he didn't retain much emotional memory of the events. The best way to know he'd done something important and powerful was to make a record of it that he could return to again and again as a reminder. Looking at the mementos he'd stolen or reading a newspaper account of the crime or his own description, he recalled the details and felt a little of the past excitement. It was better than feeling nothing, but not enough. Maybe the next murder would allow him to hold on to that sense of power and make his life seem real. Maybe starting a family would help. Wasn't that what his father had done? Wasn't that what men were supposed to do? Surely, being a parent would calm him down and make things better.

XII

In July 1973, Rader had left his job as an assembler at the Coleman camping-supply factory and after being let go from Cessna, he'd taken a position with ADT, the nationwide security company. Two years later, he and Paula's first child, a son they named Brian, was born, and the family settled into its routine in the small house on Independence Street in Park City. Paula was more occupied and distracted than ever with the baby, and at his new job Rader had permission to enter people's homes throughout Wichita and work on their security systems in an official capacity. He could see what kind of alarms they'd installed and how difficult their residences were to break into (some people were buying ADT systems to protect themselves from BTK). The work kept him busy studying new ways to sneak into houses, and he would stay at ADT for nearly fifteen years.

As soon as Brian was old enough, Rader would get him involved in Cub Scouts and become a troop leader himself, while his son would one day earn the distinction of Eagle Scout. Rader was quite strict with the young boys in his charge, just as he was a great stickler for handling the details at his job, and he made the Cubs pay extraclose attention when teaching them his specialty—knot tying. Rader had always wanted to continue his education, and by the mid-1970s he'd become a student at Wichita State University, in 1979 earning a bachelor of science degree in administration of justice. He was drawn to law enforcement, had long been interested in the kind of detective work the police did, and had even thought about becoming a cop: it might be fulfilling to hunt for lawbreakers who needed to be rounded up and punished.

Sometimes he and his neighbors got together and talked about the virtues of living in Park City, as opposed to a crowded and dangerous urban environment like Wichita. Rader said he never wanted to move down to the city because it had too damn much crime.

Just before noon on March 17, 1977, near the intersection of Lincoln and Hydraulic streets and close to a Dillon's grocery store, he settled on a plan. His initial target this morning had been a house down the street, where two women lived, but no one had answered the front door. Wearing dark slacks, expensive shoes, and a tweed coat, an outfit that he felt evoked James Bond, he was too dressed up to break into this home in the middle of the day. Someone would see him and remember his outfit. He tried another residence but no one was there either. Strolling on down the sidewalk, he ran into a six-year-old boy named Steve Vian, who'd just been at Dillon's grocery shopping for his mother. Rader spoke to the child and tried to gain his trust by saying he was a detective and showing him a photo of two people he was searching for. The two faces in the picture belonged to Brian and Paula Rader.

"Have you seen these people?" he asked the boy.

"No," Steve said, walking away from the man.

He went back home, put down the groceries, and crawled into bed with his mother.

Rader followed him and minutes later forced his way into the home of Shirley Vian and her three young children: Bud, Steve, and Stephanie. Only twenty-four, Shirley wasn't feeling well this morning, spending most of her time in her bedroom trying to rest. The intruder had barged into the living room carrying a briefcase, and when he saw two kids watching television, he snapped off the TV, lowered the blinds, and brought out a pistol from his shoulder holster, telling them to follow his orders. Shirley, dressed in a pink nightgown, heard a commotion in the next room and wandered out to see what it was. Shocked at finding an armed stranger in her home, she tried not to panic but to do whatever was necessary to protect her sons and daughter.

"Don't hurt us," she told the man.

"I'm not going to hurt you," he said, determined this time to keep things under control. "I'm gonna have to tie up the kids."

"Don't do that," she begged him.

"I've got to."

Rader unzipped his briefcase, removed a rope, and started to bind Bud's small hands. The child resisted and began to cry, so Rader herded all three kids toward the bathroom.

"Somebody's gonna come check on us," Bud said, but Rader ignored him.

The phone rang but he told them not to answer it. When he demanded that Shirley get some toys and a blanket and bring them into the bathroom, she gathered up a plastic airplane, a truck, and a car. Rader tied the two bathroom doors to a drainpipe, marched the kids into this small space, tied one of the doors shut, told them to keep quiet, and closed the other bathroom door leading into Shirley's bedroom, shoving the bed up against that door so the children were locked in. Project Waterfall had begun.

Alone with Shirley, he said that all he wanted to do was tie her up, take a few pictures of her, and have sex.

"I'm too sick," she told him.

"I know, but that's the way it's going to be."

She'd already thrown up this morning, adding to the mess inside the residence, a sloppiness that had upset Rader the moment he'd entered the house. He didn't want her to vomit again, so he walked into the kitchen to get her a glass of water, thinking it would soothe her stomach.

The children had begun crying in the bathroom and yelling for their mother—saying they were going to escape and get her help. She screamed back at them, insisting they stay put, because this would soon be over and everything would be all right. They tried to obey, but then terrible sounds started coming from the next room, and all their instincts told them to shout louder and to pound on the walls and to do whatever they could to get out of the bathroom and save their mother.

"Leave my mom alone!" Bud yelled, trying to break through the bathroom door. "Get out of here!"

Steve hoisted himself up, peeked over the transom, and looked into the bedroom. His mother was lying facedown on the mattress, her ankles elaborately tied to the bed with venetian-blind cords and panty hose. Her hands were bound behind her with black electrical tape, a plastic bag was drawn tight over her head, and a rope was tied around her neck. Stephanie also climbed up and saw her mom in this position. They screamed again and banged on the door as hard as they could, telling the man to stop. Bud pushed against a small bathroom window, breaking the glass and slicing open his hand. Blood was pouring from the wound and the kids began shouting out the window.

The phone rang again and Rader panicked, remembering Bud saying earlier that someone was coming to check on them. Working faster now, he sealed the bag over Shirley's head and wrapped it tighter with her pink nightgown, applying so much pressure that her features distorted and her face turned blackish red from hemorrhaging. The kids' voices echoed around the bathroom walls, their little fists hammered against the door, and all of it tore at Rader's nerves. He despised random noise and chaos, and now someone was coming to interrupt him before he was finished doing what he wanted to do, but it was too dangerous to stay. Half-finished, he threw some mementos into his briefcase and bolted from the house, the kids screaming in the bathroom.

It was still the noon hour so he went to his car and drove back to work at ADT. He always liked returning to the office, where everything was normal and quiet and predictable. On the job, he was known as an excellent detail man and something of a prude. It bothered him a lot when his male colleagues made off-color jokes or swore around the female employees.

Using all his force, Steve rammed his small body into the bathroom door and knocked it ajar, enough to allow him to squeeze through. He ran into his mother's bedroom and found her tied on the mattress, her blue panties laying next to her and she wasn't breathing. Steve dashed outside to some neighbors and told them to call the police. When law enforcement arrived, Shirley couldn't be revived and the three kids were quickly taken from the house to be interviewed by the authorities and later by a psychologist. Eventually, they moved to Oklahoma to be raised by Shirley's parents.

Crime-scene professionals, including those from the FBI, were as disturbed by what they found inside the Vian household as by what they'd seen at the Oteros'. While Shirley's death was similar to the Otero murders, police didn't initially think of BTK as a suspect. For the past several years, he hadn't surfaced in Wichita, law enforcement was reluctant to believe that a serial killer was on the prowl in their city, and there were differences between the crimes. While BTK had taken four lives at the Otero residence, the Vian children had apparently not been targets. When a pair of detectives working the Vian case raised the possibility that BTK might have been involved in the new homicide, they were discouraged from pursuing that line of thought. If the police didn't want to consider that BTK was back, they didn't want the media thinking that either, and it was best for everyone not to try to make that connection.

Rader scoured the papers for any linkage between BTK and the Vian homicide, but found none, once again disappointed in the WPD. He'd have to try again to get their attention.

XIII

As soon as one project was completed, Rader began putting together another series of possible hits, filled with detailed plans. He continued writing and drawing—documenting not just what BTK had done, but all the things he still dreamed of doing. On warm evenings, he went outside to the tree house in his backyard, which sat on stilts and was surrounded by sprawling elms, climbing up to the top while carrying a sheaf of papers. Alone in this quiet and peaceful setting, with the sun going down and the birds chirping around him, he thumbed through pictures and scribbled accounts of his past crimes, reliving the most exciting moments of his life and imagining new ones. Neighborhood kids saw him sitting up there absorbed in reading and found this strange behavior for a grown man, but nobody disturbed him. He was familiar to everyone in Park City, worked hard at fitting into the community, didn't call attention to himself, and went out of his way to please most people. The only place he could be himself was up in the tree house looking at old pictures and drawings, or in the middle of an attack on someone under his total domination. The only people allowed to see him for who he really was were either dying or already dead.

On December 8, 1977, less than nine months after Shirley Vian was killed, Nancy Jo Fox came home from her job at Helzberg's Jewelry Store. On the drive to her duplex at 843 South Pershing, she stopped at Wendy's and ordered a hamburger, taking a few bites on the ride. The other half of her duplex was unoccupied and she'd lived alone for nearly two years. By the time she reached her address, she'd finished the hamburger and carried the empty bag into her kitchen. Drawing a glass of water, she sat down and lit a cigarette, a habit she very much enjoyed and one she took her time with now. Putting out the smoke and entering her bedroom to undress, she heard movement in her closet and saw a man rush toward her. He'd been waiting in there quite a while, sprawled out on a chair made from her clothes.

Rader had gotten Nancy's name from her mailbox and been stalking her at home and at Helzberg's. The more he'd learned about her, the better he liked her and the closer he felt to the young woman. She was his kind of person—attractive, organized, she seemed kind, and her tidy apartment reflected a sense of pride. After breaking into her home through a rear window, he'd drunk a glass of water in the kitchen and then cleaned it until it was spotless, wiping it dry and putting it back in the cupboard, exactly where it had been. He settled into the closet and listened for Nancy to arrive. Sometimes he wished he were a lone wolf who didn't have to support others or check in with his wife all the time. He'd told Paula that he'd be out late tonight, studying for a term paper for a night class at Wichita State, and he'd been on campus earlier this evening. Leaving there before 9 p.m. and carrying his Hit Kit, he drove over to Nancy's and crawled into her closet, eager for Project Foxhunt to unfold.

"Get out of my house," she said to the man in her bedroom. "I'll call the police."

"It won't do you any good," he told her. "I already cut the phone line."

Enraged and trembling, she asked what he wanted and said she needed a cigarette.

"I just want to have sex and take some pictures of you," he said. "But I have to tie you up to take pictures."

"Get *out* of here!"

"No. It ain't gonna be that way."

They went into the kitchen and she lit a cigarette, trying not to show her terror.

As she smoked, he casually emptied her purse on the table, pocketing her driver's license and some other items.

"Let's get this over with," she said. "What are you going to do to me?"

"I'm going to tie you up," he answered matter-of-factly, "and then probably rape you."

"You're sick."

"Yeah, I'm sick, ma'am, but that's the way it's got to be."

She snuffed out the cigarette and tried to stall, saying she wanted to change clothes.

He allowed her to go into the bathroom, but only after she assured him that she couldn't escape out a window and there was no inside latch on the door.

She came out partially undressed and he began taking off his own clothes, ordering her to lie down on her bed.

She watched him put on a pair of gloves and pull out some handcuffs.

"This is ridiculous," she said. "This is a bunch of bullshit."

She protested as he slipped the handcuffs on her wrists and they got into the bed.

As he began tying her up, she tried to resist but it was too late. He leaned over and whispered in her ear that he was the serial killer known as BTK.

The next morning Rader was driving through Wichita in a white ADT van with blue lettering on the sides when he decided to make a bold move. Stopping near a market where he and his work crew often got sweet rolls and coffee, he went to an outside pay phone. Dialing the operator, he asked to be connected to the police emergency hotline.

When a female dispatcher answered, he said, "You have a homeicide at 843 South Pershing."

Then he added, "Nancy Fox."

"I am sorry, sir," the dispatcher said, using her training to distract the caller and keep him on the line as long as possible.

After apologizing, she immediately tried to reach a patrol car and send it to the pay phone's location.

"I can't understand you," she said to the man. "What is the address?"

The dispatcher didn't realize that the telephone operator hadn't yet hung up but was still listening in on the conversation, as she was also trained to do.

"He said 843 South Pershing," the operator replied.

"That is correct," the man said, dropping the receiver and running away from the phone.

The captain of the Wichita Fire Department, Wayne Davis, who'd been waiting to use this same pay phone, had stepped inside the market until the call was finished. When he came out, he saw the receiver off the hook, picked it up, and spoke to the dispatcher, who described what had just happened. Davis later told the police that the man who'd been using the phone before him was around six feet tall, had blond hair, and was wearing a bluish gray industrial uniform. From other reports that would filter into the WPD, the police came to believe that the caller had been driving a windowless van with writing or advertising on its sides.

When homicide investigators arrived at 843 South Pershing, they found Nancy Fox lying on the bed, her ankles bound together with a sweater. Several sets of her own panty hose had been tied around her neck, around her hands (cinched behind her back), and around her legs and ankles. Panty hose had also been used to gag her. She'd fought back against her attacker, clawing his testicles, but eventually he'd subdued her. For once Rader had been able to spend as much time with a victim as he'd wanted to, and Nancy's face was swollen and distorted from the prolonged torture. He'd ejaculated into one of her negligees, laying the garment by her head and cleaning up the rest of the mess he'd created before leaving her home with some jewelry and her key chain.

The DNA in the semen at this crime scene was collected by investigators, as it had been at the Oteros', and would be preserved for decades.

XIV

By January 1978, Paula Rader was pregnant again and this time with a girl. Kerri arrived a few months later, while her father stayed busy working for ADT, studying for his classes at Wichita State, and creating new writing. One day Paula found some lines of a bizarre poem her husband had put together and they frightened her.

"What are these?" she asked him.

"We're working on a BTK thing at school," he shot back, thinking as fast as he could.

She tried to ask more questions, but he said there was nothing to worry about because all the students in his class were doing similar writing. Her concern faded and they didn't talk about it again.

On January 31 of that year, he mailed an index card inside an envelope to the *Eagle,* but the paper misplaced it for several days before somebody noticed it. On the card was a poem, placed there with a child's rubber stamp, and the writing parodied the old nursery rhyme "Curlylocks." It began, "SHIRLEYLOCKS SHIRLEYLOCKS WILT THOU BE MINE"—a likely reference to the 1977 murder of Shirley Vian. When employees at the *Eagle* realized this, they sent the poem over to the police department.

Rader had been expecting a fast public response to the verse from either the media or the authorities. When that didn't happen, he sat down to write again, and this time he was much angrier.

On the morning of February 10, Wichita's KAKE-TV received a long letter, which included another poem entitled "Oh! Death to Nancy," and a drawing of Nancy Fox lying dead on her bed. The author vented his frustration at the lack of response to the "SHIRLEY-LOCKS" poem. Intentional or not, his typing, spelling, and grammatical skills were still poor:

"I find it the newspaper not writing about the poem on Vain unamusing. A little paragraph would have enough. Iknom it not the news media fault.

"The Police Chief he keep things quiet, and doesn't let the public know a psycho running lose strangling mostly women. there 7 in the ground; who will be next? How many do I have to Kill before I get a name in the paper or some national attention."

This last sentence was particularly chilling because more than three years earlier the authorities had decided not to publicize BTK's first letter to the media about the Otero murders. At the time, they'd believed that if this communication wasn't generally known, he'd be less inclined to kill again. Clearly, that strategy had failed.

"Do the cop think all those deaths are not related?" he went on. "Golly—gee, yes the M.O. is different in each, but look a pattern is developing. The victims are tie up—most have been women—phone cut—bring some bondage mater Sadist tendencies—no struggle, outside the death spot—no witnesses except the Vain's Kids. They were very lucky: a phone call save them. I was going to /// tape the boys and put plastics bag over there head like I did Joseph, and Shirley. And then hang the girl. God—oh God what a beautiful sexual relief that would been. Josephine, when I hung her really turn me on; her pleading for mercy then the rope took whole, she helpless; staring at me with wide terror fill eyes the rope getting tighter-tighter. You don't understand those things because your not underthe influence of factor)x)."

He launched into an explanation of Factor X and a rationalization for the impulses that had driven other serial killers, whom he'd obviously studied. A few of them, such as Son of Sam in New York or Ted Bundy, had lately been in the news, but others were historical figures, such as Harvey Glatman, from the 1950s, and Dr. H. H. Holmes, America's first known serial killer, who'd terrorized Chicago during the 1893 World's Fair. BTK's own sense of victimization poured out through the letter, as if he were looking not just for attention, but sympathy:

"The same thing that made, Son of Sam, Jack The Ripper, Harvey Glatman, Boston Strangler, Dr. H.H. Holmes, Panty Hose Strangler of Florida, Hillside Strangler; Ted of the West Coast, and Many more infamous character kill. Which seem a senseless, but we cannot help it. There is no help, no cure, except death or being caught and put away. It a terrible nightmarebut, you see I don't lose any sleep over it. After a thing like Fox, I go home and go about life like anyone else. And I will be / like that until the urge hit me again. It not continuous and I don't have a lot of time. It take time to set a kill, one mistake and it all over. Since I about blew it on the phone—handwriting is out—letter guide is to long and typewriter can be traced too. My short poem of death and maybe a drawing; later on real picture and maybe a tape of the sound will come your way. Before a murder or murders you will receive a copy of the initials B.T.K., you keep that copy the original will show up some day on guess who?

"May you not be the unluck one!

"P.S. How about some name for me, its time: 7 down and many moreto go. I like the following. How about you?"

After offering up several choices—"THE B.T.K. STRANGLER," "WICHITA STRANGLER," "POETIC STRANGLER," "THE WICHITA HANGMAN," and "THE ASPHYXIATER"—he was still not finished.

Showing his earlier obsession with detail, he described the recent crime scenes, starting with death the of Kathryn Bright:

"#5 You guess motive and victim.

"#6 You found one Shirley Vian lying belly down on a unmade bed in northeast bedroom hand tied behind back with black tape and cord. Feet & ankles with black tape & legs. Ankles tied to west head of the bed with small off white cord, wrap around legs, hands, arm, finally the neck many times. A off white pla stic bag over her loop on with a pink nitie was bare footed. She was sick use a glass of water and smoke 1 or Two cizrette a total mess—kids took some toys with them to the bathroom—bed against east bathroom door. Chose at random with some pre-planning. Motive Factor X.

"#7 One Nancy Fox—lying belly down on made bed in southwest bedroom—hands tied behind back with red panty hose—feet together with yellow nitie—semi-nude with pink sweater and bra small necklace on west dresser—panties below butt—many different color panties hose around neck, one across the mouth—strangled with man belt first then the hosery . . . very neat housekeeper . . . heat up to about 90 degrees—Christmas tree lights on . . . driver license gone—seminal stain on or in blue women wear. Chose at random with little pre-planning. Motive factor 'X.'

"#8 Next victim, maybe. You will find her hanging with a wire noose—Hands behind back with black tape or cord—feet with tape or cord—gaged—then cord around the body to the neck—hooded maybe—possible seminal stain in anus—or on body. Will be chosen at random. Some pre-planning-Motive Factor 'X.'"

The letter was signed "B.T.K." and another poem was included in the envelope. Its eleven lines, though not really original, were the most succinct things he'd ever composed:

OH DEATH TO NANCY

What is this that I can see,
Cold icy hands taking hold of me,
For Death has come, you all can see,
Hell has open it,s gate to trick me.
Oh! Death! Oh! Death, can you spare
Me, over for another year!
I'll stuff your jaws till you can't talk
I'll blind your leg's till you can't walk
I'll tie your hands till you can't make a stand
And finally, I'll close your eyes so you can't see
I'll bring sexual death unto you for me.

Investigators would eventually discover that the verse was based upon a folk song, "Oh, Death," taught by Professor Phyllis (P.J.) Wyatt in an American folklore class at Wichita State in the 1970s. The teacher had the song performed in one of her popular work-shops, so detectives assumed that the killer had attended WSU and taken one of Wyatt's courses, which wasn't true. While studying for his administration of justice degree at the university, Rader had stumbled on some volumes of poetry and been captivated by their language and the sounds they made—their meter and syntax and rhyme—when read aloud. He thought they might be useful in the future and had copied out a few poems.

After receiving the latest envelope and learning that BTK was planning to kill "#8," the police department felt they no longer had a choice. They needed to inform Wichita's population what it hadn't known until now: a serial killer had been living among them for the past four years. He'd murdered at least seven people and had indicated there were more deaths to come. Within days of this announcement, the city was filled with even more fear than had followed the Otero killings, and among many women the feeling bordered on panic. Once more gun purchases soared, along with the sale of security alarms and self-defense devices. Children were put under constant protection, and neighbors began looking at one another with more scrutiny and suspicion. The sheer randomness and senselessness of the killings perplexed law enforcement the most, as if the killer himself didn't know what he was going to do next until it was done.

XV

SIXTY-THREE-YEAR-OLD Anna Williams had been alone since her husband had passed away the year before. His death had been a terrible loss, and recently she'd been treated for depression and failing health. It was important for her to go out on occasion and try to carry on with her life, so that's what she'd done on this Saturday night, April 28, 1979. When Rader arrived at her home at 615 South Pinecrest, he thought the house was empty but wanted to make sure. He walked around the dark residence, carrying his black bag, looking and listening for any noise. Certain she was gone, he smashed out a basement window, wiggled in through the space, cut her phone line, and moved slowly from one room to the next, until he was positive that no person or pets were inside. It was exactly what he'd been hoping for with Project Pine Cone.

He went into the master bedroom, opening her closet and looking at her clothes, touching the fabrics on the rack. He liked the feel of women's garments, especially the softer ones, the panty hose and underwear. He rifled her dresser drawers and examined her jewelry, stealing a couple of smaller pieces. He took a scarf and $35 in cash. The longer he stayed in her home and went through her belongings, the more anticipation and excitement he felt. All his senses were heightened with both fear and the same kind of pleasurable charge that runners experience when they've broken through a wall of exhaustion or pain and can see the finish line up ahead.

Anna Williams lived only six blocks from where Nancy Fox had died. He'd been trolling in this neighborhood for some time, sneaking away from work and driving slowly through these streets, checking out the lighting of various houses, walking down sidewalks to get a closer view and a better feel, watching people come and go in cars and on foot, considering all the possibilities and risks. Which houses held families and which had only single women? Which of the single females looked more likely to resist with force? The preparation and narrowing down of choices consumed him, with countless details to be mastered before putting together a final plan.

Even though it was Saturday night, he thought she'd be home soon. He'd cleared a space in her closet and spread out some clothes to sit on, trying to imagine what would happen when she came back—the look on her face when she realized she wasn't alone. What would she say? Would she try to run away? Or just go along with him as others had done before they'd realized they couldn't escape? He wanted to embed this moment into his memory: the order of her household, the smell of her clothes, the way the room was laid out, how the bed looked and its position in relation to the other furniture. He wanted to be able to recall everything precisely later on, when he was ready to write about it. Things always seemed bigger and more significant and more lasting when you turned them into writing and could relive them, step-by-step. Once he'd completed this project, he might make a drawing or two of it, depending on what happened.

The clock was ticking and time was disappearing, but she still hadn't returned and that was worrisome. Paula and the kids were at home waiting for him; she'd have put them to bed by now and would be expecting him soon. Where was Anna—did she really think she could avoid what was coming? He'd picked her because she was too old to fight him off, but he hoped she didn't scratch his face or make it bleed because that would be hard to explain. He had to be home before midnight because he needed to get some rest and go to church early tomorrow morning with the family. They almost never missed a service at Christ Lutheran.

Stepping from the closet, he walked through the house again, opening doors and rummaging in cupboards and closets, touching her possessions and looking for something more to steal. He took a piece of clothing, nothing expensive really, just a personal item specific to Anna. Each woman was so different—one of the things he liked about females. Back in her bedroom, he reached into his black bag and took out part of a wooden broomstick handle and a piece of rope. Should he leave now or give her ten more minutes? What was that sound—was she finally coming home?

He froze but heard nothing more.

Picking up the handle and the rope, he carefully arranged them by the bed. When she got back tonight, she might not see the broken window or messed-up closet for a while, but the handle and rope would be visible as soon as she entered her bedroom. He wanted the police to see them too, after they'd come to her house to investigate the break-in. They'd find the stick and the rope and connect those things to BTK. He'd told them he was going to strike again and wanted them to know he kept his word.

At 11 p.m., Anna arrived home from square dancing and noticed her spare-bedroom door ajar and a dresser drawer open. Clothes were strung out on the floor, jewelry boxes were empty, and garments were missing. A broom handle and rope were by her bed. When she tried to phone the WPD, the line was dead so she went next door to make the call. After investigating her residence, the police couldn't be sure that the break-in was connected to any other crimes, until nearly six weeks later. On June 15, 1979, Anna received a large manila envelope addressed in block letters to Clarence R. Williams, her late husband. Inside were the stolen jewelry and scarf, plus a typed poem and some realistic drawings depicting a woman kneeling by the bed with her torso resting on a pillow. She'd been gagged and her ankles were bound with rope. The tension on the rope could be increased or decreased by manipulating a broomsticklike piece of wood that ran from her chest down to her feet. The most troubling part of the images was that the woman looked right at the viewer with wide-open, frightened eyes—making her agony real.

The poem, entitled "Oh ANNA Why Didn't You Appear," revealed the anger and disappointment of the author because she hadn't come home that night, but also showed a mixture of dread and loneliness and longing. This verse was original and the language far more elevated than in Rader's past writings, as if he were becoming not only a better stalker but a better writer. Close attention had been paid to the words, as he tried to be precise about his feelings and experience. It's an erotic poem for a thirty-four-year-old man to write to a woman almost twice his age. A weird tenderness comes through the lyrics, along with hunger for the company of a woman who can share his secret life, even if she must die in the process.

It read:

> T'was perfect plan of deviant pleasure so bold on that
>   Spring nite
> My inner felling hot with propension of the new
>   awakening season
> Warm, war with inner fear and rapture, my pleasure of
>   entanglement, like new vines at night
> Oh, Why Didn't You Appear
> Drop of fear fresh Spring Rain would roll down from
>   your nakedness to scent the lofty fever that burns
>   within.
> In that small world of longing, fear, rapture and
>   desperation, the games we play, fall on devil ears.
> Fantasy spring forth, mounts, to storm fury, then winter
>   clam at the end.
> Oh "Why Didn't You Appear
> Alone, now in another time span I lay with sweat
>   enrapture garments across my private thought.
> Bed of Spring moist grass, clean before the sun, enslaved
>   with control, warm wind scenting the air, sunlight
>   sparkle tears in eyes so deep and clear.
> Alone again I trod in pass memory of mirror, and ponder
>   why you number eight was not.
> Oh, "Why Didn't You Appear"

As soon as she received the package, Anna moved out of her home and in with her daughter. One day after she received the poem, a new envelope arrived at KAKE-TV, containing another scarf, hair clips, and more writing claiming that BTK had broken into her house. The message to KAKE pushed the hunt for BTK, which had been stagnating, back into full motion. The WPD chased down leads all over the city, and while their legwork didn't bring them closer to a suspect, they did conclude that the killer had most likely attended Wichita State in the mid to late 1970s and used one of the school's copiers for his communications. Those two pieces of information weren't much to go on, as thousands of young men enrolled at the university in those years had had access to the copy machines.

Months passed with no investigative breakthroughs, then years, and then more than two decades evaporated without any progress on the case. Throughout the 1980s, new task forces were created, new profiling techniques were employed at the WPD, and psychologists studied BTK's writings and drawings, some of which were never shown to the public. Many in law enforcement believed that at least one person in Wichita must have some firsthand knowledge of the type of individual who wrote bizarre poetry, made elaborately cruel sketches of women in pain, probably acted angrily or bitterly toward the opposite sex, and appeared to function without a conscience. It wasn't possible that over so much time a man like this would not stand out in some way or could remain completely unknown to everybody.

Following the break-in at Anna Williams's, Rader didn't contact the police again for twenty-five years. During this long silence, the common feeling in Wichita, among the police, forensic psychologists, and amateur observers of the case, was that he'd stopped killing and left town or gone into prison or died, but he hadn't done any of those things. He'd held down a job, raised his family, and gone to church every Sunday with his wife and kids. Brian became an Eagle Scout, which his father was extremely proud of, and Kerri would grow into a high school golf champion. Rader himself was a highly respected Scout leader who loved showing boys how to tie his favorite knots: the square knot, the sheepshank, the double half-hitch, the bowline knot, and the taut line hitch, used when tying down tent poles. One evening during a special scouting event, he displayed a rare flash of humor, when he and another man put on women's clothes and staged a skit for the troop. With a mop on his head and wearing a dress, Rader was a hoot and the boys couldn't get enough, greeting his performance with catcalls and howls of laughter.

When he traveled to other cities to install ADT security systems, he trolled for new victims and burglarized homes, always searching for another target. One night at a Cub Scout campout, he sneaked into the back of his truck, placed himself in bondage, and practiced the autoerotic game of hypoxia, choking himself to cut off oxygen to his brain and heightening orgasm. He'd wrapped himself so tightly in dog choke chains that he couldn't get free and began to panic, fearing he might have to call out for one of the Scouts to help him, but he finally busted loose.

Throughout the quarter century he was silent with the media and the police, the relatives of the victims he'd killed or wounded tried to go forward with their lives. The three older Otero children became adults, Kevin Bright recovered from his gunshot wounds, the Vian kids grew up, and Nancy Fox's next of kin attempted to make sense of her death, all of their suffering heightened because none of these cases had ever been solved. The survivors never had anything like closure to the murders, and their pain and loss could only go deeper inside.

Over the decades, countless words were spent describing what the slaying of the four Oteros or of Shirley Vian had meant to the sons and daughters left behind, but no words were equal to the expressions of grief that had permanently been lodged on the faces of Charlie Otero and Steve Vian (who now referred to himself as Steve Relford). The unending cost of coming home and finding a parent or sibling strangled to death, or hearing and watching a mother be tortured and murdered in the next room, had been stamped into the features of these two men, and you couldn't glance at them without seeing and feeling a piece of the trauma they'd endured. That kind of savagery leaves an imprint forever.

Charlie Otero's eyes appeared wounded, and for the rest of his life whenever Steve Relford picked up the scent that BTK had worn on the day his mother was killed, which smelled like cologne or deodorant, he became agitated and angry. These men didn't have to say or do anything to convey their experience. They would never get over what they'd been through, and it was hard to look at them.

THE SEARCH
BEGINS

———

A dungeon horrible, on all sides round,
As one great furnace flamed; yet from those flames
No light; but rather darkness visible
Served only to discover sights of woe,
Regions of sorrow, doleful shades, where peace
And rest can never dwell, hope never comes
That comes to all, but torture without end.

—JOHN MILTON, *Paradise Lost*

XVI

I F THE WICHITA POLICE Department wasn't any closer to capturing BTK in March 2004, after receiving a new communication
from him and reopening the investigation, they felt they were starting to understand more of what drove him. He wanted to share pieces
of his story with *someone,* even if those pieces weren't completely
true and the people he was sharing them with could put him in prison
for the rest of his life. Or execute him under the death penalty that
Kansas had reinstated in 1994, after a twenty-year absence. In
March, the WPD, with critical input from the FBI, made two important decisions. The first was to establish fifty year old, bespectacled,
silver-haired Lieutenant Ken Landwehr as the official face and voice
of the investigation. That voice was a little husky because he was a
heavy smoker who liked caffeine as much as nicotine. Mountain Dew
kept his mood up and his energy high. His forehead was lined and
his eyes a little tired, as if the toll of his job had left its mark on them.
He had more knowledge of the case and more invested in it than anyone else in law enforcement. He'd been working on the murders since
1984, and when BTK resurfaced in 2004, his wife and his mother
both expressed deep personal fear of the man.

From now on, whenever the officer delivered a public comment
about the case, he might seem to be addressing the media and local
citizens, but he wasn't. He was talking directly to the serial killer himself. Landwehr's soft-spoken manner and rather bland exterior concealed his passionate commitment to his job and how much he
despised BTK. His goal now was to appear friendly and open. Law
enforcement hoped to create a personal connection, perhaps a dia-

logue, between the lieutenant and the killer. They believed if he was speaking one-on-one with Landwehr, he might be less inclined to murder again. Second, the police chose to reveal little of what they were doing, thinking this could motivate the suspect to communicate with them more often.

All this strategy was in place on March 25, when Landwehr went before a crowded City Hall press conference to announce that the investigation was officially back on. A new task force would look into other unsolved murders and check out potential suspects, particularly men in their fifties and sixties who'd recently left prison. Public hotlines were being set up for people to phone in leads, along with a special police department e-mail address. In the coming months, forty-five hundred tips rolled in.

Detectives went door-to-door swabbing the mouths of white males in Wichita, checking out men who'd worked at the Coleman Company factory when Julie Otero and Kathryn Bright had been employed there. They swabbed former Wichita State University students who'd taken P. J. Wyatt's folklore course and ex–U.S. Postal employees from the 1970s. They tested ex-cops and a former Wichita mayor, Bob Knight, but none of the samples matched the DNA preserved from the old crime scenes. The great majority of people who were asked for DNA samples participated willingly to have their names cleared, and there was a growing sense in Wichita that this wasn't just a police effort or an FBI investigation, but that the whole community needed to get involved if they were ever going to find the person who'd tormented them since 1974. Worshippers at churches throughout the metropolitan area, including Rader's own, had begun offering prayers for BTK's capture.

Every place task force members went, people gave them their opinions about the killer's identity and where he was living or working; if only the cops would conduct surveillance on this suspect or that one, the case would be solved. The detectives listened and nodded politely, wondering how many reruns of *Law & Order* these folks had been watching. If law enforcement hadn't been able to catch

BTK after thirty years and with help from the best minds in the serial-killer profiling business, things probably weren't going to get wrapped up by the top of the hour. As March gave way to April, Lieutenant Landwehr kept delivering the same message to his investigators: patience was critical, along with a steady commitment to the legwork in front of them. Keep taking tips, swabbing, and pursuing leads. Something would break. In early April, Landwehr asked the public for new information in the Otero murders. Despite the three-decades-old evidence and eyewitness testimony, the police believed this remained the most important crime in terms of cracking the case.

"Since this was the first in a string of homicides related to BTK," Landwehr said, "we believe that it has special significance, and we want to hear from anyone who may remember anything related to the Otero homicides. We want to hear specifically from anyone who may have seen someone around the Otero residence or around their vehicle at the Dillon's parking lot."

The lieutenant then revealed the breadth of the emerging investigation:

"We are using all available resources, and we continue to work closely with the FBI, the KBI, the Sedgwick County Sheriff's Department, the Sedgwick County Forensic Science Center, and the Sedgwick County District Attorney's Office. We also appreciate all the leads and tips we have received from the public. The overwhelming response we have received from citizens is reflective of our city's community-policing philosophy, and we could not effectively pursue this investigation without their help."

His words were aimed at BTK, and they soon paid off. The police had correctly intuited one thing: the killer was lonely and looking for someone to bond with and write to.

On May 5, an envelope arrived at KAKE-TV, with a return address of Thomas B. King: TBK, a variation on the name the killer had given himself. Detective Kelly Otis met with station manager Glen Horn, who handed over the envelope. Six days later, after the FBI had scrutinized the contents of the package, the authorities went public with this development. Called "Communication #2," the envelope contained photocopies of a cryptic, computer-generated word puzzle, a piece of paper with photocopies of two identification cards, and a document entitled "The BTK Story," with a list of thirteen chapters:

1. A Serial Killer Is Born
2. Dawn
3. Fetish
4. Fantasy World
5. The Search Begins
6. BTK's Haunts
7. PJ's
8. MO-ID Ruse
9. Hits
10. Treasured Memories
11. Final Curtain Call
12. Dusk
13. Will There More?

Experts were brought in to study the puzzle and saw that it was divided into three sections: MO, ID, and Ruse, representing BTK's mode of operation, his use of false identification cards to get into victims' homes, and his posing in different roles to allow his target to be tied up. Rader's name (DRADER), address, and other clues (DNA) were buried deep inside this alphabet soup, but at the time the puzzle seemed to reveal little about his actual identity. It was gratifying to him that he could invent something this mysterious, and that even when trained police eyes were looking right at the puzzle, they missed the most important hints. He was having a lot of fun preparing these packages in the evenings at home or when he slipped away to his office for a couple of hours to get away from his wife. By May, he was glad he'd restarted this cat-and-mouse game with the cops because it was the most creative and imaginative thing he'd done in a long time, and the old excitement had been rekindled.

Six weeks later, on June 13, a Wichita citizen named Michael Hellman found "Communication #3," a brown envelope, labeled "BTK Field Gram," taped to a stop sign near downtown, at the intersection of First and Kansas. Hellman gave the police the package and its contents were entitled "C1 Death on a Cold January Morning," which included six pages of writing plus a sketch of a nude female, bound and gagged and hanging by a rope. Accompanying the drawing were the words "The Sexual Thrill is My Bill," and in the lower right-hand corner was a symbol made from the letters *B, T,* and *K.*

The pages contained a graphic narrative account of the Otero strangulations composed way back in February 1974, just weeks after the murders. After capturing the experience in words when it was fresh in his mind, Rader had kept these pages locked away in his Mother Lode of information for thirty years, moving them around his house and from job to job. He clearly regarded them as a treasure, and they revealed for how long and how deeply he'd felt the need to express himself in writing and to tell the story that only he could tell. Filled with misspellings, the author had made an amateurish effort to present the killings as part of a novel. He'd tried to turn his real violence into a fictional art form, and his prose came under the influence of the detective magazines he'd looked at as a boy, spy thrillers, and pulp fiction. Referring to himself in the third person, he wrote that "a fantasy of having a pretty bound victim before his hand" was a long-standing desire and had grown "each day inside his body . . . just the thought of a girl being bound was enough. He could play with himself and think and immediate have an ejection. . . . Eventually, the long yaers [*sic*] of fantasy, the thinking and desire boil over, and in one night he began to stake his prey."

After recounting the gruesome details of the murders, he concluded with a sigh of relief and fulfillment and broken grammar:

"The dream had alast came true."

XVII

As BTK WAS PUTTING together and mailing out round after round of communications in mid-2004, Dennis Rader became the vice president of Christ Lutheran Church. Over the years, his faith had grown increasingly important to him. In the early sixteenth century, a German monk named Martin Luther had rebelled against the Roman Catholic Church and founded both Protestantism and the Lutheran denomination. Luther's break from Catholicism had come from his struggles with papal abuses, the sale of indulgences, and his differing concept of salvation. The Roman Church had encouraged good works among its worshippers and counted those works toward being saved by Jesus Christ and rewarded with a place in heaven, but to Luther, this was a vague and troublesome notion. How much was each good work worth? How many works did you have to complete before you were saved? How would you know when you'd done enough? Tormented by such questions, he came to believe that Catholics were simply wrong. A Christian did not achieve salvation through either the blessings of the Roman Church or the number of good deeds performed, but through faith alone. The depth of one's spiritual convictions and the fervent belief in Jesus as the Son of God qualified one for heaven—not what one did in daily life. You could always be forgiven for your sins if your faith was deep enough. This distinction had created scores of Protestant offshoots and was the historical root for the many different denominations found today in a town the size of Park City.

Rader may have done unspeakable things during the past three decades, but his religion had conveyed to him that if he believed in

Jesus Christ as his savior and devoted himself to that belief, this was enough to achieve salvation and a place in heaven after his death. Jesus had been crucified for humanity's sins and paid the final price, once and for all, for entry into the afterlife for everybody who followed him. Faith was the key, and Rader's faith was intact: God would protect and keep safe the true believers. Rader's commitment to Christianity and dedication to church work made him the natural choice to become vice president of the congregation and president a year later.

In the 1970s, Christ Lutheran had been located a few miles south of where it stands today, near Wichita State University. The old church was a wooden structure without air-conditioning and was surrounded by a neighborhood that had become progressively more racially diverse. Church leaders didn't feel as comfortable there as they once had, so they decided to move north, but the building was too big to haul up the road. They cut it into thirds, took the sections up near Park City a piece at a time, and glued them back together. In the mid-1990s, they tore down the old building and put up their new church, which was not only larger but had air-conditioning and the congregation had seemed happier ever since. In the final decade of the millennium, Christ Lutheran was led by a female minister, Sally Fahrenthold, who stayed until the close of 2000 and was replaced by Pastor Michael Clark.

He'd grown up in Council Bluffs, Iowa, and been baptized in the Methodist Church, but his religious affiliation had never meant that much to him. When Mike was a teenager, his girlfriends usually belonged to a different denomination from his, and he was eager to attend their church services so he could spend more time with them. Other things from his childhood, locked beneath the surface of his quick-witted and humorous personality, were more important than his faith.

When he was eighteen months old, his parents already had three small children, his mother was pregnant again, and his father decided he couldn't support such a large family. He put Mike up for adoption and the boy was taken in by his father's brother, becoming the brother *and* the cousin of his other siblings. As he grew older, he tried to fit into his adopted home as an only child, but his feelings about being given away by his real parents were entangled and raw, always festering within. His adopted family moved from Iowa and resettled in Nebraska, where his new father was employed as a steam-pipe fitter for the Omaha Public Power Company. He inhaled a lot of steam on the job, while smoking two and a half packs of unfiltered Camels a day. One morning, a coworker popped opened a steam valve near the man, severely burning the lower half of his body and scorching his lungs. He spent months in the hospital and never recovered from the burns or the cancer that had been eating away at his health. When he died, Mike was thirteen, as confused and angry about the abandonment by his biological father as he was by the illness and death of his adopted father.

He liked three things—sports, girls, and animals—so he threw himself into football and wrestling, began dating, and decided to become a veterinarian. While playing football, he lost a tooth and replaced it with a gold one that flashed whenever he told a joke or smiled. In high school he worked for a vet and loved being around four-legged creatures, but he was a lousy student, which precluded becoming a vet. After graduating from high school, he attended Iowa State University in Ames and flunked every course except English literature.

"With my tail between my legs," he says, "I left ISU for the University of Omaha."

He now wanted to study criminology and become a prison warden, but ran into another problem. He learned how to play snooker, was pretty good at it, and found himself spending a lot more time bent over a pool table, cue in hand, than going to the library and hitting the books. At the University of Omaha he had a 1.2 grade point average on a scale where perfection was a 4.0.

"The school really didn't need people like me around," he says. "I was in a fraternity and went through all that crap for a semester, but I couldn't become an active member because my grades were so low."

He quit college and got a job with the Union Pacific railroad as a file clerk. He worked there three years, supporting himself and his adoptive mother, and fell in love with a former high school classmate named Jan. A student at Drake University in Des Moines, she'd go on to become a psychologist. Her religious background was Lutheran, which was enough to push her fiancé in that direction, and the two were married in the spring of 1965.

The young husband was growing dissatisfied working for the railroad; he couldn't get promoted in the office until people above him died. One day he read in the *Des Moines Register* that a Chicago pharmaceutical company was looking for a sales rep in this part of the Midwest. The company offered two lines of products—gynecological creams and condoms—and he applied for the job.

"For many years," he says, "this was my claim to fame. I was a Lutheran minister who'd once sold condoms. For three days a week, I'd travel around the eastern half of Iowa and call on drugstores. I sold almost nothing and had to return a lot of products to the manufacturer because they were too old to be used. I did the job for two or three months, but didn't like being away from home this much. I thought it was time to get serious."

He applied to Drake but was denied admission because his previous college grades were so bad. He made an appointment at a Lutheran junior college in Des Moines and did everything but get down on his knees while begging an official to let him attend summer classes. He was offered a deal: if Mike took nine hours of courses and got all A's and B's, the school would let him enroll as a regular student in the fall. Inspired at last, the young man sought advice on how to study and came through the summer with good grades. With his wife now teaching school, Mike went full-time to Grand View junior college, scrubbing windows and washing floors to make ends meet. He soon transferred to Drake and made the dean's list, graduating in 1970 with a degree in elementary education and becoming the first male in the Des Moines school district to teach in the first and second grades. After working there a couple of years, he wasn't earning enough money to start a family.

He shifted into real estate and was good at it, taking over as office manager of Des Moines' third-largest real estate business. He and Jan had a daughter, Michele, then a son, Tim, and things were fine for a while. Mike tried to be content but something was nagging at him, a combination of unresolved feelings from childhood and a more mysterious calling or sense of emptiness and dissatisfaction, sensations that grew stronger over time. He thought about going to his pastor at Grace Lutheran Church, but kept putting it off. One Sunday, after coming home from attending church with his daughter, he sat down on the bed with his back to his wife.

"You know what I've been thinking about doing?" he said to Jan.

"Going to seminary," she told him.

He whirled around and stared at her.

"I just about fell off the bed," he recalls. "She had no idea what I'd been thinking about. At least I didn't think she did. This blew my socks off."

He spoke to his minister, who told him to go over to Wartburg Theological Seminary in Dubuque, a two-and-a-half-hour drive from Des Moines. The Clarks met with the Wartburg admissions people and Mike was accepted. He was concerned about being separated from his wife and kids and equally concerned about his financial future, but decided to go forward. He was so old compared to most of the seminarians and had done so many different jobs that he referred to himself as a "retread."

"I went to seminary," he says, "because the Lord has a sense of humor and is very patient. I did a lot of praying to see if it was the right thing to do, and it was. My call to the ministry was very slow and gradual. I was well in my thirties when I decided to answer it."

Near the end of his studies for the ministry, he took a class with a psychological/spiritual counselor. The man told the students that before they entered the pulpit, they needed to deal with their own inner troubles and jagged emotions, especially those left over from childhood or adolescence, before they could attempt to help other people. Mike knew he had haunting and painful issues in his background—things he'd never faced. For years he'd tried to ignore or dismiss them, but that hadn't worked, nor had trying to handle his feelings with humor. He was hurt and angry and had been since age two. No matter now much he told himself he shouldn't be this way, he was quietly enraged, and that was never going to change unless he did something about it that he'd never done before. Therapy might help, or speaking with this counselor, but it wasn't enough. He couldn't change the past and couldn't change those who'd made the decisions that had permanently altered his life, so what could he do? He didn't want to enter the ministry with all this in his heart and didn't want to give up his spiritual calling.

"One day I was in the counselor's office talking about all this," he says. "I had so much anger at my biological parents that if my father had been in that room with me, I'd probably have gotten up, walked over to him, and strangled him. I was angry at both my biological parents, for making my life different by giving me away. I was stuck and had to do something about it. The anger was breaking my relationship with God. Everything in life is about our relationship with God and paying attention to what He wants for us. Sin is nothing more than a broken relationship with God."

He turned to his faith in a way he'd never done before.

"I prayed about this," he says. "I went really deep into prayer and listened for anything in the silence that could help me. The answers didn't come immediately, but they did come. Jesus told me, 'Make amends with people. Find a way to deal with your problems.'"

After thinking about this, he drove to the home of his biological parents and said he had something important to tell them. They looked at him strangely and could see he was upset, wondering if he was going to confront them about the distant past. But when he began to speak, he didn't accuse them of anything or offer to forgive them for what they'd done all those years before. Openly and humbly, he asked them to forgive *him* for carrying around so much anger for so long. He'd done what he had to, and the pain that had been building inside him since early childhood cracked apart.

"After receiving their forgiveness," he says, "I walked out to my car and saw what looked like a long, dark, narrow hallway in front of me. At the end of that hallway was a brilliant light, and I saw a man going down that hallway toward the light. He jumped up in the air and clicked his heels together in joy. I was that man."

Approaching forty and keenly aware that Moses himself had spent four decades wandering in the desert with the tribes of Israel before coming to the promised land of milk and honey, Clark was finally free to join the ministry and do the work he most wanted to do. Now he could mount the pulpit with the full and clean knowledge that he was emotionally armed to do this, and maybe he could offer something more to others than he might previously have done. He was ready to serve a congregation.

During an internship in Galena, Illinois, he took in two of his brother's teenage children. Raising two extra kids, in addition to his own two, provided a new series of trials for Pastor Clark and his wife, but they overcame them and were preparing themselves for what lay ahead. Life was by no means finished throwing them major difficulties, or as the sign in his office puts it, "The road to success is always under construction."

His first ministerial job was in a town of four hundred in south-central Nebraska, then he spent a few years in Pittsburg, Kansas, followed by seven more in Beloit, Kansas. In late 2000, when he received the call from the Lutheran Synod to come to Park City, he was prepared for the new position.

"The people at Christ Lutheran know why they're in church," he says. "They have a good foundation and that's what you're looking for. They have a strong sense of what they're doing with their spiritual lives and that makes my work a lot easier."

When he took the job, he couldn't have known who was sitting out there in the pews on Sunday morning or kneeling down and taking Communion from his hand. He couldn't have guessed that within a few years his claim to fame would no longer be that he was a preacher who'd once sold condoms. Or imagined that he'd receive national attention for doing what he most wanted to do—minister to the deepest problems and needs of a believer.

XVIII

Downtown Wichita is small and feels intimate. All the major government buildings—the police department, City Hall, the district courthouse, and the Sedgwick County Detention Facility—are within a few blocks of one another, and the scale of everything makes the area seem wide open and friendly. If you visited here often, you'd start to see the same people again and again. After work or during a daytime break, Rader enjoyed cruising past City Hall—buzzing the WPD and the courthouse before getting back onto a main artery heading north and being home or at the office within minutes. It was exhilarating to be this close to people who were now searching for him twenty-four hours a day and had been, off and on, for more than thirty years. They were looking right at him as he zipped past the detention facility, which was surrounded by police cars and personnel, but they didn't know what they were seeing. It was thrilling to be able to hide in plain sight, so much more fun than his job.

The police always looked at things based on statistics or probabilities or what they were convinced had happened in the past. They liked to bring in FBI profilers to examine the pattern of events that might point toward what a killer would do next. Rader had read the same books the experts had. He'd studied the entire history of serial killing from Jack the Ripper to the Boston Strangler to Ted Bundy, the Son of Sam, and others whose names were in this hall of infamy. Two of the books in his collection were *The Criminal Mind* by Katherine Ramsland and *Serial Killers* by Peter Vronsky. Published in 2004, *Serial Killers* included Rader in its pages, reprinting one of BTK's letters to the WPD. He sat at home at night and read about himself in this book, as he thought up new messages to send to the police. This was a heady experience, seeing his chosen criminal name in a work alongside those of other notorious murderers. *Serial Killers* also featured a section on the detective magazines that had so fascinated Rader as a child.

In the mid-1980s, these magazines were the subject of a detailed study of serial homicide, child molestation, rape, and autoerotic deaths. Their covers usually featured a luridly illustrated or photographed image of a frightened, bound female, thrown to the floor or ground, skirt hiked up or blouse torn. Her assailant was a male who loomed over her but was indistinguishable, lurking just beyond the edges of the page as the victim stared up at the reader in anguish. No explicit violence or nudity was depicted, but numerous serial killers, including Ted Bundy, reported being excited and inspired by such publications. Because nudity wasn't present, the pictures could function as a stimulant rather than a release of sexual fantasy. The magazines were directed at adolescent and teenage males, and the reader had to "fill in" the action himself and imagine what he would do with this tied-up woman.

After reading about the lives of other serial killers, Rader believed he was smart enough to learn from their mistakes and avoid being caught. If profilers were searching for behavior that was predictable, it was a bad idea to repeat the past, but he couldn't always resist doing so. In October 1974, he'd called the *Eagle* and told the paper to go look for a letter at the downtown branch of the Wichita Public Library. It was the first time he'd introduced himself to the media or police as the person who'd murdered the Oteros, and it had felt good to step out of the shadows a bit and take credit for what he'd done.

At 8:30 a.m. on July 17, 2004, the WPD was again summoned to the downtown library, a modern cement-and-glass structure just a few blocks from police headquarters. An employee, James Stenholm, had found a suspicious-looking plastic bag in a drop box outside this branch. On papers inside the bag Stenholm saw the letters *BTK* and turned them over to his superiors. The library called 911 and Detective Kelly Otis collected the five pieces of paper, whose first page was entitled "BTK FLASH GRAM." The FBI authenticated these contents, and within days Lieutenant Landwehr was making another public announcement about the killer's recent communications and warning the local populace on ways to protect itself.

"In a letter received by KAKE-TV on May 5, 2004," Landwehr said, "BTK indicated that he has used fake identification in the past to either conduct surveillance or gain entry to residences. We don't want any of our citizens to fall prey to this ruse.

"Based on the information provided us by the FBI, and the fake IDs and fake badge that were sent to KAKE by BTK, we think it is important to continue to practice personal and home crime-prevention techniques. We want parents to teach these skills to their children also."

Landwehr had a few specific suggestions: put dead-bolt locks and peepholes on entry doors and secure windows; install good lighting around residences; do not open doors for strangers; if solicitors show up, tell them to leave and call the police; join or start a neighborhood watch; and never enter an empty home or apartment if something looks wrong—a ripped screen or broken window or pried-open door.

Rader watched the news conferences and followed the police moves closely, relishing how much reaction a couple of letters could produce. The terror Wichita had known in the 1970s was back full force. Men were taking Landwehr's advice about making their homes safer, women were glancing over their shoulders when getting out of cars or entering houses, and children were kept under adult supervision.

The unspoken, underlying message of all the police pronouncements was the same as it had always been: the WPD had no idea whom they were looking for or where he might live.

The July 17 package from the library was marked "Communication #4." It contained four pictures of a man in bondage, as well as two pages about the bizarre July 2004 death of a nineteen-year-old man, Jake Allen of Argonia, about forty-five miles south of Wichita. After investigating this case, the police decided that Allen had not been murdered but had killed himself by lying down on the railroad tracks near his farm home and letting a train end his life. The two pages were entitled "JAKEY" and claimed that the author had been guiding Allen toward his death. According to "Communication #4," BTK had lured the young man out to the tracks by acting like a private investigator who was hunting for a serial killer.

"The letter talked about how BTK was there when Jake died," says a member of the task force, "and how exciting it was for him to watch this. He talked about the fear in Jake's eyes and how the police should have checked his mouth and anus for semen. BTK said that he'd always been sexually motivated by the sound and motion of the trains. He talked about tying a string around his penis and attaching another piece of string to the railroad tracks and connecting the two pieces. The shaking of the train as it went by would make him ejaculate. We thought BTK was someone who was really interested in trains. Jake Allen had had surgery, and BTK said that he'd met him through hospitals, so we also thought that BTK might have been a physical therapist. He wrote about how much work it was to stalk and kill a kid and then acted like this would take a lot of planning. He sounded exasperated and said something like 'Details, details, details.'"

The police informed the public about the arrival of the new package but not its contents. The graphic "JAKEY" section was disturbing, but not the only unsettling thing in "Communication #4." BTK claimed that he'd also selected his next victim: "I have spotted a female that I think lives alone and/or is a spotted latchkey kid. Just got to work out the details. I'm much older (not feeble) now and have to conditions myself carefully. Also my thinking process is not as sharp as it uses to be. . . . I think fall or winter would be just right for the HIT. Got to do it this year or next! . . . time is running out for me."

In the late 1980s, Rader had lost his job with ADT Security and then worked briefly for the Census Bureau, but for the past thirteen years he'd been employed as a compliance officer. His office at Park City's City Hall was just a few blocks from his house, and he drove home for lunch nearly every day. He had lots of time now to ride around town in an official vehicle looking at people's properties and memorizing their routines. He enforced housing codes, made sure gutters were kept clean, and noted whether dog owners were obeying local laws. He relentlessly checked to see if people violated minor laws by putting up advertising signs or garage-sale notices or kept too much junk in their yards. Most compliance employees in Park City cut the citizens a lot of slack, since everyone in the small town was everyone else's neighbor, but not Rader. He was known for busting locals, especially women, if their grass grew too high, and he had been seen stepping out of his truck, getting down on both knees, and measuring the length of their lawns with a ruler, then writing up a ticket. If he didn't like you, rumor had it, he'd release your dog from its pen just so he could round it up and fine you. Enough of those fines could result in the loss of your dog. Yet he was also known for going out of his way to take wounded pets to the vet and saving their lives, just as he was known for helping certain of his neighbors with any request, be it early in the morning or in the middle of the night. He was selectively cruel.

In the late 1990s, Mary Capps took a job as a Park City compliance officer, and from the start Rader made her miserable, demanding that everything she did be perfect as he defined that term. He constantly hounded her about details, harassing her so relentlessly that she eventually filed four formal complaints against him, but no one took any action to discipline him. It was a small office in a small town, and who wanted to make the kind of waves necessary to tone Rader down? He may have stopped killing by the mid-1990s, but he hadn't stopped victimizing women. He still wanted to control the untidy and uncomfortable feelings they created inside him; whenever he felt most out of control inside himself, the need to control others surged. He once went to trial over a $25 dog-running-loose ticket; instead of treating it as a casual offense, he walked into the courtroom armed with audiotapes, videotapes, a half-inch-thick stack of documents, and an elaborate legal presentation that stunned the defendant's attorney. Rader won.

Cindy Plant also worked alongside him and didn't see any cruelty or rage, but observed his neatness, extreme organization, and always professional appearance. He overdressed for the job, wearing crisply pressed Polo shirts and Dockers instead of blue jeans. His pens were lined up straight inside his leather Day-Timer, his papers stacked with the edges aligned, and his personal space well ordered and spotless, as was his city truck. Holding himself aloof from the other workers, he sat alone on breaks eating Krispy Kreme doughnuts (which he didn't offer others) and clipping articles from the paper about BTK. These were categorized, filed in marked plastic folders, and deposited into the Mother Lode, a storehouse of secret scribblings and draw-ings that he kept locked beside his desk. If his clothes and surround-ings were immaculate, the Mother Lode held an incredibly messy reality, captured in writings, sketches, and photos. Just as messy as when he went on the road for his job and visited shops selling female masks, which he painstakingly decorated to resemble a pretty woman with delicate features, a fine-shaped nose, and red lips. He liked to wear the masks and a blond wig when he got dressed up as a woman and snapped pictures of himself. On his travels, he often stalked women at night, breaking into their homes and stealing mementos, or laying plans to kill.

"I was omnipresent," he said once, when describing his activities outside Park City. "There was no place in Kansas you were really safe if I was on the prowl."

Cindy Plant never saw any of these things about Rader but noticed a softer side when he spoke to his relatives or took a call from one of them at work. Always concerned about the well-being of his wife and children, he seemed like a model family man. Cindy was impressed enough with Rader to recommend he be placed on the Sedgwick County Control Advisory Board, which he was in 1996.

Rader kept especially close tabs on women who lived alone or were home by themselves during the day, focusing a lot of attention on an attractive blonde named Misty King, until she got a boyfriend. One day she saw the compliance officer looking in her front window and asked what he was doing. When he told her to get rid of her boyfriend, she thought he must be kidding, but he wasn't. She won-dered if he was dangerous but wasn't sure what to do. The man was, after all, a city worker employed in a kind of law enforcement, and she didn't want to make him any angrier than he was. When he issued veiled threats against her beloved Saint Bernard–chow dog, Jasmine, she doubted he would follow through, but Rader rounded up Jasmine without Misty's knowledge and put the dog to sleep. The woman was so upset she left Park City.

In "Communication #4," BTK didn't tell the police that he'd lately been driving by the home of another Park City woman with small children. She appeared to be unmarried and unattached to a man—crucial for a new project. He'd been watching her carefully, taking pictures of her and her house, studying her habits, and weighing how much resistance she might offer during a surprise attack. The woman had become aware of him and was increasingly upset by the presence of a strange man lurking near her home and kids, but she hadn't yet called the police. Sometimes he drove a dark-colored truck past her house and parked it, looking at her residence. She was determined to figure out the pickup's owner, but hadn't done that yet either.

The threat in "Communication #4" was so strong that the WPD, under the leadership of Chief Norman Williams, felt it had to take special action. Within days of receiving the package, the department enlisted the assistance of Representative Todd Tiahrt, a Republican congressman from Goddard, who quickly sought and obtained $1 million in federal funding to expand the investigation. The task force, which would grow to nearly thirty officers, needed more office space, more computers, more unmarked rental cars, and more overtime pay for detectives. Every day on the sixth floor at City Hall, task force members met with the top WPD brass and advisers from the FBI, then went out and searched for an invisible man and monster.

XIX

THE CUSTOM AT Christ Lutheran was for the vice president to serve twelve months and then assume the presidency of the congregation and set the agenda for the upcoming year. Throughout 2004, Rader's main job was to prepare himself for taking office in 2005, but as vice president he was more active than that. The church was growing modestly, and the membership had been talking about building Sunday-school classrooms on the second floor. If every small Kansas house of worship lived in fear of watching its congregation (and financial resources) shrink, the more specific fear was not being able to attract enough young people to assure a church's long-term future. With half a dozen other churches within a few miles of Christ Lutheran, the challenges became even greater.

"We just couldn't make ends meet," said a member of Christ Lutheran, whose former church had closed its doors because of a lack of funding. "It was like tryin' to push a wet rope."

Since early 2001, Pastor Clark had done well in expanding the congregation, and many worshippers felt that building the Sunday-school rooms would continue that process. Rader was one of the main supporters of this addition and worked hard to make it happen, as he had in carrying out all his other duties at the church. He seemed to be doing more now for Christ Lutheran and Pastor Clark, in part because he had more time. Brian and Kerri Rader, who'd gone to the church as youngsters, had left home. After attending Kansas State University, Kerri had moved to Michigan, while her brother was serving in the military in Connecticut. With their children gone, Dennis and Paula faithfully went to church every Sunday morning, preferably the second service, which began at 10:45. Paula sang in the choir and her husband performed the small tasks that made everything run smoothly: greeting worshippers at the front door, handing out programs for the day's service, checking the sound system to make sure it was loud enough without feedback, lighting the candles on the altar, taking the collection, and doing everything he could to help Pastor Clark. Rader hovered around the minister, and the preacher had come to rely so much on his vice president that sometimes he asked Rader to take care of a chore without even turning around to make sure the man was nearby. He knew Dennis would be there for any request he could make.

The two were opposites in many ways. The minister was outgoing and funny, Rader quiet and reserved; the preacher was spontaneous, but the vice president expected everything to go precisely to schedule and a detailed plan. Pastor Clark and his wife, Jan, weren't quite friends of the Raders'—Dennis and Paula were close to few people at Christ Lutheran. The Raders occasionally invited other churchgoers into their home but had always maintained a certain distance. Everybody liked Paula, who was warm and friendly, but Dennis only loosened up when talking about one of his interests, such as college football, and his favorite team, the Kansas State Wildcats up the road in Manhattan. Football brought him out of himself, as almost nothing else could.

Pastor Clark had come to rely so heavily on Rader because he had a lot to do to get ready for Sunday mornings, both mentally and emotionally. In addition to writing his sermon and preparing to deliver it, he felt a special pang whenever he looked out at the congregation for the 10:45 service and his eyes settled on the back row. His son, Tim, was in the last pew, sitting in a wheelchair. Next to Tim was the person employed this morning to assist him—a rotating group of four adults shared this job—and Tim's Seeing Eye dog, Tai. The pastor's son could only be left alone when he was sleeping.

February 2, 1998, had been a foggy night in Beloit, Kansas, a balmy evening for the middle of winter. Driving visibility was poor and it was best to stay off the highways, but Tim had taken his Dodge Dakota out for a spin. There wasn't much traffic and the twenty-two-year-old was moving easily through the fog, but couldn't make out the approaching embankment at the end of the road. At the last moment, trying to adjust the steering wheel and slamming on the brakes, he lost control of the truck and it rolled end-over-end three times before landing right-side-up. Tim was thrown from the cab, landing in a plowed cornfield, but not before banging his head on the interior. The blow instantly caused brain trauma and he was near death.

"We got a call from the hospital," says Pastor Clark, "and they told us we'd better come there right away."

In the emergency room, Tim's heart stopped twice but started beating again. For the next ten days, the doctors weren't sure he would live, but slowly he began to pull through, and the medical staff assessed the long-term damage. Tim's cognitive skills were seriously diminished: he was aware of his surroundings and could talk to people, but not form complete sentences. His short-term memory was limited, he would be confined to a wheelchair and could walk only if another person was supporting him. A muscle flap in his windpipe had stopped responding, and occasionally he had to be reminded to swallow to avoid choking. All the fluids he consumed had to be the consistency of runny pudding, his meals had to be specially made, and he needed care throughout the sixteen hours a day he was awake. He was vulnerable to bacterial pneumonia.

Pastor Clark's faith had been tested once in seminary, when he'd chosen to confront his birth parents about his childhood anger, and a second test had now arrived.

"Not once," he says, "did I ever question *why* this happened, but I did at first have trouble understanding where God was in the midst of all this chaos in my life. In the state of shock we were in, you can only see and feel chaos and pain. When Tim was in intensive care, I could have yelled in anger at God or accepted what had happened and that it wasn't God's fault. God wasn't the one getting angry—I was. I'm the one who had to reconcile all this. My pride and my ego were in the way, and I had to get over that.

"My faith got me through this—I knew there was a loving God who cared and He was not causing this evil to happen. It wasn't because I was a minister that I believed this. It was because I could begin to see God in the actions of the people reaching out to help my family in a time of crisis. They sat with us in the hospital and relieved us when we were spent from being there with Tim. They cared for us when we were coming unraveled.

"One night we went out to dinner, and when we came back to the hospital, I knew something was wrong. The oxygen supply wasn't working on his tracheotomy tube and the ventilator had no exhaust in it, no vapor. Nothing was happening and he wasn't getting any oxygen. Nobody was doing anything about it and he was going to die. A resident was in charge and he wanted to move Tim to a new room and try to fix this. My son was in a semi-coma and his body was producing a bacterial infection in his lungs that had to be treated or it could have killed him. I told the resident to get someone in there who could help him—now! So he did. A resident was never going to learn how to be a doctor on my son."

For thirty days and nights, the Clarks stayed beside Tim in the hospital, before he could finally be removed from his bed. He was taken home, and an entirely new routine—an entirely new life—began for the parents and the patient. Nothing would ever again be the same for Tim's father.

"A lot of things died on the night of February second, 1998," Pastor Clark says. "I lost a son."

While recovering from his own pain over the accident, the minister decided that something in his life had to change and the best solution was to take action—do something unpredictable. He commenced studying how to be a clown, so he could entertain adults and children and help those struggling with grief, and was soon wearing a polka-dot outfit, a yellow mop on his head, a red ball on his nose, and performing jokes or tricks in public, as Rufus. The minister may have laughed at the clown's antics more than anyone else. He played Rufus during the last two years of his ministry in Beloit, before receiving the call to come to Park City and take over at Christ Lutheran. He almost never started the new job.

On December 30, 2000, he'd just finished writing his final reports for the Beloit church when he felt what he thought was a bad case of indigestion. This didn't entirely surprise him. He hated doing paperwork, and whenever he was forced to, it put him in the kind of testy mood that could bring on stomach pain. Eating was clearly the way to solve this, but once he'd had something to eat, the pain didn't go away. In fact, he felt worse.

"At nine p.m., I went to the emergency room at the Beloit hospital and the doctor told me I was trying to have a heart attack," he says, laughing. "There was blockage in the lower back side of my heart, and my blood pressure was bumpin' the ceiling pretty tight. This doctor was in my congregation and he said, 'We better get you out of here 'cause you might need bypass surgery.' He wanted to fly me to Wichita, but I don't like flying. Not even when I'm having a heart attack. They put me in a car and two hours later I was in a Wichita hospital. The driver was pushin' it hard.

"My first week in Wichita I was supposed to be at my new job but I was in a hospital bed recovering. Many of the folks at Christ Lutheran came by to see me. Dennis and Paula visited and were wonderful."

XX

By mid-August 2004, the Wichita authorities were becoming frustrated over the lack of progress in the case and considering new actions. On August 20, the WPD released information about former Wichita State professor P. J. Wyatt and the poem "Oh! Death to Nancy," which BTK had mailed to KAKE-TV back in 1978. A week later, Lieutenant Landwehr publicized the poem BTK had written to Anna Williams in June 1979. For a quarter century, the police had kept these writings secret.

"This poem," Lieutenant Landwehr said, referring to the one addressed to Anna Williams, "appears to be an original writing, as an extensive search has not found this to be a known, published work."

The lieutenant's latest statement was met with a collective groan all over town. Many longtime observers of the case felt certain that it reflected just how little headway the police had made in finding the killer, five months after BTK had resurfaced. If they had anything resembling a solid lead, would they be talking publicly about a twenty-five-year-old verse? If they had a DNA match to any suspect on a list that now ran into the thousands, they wouldn't be fooling around with the overheated words of a frustrated poet. Despite the recent communications BTK had sent to the media and the police, the investigation was stalling out once again, even though detectives kept swabbing local white males and doing other legwork. If all this weren't troubling enough, vandals in Wichita had started spray painting or writing BTK on surfaces across the city. They too were mocking law enforcement.

The WPD and FBI didn't have a solid lead but were encouraged that the killer had continued speaking with them through his writings, puzzles, and drawings. The plan remained the same as it had been last March—don't upset or aggravate him into committing a crime; don't drive him away by appearing too hostile or hungry to make an arrest; let him feel comfortable sending in messages to the police; keep him building a relationship with Lieutenant Landwehr and let him come to us. Part of Lieutenant Landwehr's job was maintaining an air of hope and optimism, not just for those working below him but for the city at large. With his thick swatch of silver hair and pleasant but serious demeanor, he tried to convey a feeling of patience and determination, of getting neither too high nor too low no matter what came next. Waiting was a necessary part of the game, and by August 2004, Landwehr had waited twenty years to engage in a dialogue with BTK. He'd have to wait two more months before the man reached out again. Throughout this long silent stretch, Landwehr had to wonder if their strategy was working and if he'd made any connection with BTK. He couldn't have known that his trusting voice was sinking into the man slowly and taking hold. In the meantime, plenty of cigarettes and Mountain Dew kept him going.

On the night of September 16, the anniversary of Vicki Wegerle's 1986 murder, the police conducted round-the-clock surveillance at her grave at Resthaven cemetery and repeated this the following night. BTK was never known to frequent graveyards, but the police felt they had to check out this possibility because in the past few years, in mid-September, Vicki's family had told detectives, flowers had been stolen from her plot. Investigators spent hours parked in the shadows of the cemetery, but nobody came near her resting place.

XXI

A S HE'D GOTTEN TO KNOW the congregation at Christ Lutheran, Pastor Clark was pleased about taking this new position. Everyone at the church was good to him and concerned about his health and that of his son. Each February the membership put on a Sweetheart Banquet—a fund-raiser held in conjunction with Valentine's Day, with the money going for religious activities. One year he and Jan sat across from the Raders at the banquet and enjoyed their company. Paula and Dennis were friendly without being open, but always eager to talk about the goings-on at Christ Lutheran. The small church had an undeniable sense of informality and intimacy and a down-home atmosphere. In the summer of 2005, a notice in one of the bulletins read, "If anyone has a light-weight, portable sewing machine to donate to our quilting ladies, please contact . . ."

At the same time, Christ Lutheran had tried to stay current with the latest trends in faith-based therapy by offering assistance to members who were struggling with personal issues and problems. One arm of the church called the Stephen Ministries produced a brochure—"Stephen Ministries Are Ready to Care"—available in the lobby. The cover read, "Hurting? Struggling? Discouraged? Stressed? Confused? Broken?" Inside, the brochure explained, "Our congregation's Stephen Ministry equips lay people to provide confidential one-to-one Christian care to individuals in our congregation and community who are experiencing difficulties in their lives." A Stephen Minister was "A Child of God who walks beside a person who is hurting" and a layperson with at least "50 hours of training in providing emotional and spiritual care." Church elders also offered a special laying-on-of-hands ceremony, taken from the Bible and designed to heal feelings. Unlike Pastor Clark, Rader never felt compelled to speak to anyone about his inner life or demons and could deal with things alone. During church or a social activity, he was a model of strength and consistency, opening doors for elderly women and passing out crayons to young kids so they'd stay busy and quiet throughout the sermon. Every detail he handled helped the operation run more efficiently and made Pastor Clark's job easier, so he could focus on delivering his Christian message.

The minister was a born entertainer, and at Sunday-morning services he moved around the sanctuary a lot, walking up and down the center aisle and evoking an emcee at an awards dinner. His outgoing personality stood in sharp contrast to the church's quiet congregation and spare decorations. From the beginning, Lutherans were determined to be different from Catholics in several ways. Catholicism had long been distinguished by its art and architecture: Europe was covered with brilliant examples of cathedrals, paintings, sculptures, and other aesthetic treasures created by this faith. The Lutherans decided to pare down the trappings of their religion, and the results of that decision could be seen nearly five hundred years later in the small church outside Park City. Christ Lutheran had a vaulted wooden ceiling and walls made of cement blocks painted white. No art was present inside the sanctuary, which was bare except for a few crosses and three tall, white candles. Like the landscape around the church, with its open fields and pasture, the sanctuary was uncluttered and worshippers no longer got dressed up for the services. None of the men wore ties.

When new members came forward to be baptized, they stood before Pastor Clark and he asked them one daunting question: "Do you renounce all the forces of evil, the devil, and all his empty promises?"

The answer was always "I do," and the minister welcomed the worshipper into the church.

Catholicism had institutionalized the ritual of confession—of privately going to a priest and formally declaring one's sins so they could be absolved. The Lutherans abolished this sacrament, and at Christ

Lutheran each Sunday, the entire congregation said out loud, "Lord, we confess our sin. You have promised to provide all of our needs, and yet we mistrust your promise. We know the futility of our own ambitions and our inability to do that which we desire. Today we recognize the sin within us and ask that You forgive us . . . and cleanse us so that we are pleasing in Your sight and minister in Your service."

Pastor Clark responded with "Our God Is a great God. He provides for all our needs. He gives us daily bread and meets every spiritual need. Our sin no longer controls us. Our response to His love is the focus for our lives. The death of His Son, Jesus Christ, has paid the cost of our sin and has set us free to live in victory. We are forgiven. We are sons and daughters of the King. We are ministers to each other. Praise God for His daily provision for our every need."

Rader spoke these words and listened to the minister's assuring message, safe and secure in the knowledge that his sins had been paid for—no matter what they were or how close they came to his church.

In 1985, he'd begun stalking a fifty-three-year-old woman living six doors down the street from him. He hadn't fulfilled a project in years, in part because he'd been so busy supporting and raising his family or going to church and becoming a Cub Scout leader, but this lady had gotten his attention. Marine Hedge was a neighborly presence on the block, always smiling or waving at others and willing to chat with those passing by. Paula and Dennis had known her for years even though he'd rarely spoken to her. Born in Arkansas, she had a friendly Southern manner and remained connected to her background through her cooking, by making catfish and hush puppies, and in her tone of voice, which reminded some people of country singer Dolly Parton. Less than five feet tall, she always dressed well in a petite size, with her shoes, jewelry, and accessories meticulously coordinated. The mother of four grown children, and now a grandmother, she was recently widowed and employed at a coffee shop at nearby Wesley Medical Center. She filled her spare time working in her yard, playing bingo at a local parlor, and attending the Baptist church.

Rader had always avoided carrying out a project this close to home—"in his own habitat," as he put it to himself—but stalking Marine had its advantages. Her address made it easy to study her routines, and she was the right age. After fighting with Nancy Fox and getting clawed in the testicles, he no longer wanted to target a younger woman who might be able to cause flesh wounds or leave marks on his face. Marine was thirteen years older than he was, lived alone, and did not have a dog; Rex did not like dogs. Rader had been watching her to see when she had company, especially male companionship, but didn't think she entertained men very often. By springtime, after trolling and stalking her for months, he was ready for Project Cookie.

On the evening of Friday, April 26, 1985, he put on his Cub Scout uniform and drove out of town with the other scouting fathers and sons to attend an all-night camping event. April showers had come in abundance this year and the ground was muddy. He stayed with the others for a while at the campsite, but complained of a headache and said he was going home. Stopping on a country road, he changed from his Cub uniform into dark clothing. He went to a bowling alley, where he ordered a beer and deliberately spilled it on himself so he would smell of alcohol and appear drunk, then called a taxi and had it drop him near his home.

"I need to walk a little bit," he said to the cabdriver in a slurred voice. "I need to wear this off."

Carrying a bowling bag, he made his way down to Marine's house, taking a roundabout route that led him through Paula's parents' yard. Snipping Marine's phone line with a wire cutter, he broke in through the back door with a screwdriver, but Marine wasn't there. He was surprised, because her vehicle was in the driveway, and wandered around inside her home for a while, studying the layout, until he heard a male voice and a car door slam. As Marine and her boyfriend came into the house, he ducked into a closet in her bedroom and settled down to wait. In the past, he'd used ropes or belts or panty hose or cord for a project, but this time he'd decided on something outrageously new.

The man stayed a long time as Rader grew more and more restless and upset. Following the Otero and Bright killings, he never wanted to encounter a male again in the middle of a project. He thought about shooting or knifing the visitor, but that wasn't part of the plan. He wasn't on the clock tonight, in terms of getting home to Paula, so he forced himself to be patient and eventually the boyfriend got up to leave. After hearing the car drive off, he waited some more, until Marine came into the bedroom and began undressing and preparing for sleep. Still, he didn't make a movement or sound, trying to breathe more quietly than normal. She lay down, turned off the night-light, and quickly lost consciousness. He stepped out of the closet and flipped on a bathroom light, but this didn't wake her, so he got on the bed. Tonight would be different from all the rest. He'd made so many plans and rehearsed this so many times in his mind that alive or dead she would go along with it until his fantasies were fulfilled.

"What in the hell is going on?" the terrified woman said as she came to.

He wasted no time with conversation, grabbing her neck and choking her with both hands, as she tried to fight back. When she was partially subdued, he handcuffed her and tightened his grip on her throat, but then his hands began to cramp. He tried to shake off the numbness, but the cramps intensified. He should have planned for this and been exercising with that rubber squeeze ball he'd once used to build up endurance in his hands. Bending over her, it took all his strength to refocus his energy and kill her, and once that was done, he sat down on the bed and gathered himself, amazed at how much resistance she'd offered.

People didn't die easily in real life, Rader reminded himself, the way they did when getting strangled in the movies.

He gathered up her keys, some coins, and her driver's license, then stripped her, wrapped her in blankets, and dragged her outside to her car, a 1976 Monte Carlo. In all his years of completing projects, he'd never moved a dead body before and couldn't believe how heavy and awkward this one was, even though Marine weighed only a hundred pounds. He put her in the trunk of her car and started the engine, wanting to take her to a barn, as he'd once done with cats and dogs as a child, but that was too risky because barns were always on someone's personal property. Instead he drove over to Christ Lutheran—the old Christ Lutheran church—located where the new one would be built a decade later. He had a key to the entrance and let himself in.

Weeks earlier, he'd stashed rolls of black plastic at the church, along with thumbtacks. After tacking the plastic over the windows so that no one passing by in the middle of the night would see lights burning within, he pulled Marine from the trunk, dragged her into the church, and took her down to the basement, laying her out on the floor on a blanket. Wrapping part of her nude figure in black plastic, he tied her hands behind her, put black high heels on her feet, and a gag in her mouth. Posing her facedown, he brought out a Polaroid camera from his bowling bag and took a series of pictures of her in bondage positions. He got so busy arranging her body, trying out new ideas for snapshots, and creating these images that he lost track of time. This was his artwork—the kind of thing he'd always dreamed of doing—and he wasn't going to quit until he was satisfied. When he'd finished photographing her and cleaning up the basement, he looked outside and felt panic: the sun was already coming up and he had to rejoin his Scout troop at daybreak.

Unwrapping her, he hauled her outside, put her in the trunk, drove to a remote area, took a ring off her finger, and dumped her body in a culvert in a drainage ditch, alongside a couple of dog carcasses. After covering her with debris, he was drenched with sweat and went back to the church to wash up and change into his Cub Scout uniform. Driving fast to the campsite, he got there just before 7:30. When he arrived, nobody asked where he'd been and he tried to act normal, but throughout that day he felt agitated because he'd left a small piece of cord near the culvert, and if anyone found it and gave it to the police, they might connect it to BTK—a stupid oversight. He'd gone out of his way to change his mode of operation for this project, leaving the body outdoors rather than indoors, but the cord could give him away. When the scouting event ended, he returned to the culvert and was filled with relief; the evidence was still there.

On Monday, Marine didn't show up for work at Wesley Medical

Center and her relatives began searching for the woman. No one stumbled onto her body for several days, and by then it had started to decompose. Because of where the corpse had been found, near Park City, and because of the exterior location of the victim, neither the local police nor the WPD viewed her death as part of the unsolved BTK murders. They would come to the same conclusion the following year about another homicide in Wichita.

In September 1986, Rader's employer, ADT, was going through management upheaval and his bosses were out of the office much of the time. Free from supervision, he decided to pursue things other than working. In the past three weeks, he'd been walking past the same house over and over, listening to the sounds of a piano coming from an open window. The musician was talented and the beautiful chords and notes appealed to him. At ten o'clock on the morning on September 16, the piano player, Vicki Wegerle, had just returned home from driving her nine-year-old daughter, Stephanie, to school, and was taking care of her two-year-old son, Brandon. As Rader knocked at her address, he heard her at the keys, but she stopped to answer the door. He wore a hard hat with an SBC logo, which stood for Southwestern Bell, and showed Vicki a fake Southwestern Bell ID, saying he needed to check her telephone terminals because of a static problem. She let him in but then said that her dogs, running loose in the backyard, should come into the house. Rader talked her out of that while conducting a fake test of her phone. As Brandon played near them on the floor, Rader dropped the testing equipment into his briefcase and pulled out a gun.

"Let's go to the bedroom," he said, in a flat matter-of-fact manner.

She began to cry and moved toward her son. "How about my kid?"

"I don't know about your kid."

"My husband's going to be home pretty soon."

"I hope he won't be home too soon."

He forced her into the bedroom and started tying her up with leather shoestrings, but she fought back against him on the bed and they crashed onto the floor. She scratched his face, as the child yelled in the next room and the dogs yelped in the backyard and Rader struggled to gain control over her, fearing that her husband would walk in at any moment. Overcoming her, he began strangling her with a pair of her own nylon stockings and the leather laces, as Vicki begged for her life and then prayed in front of him, while her son played in the living room. As she neared death, he snapped the pictures of her that he would hold on to for the next eighteen years, before mailing them to the *Wichita Eagle* and reigniting the BTK investigation in March 2004.

At noon, Vicki's husband, Bill, came home for lunch, but it took him fifteen minutes to find the tied-up victim in the next room.

He called 911.

"Vicki, Vicki, Vicki, Vicki, Vicki," he moaned to the dispatcher, staring at his partially naked wife on the bedroom floor. "Oh, God. Oh no, no, no, no!"

He told the dispatcher that on his ride home he'd seen a man driving what looked like his own vehicle, a 1978 gold Monte Carlo, in the opposite direction. Rader had stolen the car and dumped his briefcase and hard hat, after tearing off the SBC logo and pocketing it for his archives. Abandoning the Wegerle car at a shopping center, he walked to his truck and drove off, seeing Emergency Medical Services responding to the crime scene.

If stopped by law enforcement, Rader decided he'd have to shoot to kill, but no one noticed him and Project Piano was complete.

For the next eighteen years, Bill Wegerle was under suspicion in the death of his wife, in part because he took—and failed—two polygraph tests about his involvement in the homicide. During that time, his children were taunted at school by other kids who said their father was a murderer.

XXII

A T ONE POINT IN THE Sunday services at Christ Lutheran, Pastor Clark liked to ask all the young children to walk up to the
front of the sanctuary and gather round him, while he sat down on
the floor beside them. Surrounded by boys and girls, he talked to
them gently about love and family and faith, about their joys and
fears, telling them that sometimes he was afraid of things and it was
okay for them to admit they were afraid too. If they got scared at
night, it was all right for them to hold on to a stuffed animal or go
jump in their parents' bed. As a child, he'd been frightened of the distant sound of trains, and it was normal to feel fear, but the kids
should always remember a couple of important things. They could
trust Jesus to protect them, they could trust their parents to do the
same, and they could trust the church to protect them too. The minister had a light touch with the youngsters, and it was moving to see
them look up at him with their big eyes and ask their off-beat questions or gaze away from him and tie their shoes. It was a naturally
funny situation, and Pastor Clark used humor every chance he got as
part of his mission at the church.

Each Sunday, all the congregants took a few moments for the
Sharing of the Peace, when everybody turned to his or her neighbors
in the pews, smiled, shook their hands, and said, "Peace be with
you." During this ritual, Pastor Clark went up and down the center
aisle, addressing each row with these same four words, and calling
everyone in the church by a first name. The unpretentious, homey
atmosphere of Christ Lutheran was never so strong as when you were
looking into the eyes of those standing next to you and speaking this

sentence. Even if you were a stranger and only visiting the church, it was impossible not to feel genuinely welcome here or feel warmth and friendliness toward those shaking your hand. Less than a hundred people were usually in the sanctuary during this moment of closeness.

Every Sunday at the 8:30 a.m. service and twice a month at the 10:45 a.m. service, Pastor Clark gave Communion. Row by row, the worshippers stood and the pews emptied out as people came forward and knelt at the foot of the altar, candles glowing above their heads, while the minister reached down and gave them the bread and wine representing the body and blood of Christ. A distinguishing trait of the Lutheran faith, compared to many other Protestant denominations, concerned the "transubstantiation" that took place during Communion. For Lutherans, the bread and wine were not merely symbols of Christ's flesh and blood but, once blessed by the minister, *became* these parts of the Savior Himself.

As Pastor Clark offered the sliver of bread and tiny container of wine to each of the faithful, he again addressed the kneeling men, women, and children by their first name:

"The body and blood of Christ, Dennis. . . . The body and blood of Christ, Paula."

It was a terribly intimate gesture, as the preacher's fingers went right up to the worshipper's lips, as if everyone partaking of this blessing had entered into a profound circle of shared belief and trust—a family really.

XXIII

O N OCTOBER 22, 2004, three decades to the day after BTK had first made contact with the media and taken credit for the Otero murders, Rader hoped to carry out a new project that had long been building in his imagination. Communicating with the police after twenty-five years of silence had stimulated him to do more than write or draw. Since the WPD hadn't made anything resembling a connection between himself and the killer, why not find another victim and make it his grand finale? He'd already finished trolling and stalking for this new project, narrowing down his choice to a locked-in target and planning to do something spectacularly grotesque. He'd break into her home, strangle her, wrap her in see-through plastic, and hang her from the ceiling with pulleys and ropes, reminiscent of what Hannibal "the Cannibal" Lecter had done to a security guard in the movie *Silence of the Lambs*. Rader called his projects BTK Productions and had always identified with film stars, especially James Bond (in how he dressed for his projects) or John Wayne (in how he handled a gun). When the police came to this new crime scene and found the victim stretched out over their heads, it would be unlike anything ever done in real life, but the murder was too complex to bring off.

Instead, on October 22, he left a plastic bag containing an envelope at a UPS drop box near the Omni Center and not far from downtown. UPS employees often found unmarked packages with mailing instructions and a check inside, but not tonight. The envelope was labeled "BTK FIELD GRAMS" and contained a plastic Baggies filled with three-by-five-inch cards, each card holding either a photograph or writing. The words were too small to make out easily, but not the photos. Some were collages of pictures of children, cut from magazines, with Rader's own drawings of bindings across their faces and bodies. Another picture showed a woman kneeling on the floor, her hands bound behind her and a rope in her mouth, terror frozen in her eyes. The images were so disturbing that the UPS workers immediately called the police, and the next day Detective Otis met with them. He didn't specifically bring up the BTK investigation, but told them to be on the lookout for a man in his fifties or sixties with a medium build and gray hair.

In this package, one piece of writing was a poem addressed to "Detective Ken Landwehr" and threatened the BTK detectives with death. Other words were so tiny they couldn't be read with the naked eye and had to be magnified before police could discern that BTK had sent in more chapters of his book. The package was given to the FBI, which verified it was from the killer. The threats and new chapters intensified the investigation, which had been wavering from a lack of progress. In early November, the WPD and the FBI started working together full-time on the case. As the task force continued swabbing and running down tips, Agents Ray Lundin and Larry Thomas of the KBI left their Topeka office and took up residence in Wichita. The feds installed surveillance cameras where "Communication #3" had been dropped off the previous June at First and Kansas and where the most recent package had shown up in late October.

One November evening, as the task force was working downtown, Rader heard a ruckus in his backyard and went out to look around. Behind his home was a metal shed, holding a number of accessories he'd used on projects over the years: panty hose, duct tape, cords, and rope. The noise was coming from the shed, and when he opened the door, he saw two young people making love among his personal items. He startled them and said they were breaking the law—a sticking point with him and something he couldn't tolerate. The offenders had to be punished, so Rader called the police, who drove out to his home, interviewed the couple, and arrested the man. When the cops inspected the property for damage, they didn't notice the panty hose or cord in the shed.

In November, WPD chief Norman Williams flew to Quantico, Virginia, to FBI headquarters to consult with serial killer experts. While he was on the East Coast, Lieutenant Landwehr kept working with federal agents in Wichita, whose office was on the fourth floor of the Epic Center downtown. The media followed every police move, and the case was still generating a lot of public attention, which spiked every time BTK sent a new communication to the press or the police. Speculation was running high that the killer might want to be caught. Perhaps he had a terminal illness, only months to live, and didn't want to die without getting recognition for his criminal career. The push was on now from every side to break the case, and a feeling was rising that they might find him by the end of the year.

After careful study of the writing in the October package, Lieutenant Landwehr held another press conference on November 30. The authorities had concluded that the apparently autobiographical material contained in this communication might be useful, even though it was risky to assume BTK had told them the truth. He obviously wanted to be in control of this situation, and to control the actions of others, but the police didn't see many other options.

Once again, Lieutenant Landwehr directed his remarks not just to reporters and Wichita citizens, but to the killer:

"Since March 2004, BTK has sent numerous communications to the media and the police. In these letters, he has provided certain background information about himself, which he claims is accurate. Based upon a review of that information, the following facts about BTK are being made available to the public in the hopes of identifying BTK.

"He claims he was born in 1939, which would make his current age sixty-four or sixty-five. His father died in World War II, and his mother raised him. His mother was forced to work, so his grandparents cared for him. His mother worked during the day near the railroad. He had a cousin named Susan, who moved to Missouri. His family moved a lot, but always lived near a railroad. His grandfather played the fiddle and died of a lung disease. His mother started dating a railroad detective when BTK was around eleven years old. This relationship would have occurred during the years 1950–55.

"In the early 1970s, he built and operated a ham radio. He has participated in outdoor hobbies including hunting, fishing, and camping. As a youth he attended church and Sunday school. He had a female Hispanic acquaintance named Petra, who had a younger sister named Tina. Around 1960, he went to tech military school. He then joined the military for active duty and was discharged in 1966. He has a basic knowledge of photography and the ability to develop and print pictures. In 1966 he moved back in with his mother, who had remarried and was renting out part of her house. His first job was as an electromechanic, requiring some travel. After attending more tech school, he worked repairing copiers and business equipment. This sometimes required travel and he was away from home for extended periods.

"He admits to soliciting prostitutes. He has a lifetime fascination with railroads and trains.

"Based upon the investigation to date, police believe that BTK frequented the WSU campus in the early 1970s and was acquainted with P. J. Wyatt, who taught a folklore class at WSU during the 1970s; has written or still writes poetry. An example of this is the 'Oh, Anna, Why Didn't You Appear' poem and the 'Oh! Death to Nancy' poem that were released in earlier media advisories. And he has utilized fake identification to gain access to people's homes or to conduct surveillance.

"Based on the information contained in the letter, police are again asking for help from the public. Police want to talk to any citizen who currently knows or recalls anyone having a similar background to the one described above."

The problem was that this background was largely misleading, with almost all of the dates wrong. Rader wasn't born in 1939, but 1945, and his father hadn't died in the Second World War. In a part of the letter that Lieutenant Landwehr had omitted from the press conference, BTK claimed that his first sexual experience had come in 1955, when he would have been ten years old. The authorities also decided not to disclose that BTK had written that one time in Texas he'd watched the making of a "snuff film," in which the death—or staged death—of a person was captured on camera. During the shooting of this film, he'd seen a Hispanic woman being tortured and killed, and for him this was a sexual turn-on. He claimed that this event had occurred before he'd committed any serious crimes and was a formative experience leading to his desire to combine sex with violence. Whether he was fabricating all this is unknown, but no record exists of his associating with the kinds of people (angry drug dealers or very far underground moviemakers in Los Angeles or Mexico) who might create a snuff film.

BTK's family hadn't moved after settling in Park City when he was young, and his mother hadn't raised him alone. Rader didn't have a lifelong fascination with trains, but one of his younger brothers did. He didn't leave the army in 1966, but 1970, and didn't solicit Wichita prostitutes—something the police strongly hoped he'd done because one of these women might have been able to identify a man with such unusual erotic habits. Prostitution wasn't his style. He was cautious when spending money and wary of diseases, but beyond that he may have considered that having sex with another woman besides his wife was immoral and outside the boundaries of his religious beliefs. He'd never actually engaged in direct sexual activity with any known partner other than Paula. As those who'd worked with him at ADT and later as a compliance officer in Park City had discovered, he was a humorless prude.

The letter was filled with falsehoods, but in the eyes of law enforcement it still had value. BTK was continuing to write the police and revealing more than he realized. The most striking psychological factor in the letter was that he appeared not to have been raised by a father—leaving the man for dead in World War II. Those with expertise in studying serial killers jumped on this lie because it fit the pattern of many sex offenders or other sociopaths who'd come of age without a father. Rader wasn't fatherless until 1996, when he was past fifty, but his strongest parental identification was with his mother. The letter focused much more on the person who'd given birth to him, disciplined him, and spanked him until he became aroused. For decades his obsession had been with women and having power over them, using them for sadistic fantasies, and ending their lives. The men who'd crossed his path during the crimes—

Joseph Otero, Kevin Bright, and the two sons of Shirley Vian—were there by chance or mistake.

It was the women in his neighborhood whom he barely spoke to if he was having a conversation with their husbands; and women he went out of his way to intimidate and ticket if he felt they were violating the least significant laws in Park City; and women whose clothes, wigs, masks, and makeup he put on after driving to his parents' house, going down into their basement, and taking pictures of himself with a rope around his neck.

In the absence of a DNA match or any solid lead, the WPD was forced to take seriously the contents of the letters and steer their investigation in the directions the killer was pointing. The details from Lieutenant Landwehr's latest pronouncement that made the largest impression on the public concerned trains. On December 1, less than twenty-four hours after releasing this information, the police received a call about a Hispanic man whom the tipster was positive was BTK. He was the right age, fit several other parts of the profile, and lived near some railroad tracks running through Wichita. The tip seemed solid, but the police took the cautionary steps of interrogating the informant several times and passing his personal information through a national background checking system known as the Interstate Identification Index. This produced no red flags and further convinced them to pursue the suspect. After eight months of exhaustive work, a solid lead had finally arrived. Optimism was surging on the sixth-floor City Hall offices of the WPD as the task force instantly swung into action, setting up surveillance at a business near the suspect's residence. Throughout December 1 they moved around the neighborhood gathering data on the man and preparing to close in. When the *Eagle* learned of this development, the paper sent a team to the location to cover the breaking story, which did not thrill law enforcement. Rumors were spreading to the national media that something big was up in Wichita—more than thirty years of hunting for a monster were coming to an end.

Five investigators, including a uniformed sergeant, knocked on the front door of the suspect's house, the back door, and the sliding doors, announcing loudly who they were. Receiving no response, they drew their guns and forced their way inside, where they located the man, handcuffed him, and showed him a search warrant. After some persuasion, the suspect opened his mouth and let himself be swabbed for DNA. As one set of officers dealt with him, another began looking though his home and snapping photos.

By evening, the man had been taken into custody, booked, and charged with the minor offense of trespassing. The initial point of the arrest was simply to let the authorities question him and get a DNA sample, while they searched his home and surrounding property. The next morning, the *Eagle* ran a small piece on the arrest but didn't report the suspect's name or connect him to the BTK investigation as everything rode on the outcome of the DNA test now in progress. Task force members were trying to stay calm, but the arrest had set off an atmosphere of near celebration inside the police department. Some of the most excited officers had only been working on the case for several months, but Lieutenant Landwehr, after two decades of unsuccessfully chasing BTK, warned them not to get carried away. Media personnel already had satellite trucks in town or were making plans to fly journalists into Wichita. The story had been building momentum since last March and was ready to erupt, but the test came back negative.

Instead of announcing the arrest of BTK, the WPD released the suspect and dismissed the trespassing charge (the man's name would eventually be publicized and he would sue). At 4 p.m. on the afternoon of December 2, Police Chief Norman Williams appeared before the media.

"We have not," he said, "and I repeat, we have *not* made an arrest in connection with BTK."

He did his best to play down the notion that the previous day's activities had had anything to do with the hunt for the serial killer, but it was a bad moment for the Wichita Police Department and the entire investigation. They'd been waiting for BTK to make a mistake, but now they'd made one and the press was losing patience. Many journalists covering the story were certain that Chief Williams wasn't speaking the whole truth, and some began making cynical jokes about those looking for BTK. If the police hadn't caught him by now and had started arresting the wrong people, what chance did they ever have of finding the right one? The case was just as cold as it had been last December, when BTK was still holding on to his twenty-five-year silence.

Lieutenant Landwehr had tried to warn the task force against congratulating itself before the killer was locked up, and the announcement by Chief Williams caused an inevitable letdown. It was dismal enough not to be able to find the killer, but to be ridiculed for their efforts made the situation worse. Landwehr told them to brush off the disappointment and get back to work.

XXIV

Eager to put the memory of the failed arrest behind them as quickly as possible, five days later the WPD launched another offensive by delivering a new public statement:

BTK MAY CHANGE REGULAR ROUTINE

Since the November 30 media release, police have received 350 tips. Since BTK resurfaced in March 2004, the Wichita Police Department has received more than 4,500 tips.

The Federal Bureau of Investigation Behavioral Analysis Unit told Wichita Police today, "Since the media release on November 30 outlining BTK's life story, and the subsequent community focus on the investigation, there may be observable changes in BTK's behavior."

The FBI indicates these behavioral changes could include disruption in his normal habits and routines. He may have minimized his contact with others; he may have unscheduled absences from work or doctor's appointments; and he may not be interacting with people as usual.

Police encourage any citizen with information to contact them.

As if to prove the authorities wrong again, Rader did not change his habits or stop his gamesmanship with law enforcement. It was deeply gratifying to see that he could create a piece of writing, send it out to the media or police, and see parts of it published in the newspaper or broadcast on television. If the WPD was getting what it wanted by building a dialogue with him, he was getting the satisfaction of delivering his ideas and words to the world. No one noticed any changes in him. He continued going to his job each day, prepared himself to assume the presidency at Christ Lutheran, and thought up new ways to torment the cops.

December 8, 2004—one day after Chief Williams's latest press release—marked the twenty-seventh anniversary of the murder of Nancy Fox. That evening, Rader went to a pay phone and called the Quik Trip convenience store near the 1977 location of Helzberg's Jewelry, where Nancy had worked. When an employee picked up the phone, he was told about a package near the intersection of Interstate 35, the north-south highway running through Wichita, and Ninth Street. The clerk didn't seem interested in this information, so Rader slammed down the receiver. It had probably been a crank call, but the clerk told his supervisor about it, and they phoned the police, who drove to the intersection and looked around with flashlights. They searched primarily two addresses, the University of Kansas School of Medicine building and the Sedgwick County Health Department, but saw nothing. They dug through some trash cans, one more dead end.

Across the street from the med school was a grassy plot known as Murdock Park, between Kansas and Minnesota avenues. Five days after the police had come up empty at the intersection, William Ervin was walking across the park and spotted a white plastic bag under a tree, but didn't stop. He was on the way to his brother's house and in a hurry, but on the walk home he spied the bag again and picked it up. Inside was a clear plastic bag holding a driver's license belonging to Nancy Fox, several pieces of paper, and a bound doll. The doll, with makeup on its eyes and lips and its arms tied behind its back with tan panty hose, was wrapped in a clear plastic bag, and the license had been attached to the doll's ankles. Two pages in the bag were entitled "CHAPTER 9: HITS: PJ FOXTAIL—12-8-1977," and described the death of Nancy Fox.

After Ervin took the bag home and called KAKE, the TV station contacted the police, who gave the new materials to the FBI for analysis. On December 15, the *Eagle* reported on the latest BTK communication, while detectives canvassed the city to learn where to buy this kind of doll. It had come from a Dollar General store, and Sedgwick County had twenty-six of these franchise outlets. The police studied video surveillance of people buying the dolls at local Dollar Generals, but everybody who'd recently bought one and been caught on tape was female. The white bag holding this communication had come from Leeker's grocery store in Park City, where Rader's mother and wife had both worked. For the first time ever, the police could connect a piece of BTK evidence to the small town north of Wichita, but at the time the bag didn't seem very relevant.

As 2004 came to a close and Rader enjoyed a quiet holiday season with his family and his beloved dog, Dudley, task force members were spending more time away from their relatives, conducting round-the-clock surveillance at Murdock Park and the main branch of the public library; at First and Kansas, where Rader had dropped off "Communication #3" back in June; at Second and Kansas, where "Communication #5" had been left in late October; and at Third and Kansas, which seemed a likely candidate for a new package (BTK wasn't that predictable). At Murdock Park, police stopped numerous middle-aged, white males lingering in the area or driving their cars slowly around the perimeter, but nothing came of these efforts.

On December 30, trying to end the year on a positive note, Chief Williams met with reporters, updated them on the case, and asked the public for more tips. He promised to bring closure to the survivors of the victims, spoke of how stressful the investigation was on his detectives, and added that he'd encouraged them to try to be with their families over Christmas.

"This is a very thorough, systematic, patient investigation," he said. "There is a continuous dedication of resources, seven days a week."

Journalists were respectful toward Williams, but the botched arrest last December 1 hung in the air above the press conference. The year 2004 was concluding the way every other year had since 1974, with the WPD no nearer to catching BTK than it had been for three decades. A lot more than cheerleading was needed to convince reporters or anyone else that the task force could ever succeed.

XXV

I N THE LAST WEEK of the old year, a tsunami hit Southern Asia and killed roughly 250,000 people in the worst natural disaster in recorded human history. On the other side of the world, a different kind of weather was settling in. During the first week of 2005, an ice storm blasted eastern Kansas—caving in roofs and wrecking cars, knocking out electrical power, and sending heating bills soaring. Dorothea Rader, Rader's seventy-nine-year-old mother, who still lived in Park City, lost her electricity and was without heat or lights for several days. Like Pastor Clark, she knew that she could count on her oldest son to take care of things, no matter how bad they got. Dennis and Paula took turns staying with her so she wouldn't suffer any more worry or inconvenience than was necessary. Dennis had always been a dutiful husband, son, and father, regardless of what else he was doing. One of his younger brothers, he liked telling people, had been the black sheep of the family.

As Rader looked out for his aging mother, he was welcomed into office as the new president of Christ Lutheran, chairing his first meeting of the twelve-member council. He was as prepared for these duties and as efficient in this role as he'd always been at the church; his transition from vice president to president went off without a hitch. Everyone on the council, including Donn Bischoff, a former church president who'd known and admired Rader for years, was delighted he'd taken the job. In the midst of all these developments, he still found time to create a new message for the WPD and planned his next drop-off, not far from home. Almost everything he did as BTK now was in the vicinity of Park City, and had been for some time. In 1985, he'd killed Marine Hedge, who'd lived just up the street from him. Six years later, he'd repeated this pattern.

In January 1991, he began trolling and stalking sixty-two-year-old Dolores Davis, whose house was a half mile east of Park City, near a dog kennel. A handsome grandmother who'd retired from an oil and gas company, she lived alone and worked part-time selling Mary Kay products to her friends and neighbors. Dolores liked the Mary Kay line for ethical and political reasons: the company didn't test its products on animals. Raised on a Nebraska farm, she very early developed a love for dogs and cats and horses. As an adult, she became a passionate defender of animal rights and liked nothing more than sitting on the couch with her grandchildren and watching movies about four-legged creatures.

Rader's plan for Dolores—Project Dogside—was his most complex and ambitious to date. He'd studied her residence by riding his bicycle into the countryside, back and forth past her small, white house, and making mental notes about the best approach. One night he sneaked up to her window and peered in, but her cat heard him and slapped the window with its paw, scaring him off. At least there wasn't a man in the house. Rader needed time to do everything with Dolores that he wanted to do, so he again employed the ruse of going on a midwinter, weekend camping trip with the Scouts, the annual Trappers Rendezvous held at Harvey County Park West.

The first evening, a Friday, he stayed with the Scouts long enough to set up camp before slipping away from his troop. He rode back to his parents' home—they were out of town—and changed into dark clothing. Driving to the Park City Baptist Church, he left his car and walked east toward Dolores's home, thumbing through the final preparations in his mind. Even though his feet hurt, he didn't go straight to her house but took a lengthy detour across a wheat field and then a cemetery, building his anticipation.

He looked at the headstones and imagined what was about to happen, a madman in dark clothing wandering through a graveyard carrying a black bag full of weapons. Rex was out in full force tonight, stalking in the moonlight with the other nocturnal Kansas predators: the raccoons, coyotes, and wildcats. They all hunted in the darkness until finding something to attack and taking it down. He'd become one of them, and in the cemetery he worked himself into a frenzy of desire and bloodlust. Nothing had ever stopped him and nothing would stop him now. He was invincible. Jack the Ripper hadn't been caught and neither would he. You really could fool all of the people all of the time because people wanted to be fooled. They wanted to think the best of others and gave you the benefit of every doubt if you were just polite and seemed normal. They wanted to believe they saw things as they really were because that made them feel good and safe and protected, but nobody was protected from him. He knew exactly how to play them and had been doing it his whole life. Get a regular job, work hard, go to church, introduce people to your wife and kids, make a fine appearance, be a Cub Scout leader, say all the right things, and you could be as perverse and as violent as you wanted to be. Nobody wanted to go below the surface these days, not even in a small town, because they were all too distracted. Nobody wanted to know who you really were. Even Paula had always been too busy to notice.

Society was made up of suckers, as all good con men knew. Get it to look in one direction and you could do whatever you wanted in another. By the time anybody had figured out the game, you'd already accomplished your goals. If you were smart enough and bold enough, you could do anything and get away with it, anything at all. And tonight he felt very alive and very smart and bold. He left the cemetery and started for Dolores's home, hoping she was asleep by now.

Peeking in through her window blinds, he saw her in bed reading, but this time the cat didn't hear him. He waited till her lights were turned off and he was sure she'd fallen asleep before picking up a cinder block beside her house and crashing it through a sliding-glass door. She awoke with a start—thinking a car had rammed into her bedroom. She jumped up and ran into the kitchen, where Rader was standing.

"What happened to my house?" the stunned woman asked. "Did you hit my house?"

"Yes," he said casually, explaining that he'd smashed into the side of it with his vehicle.

He was a fugitive from the law—just what he'd told Kevin and Kathryn Bright seventeen years earlier.

"I'm wanted in California," he said. "They're after me. I need your house and your car and some money. I need to warm up in here, but then I'm going to take your car and some food."

"You can't be in the house," she said, backing away from him.

"Ma'am," he said, coming toward her, "you've got to cooperate. I've got a club, I've got a gun, I've got a knife. You take your choice how you want it."

"Okay, okay."

He reached out for her arm and handcuffed her.

"I've got a visitor coming to see me tonight," she said. "He'll be here soon."

He believed her, amazed and disappointed at how bad his luck was in almost every situation. Somebody was always showing up and interrupting his plans.

"When is he coming?"

"Very soon."

He forced her into her bedroom and went back to the kitchen alone, finding the keys to her car, pretending to look for food, and ripping the phone jack from the wall. Returning to the bedroom, he took off the cuffs and told her that all he wanted to do was tie her up with panty hose.

"Somebody is really coming tonight?" he said.

"Somebody is coming."

"They'll find you and then you can call the police. I'm out of here."

He reached into the black bag and brought out some panty hose, as she shrank back on the bed.

"Don't kill me!" she said.

He bent down, trying to wrap the hose around her neck, but she resisted.

"Don't kill me! I've got kids."

"Too late," he said, tightening the panty hose with all his force.

"Don't kill me—please! I've got children!"

Her eyes, like the eyes of all his victims, had started to bulge from the pressure of his grip. Her face had turned red. Since killing the Otero family, he'd learned how much pressure it took to strangle an adult human being, and he was much more efficient now. Within three minutes, she was dead.

Taking her keys, a camera, a large jewelry box, and her driver's license, he dragged her outside on a bedspread, put her in the trunk of her car, and drove to a lake, dumping her body in some bushes. He'd originally thought about transporting her to a barn for a picture session, the one fantasy he'd never been able to fulfill, but hadn't found the right location. After riding back to her home, he tossed her keys on the roof and walked to the Baptist church to pick up his own car. Then he drove back to her body, and with snow coming down and the night getting colder, he hid her under a bridge, before rejoining the Scout troop.

After spending all day Saturday at the Trappers Rendezvous, he made up another excuse to leave that evening. On the drive to the bridge, he pulled into a truck stop and went into the restroom to get out of his scouting uniform and into dark clothes. While he was undressing, a highway patrolman came in.

"What are you doing?" the officer said.

Remembering that Dolores's jewelry was still in his car, he thought the game was finally over and he was about to be arrested.

"I'm going to a Scout camp," he said, showing off his uniform. "I'm changing my clothes."

As the officer stared at him, Rader's heart was pounding so hard he thought the man could hear it.

"When you get finished dressing," the trooper said, "I need to talk to you outside."

He left the restroom and Rader slowly put his Scout uniform back on, walking out to face the officer. He was shaking with fear, but the patrolman asked him a couple more questions and let him go.

Rader drove on to the bridge, where he planned to pick up the body and shoot pictures, but he was in for a shock: Dolores no longer looked the same. The Kansas nighttime predators will eat just about anything to survive, especially in the dead of winter, and they'd already started on the corpse. Rader went to the car and took out a plastic female mask, which he'd carefully prepared for this moment. He'd painted the mask a flesh tone, put red lipstick on it, touched up its cheeks with rouge, colored in black marks around the nostrils, and drawn on eyebrows and lashes. He placed the mask over Dolores's face to "pretty her up," as he later recalled, and to make her look more feminine. Then he shot a series of partially nude pictures of her in bondage positions, with her hands bound at the waist by panty hose, lying on the rock-hard January ground. When he was through, he covered her with debris, drove to Christ Lutheran Church to stash her jewelry under an outside shed, and returned to the Scouts.

Two weeks later, Dolores Davis was found decomposing under the bridge, and homicide detectives began an investigation. They didn't associate the method of killing or evidence with the BTK case, which was now fading into Wichita lore. As far as the authorities knew, BTK hadn't murdered anyone since 1977. While law enforcement looked into the death, Dolores's relatives sorted through her belongings and were surprised to find scores of periodicals and newsletters from animal rights groups, including the Doris Day Animal League and People for the Ethical Treatment of Animals. She'd been trying to help four-legged creatures right up until the night of her murder. After much police legwork, the Davis case turned out to be just another unsolved crime.

Fourteen years passed before Rader made his first mistake.

XXVI

O N T H E B R U T A L L Y cold night of January 8, 2005, the task force conducted surveillance at the Murdock Park and Kansas Avenue locations. Ice still covered the streets and the temperature fell below zero. Detectives who normally went home at dusk were pulling all-nighters, biding their time in rented apartments, driving rental cars through these neighborhoods, and checking in with their loved ones until it was too late to call. In comic movies like *Stakeout,* investigators spend their tedious surveillance hours playing tricks on one another, but this was not a time for practical jokes. They watched and waited in the cold, night after night, looking for a break that had never come.

On the eighth, Rader didn't drive to Murdock Park or Kansas Avenue, but left Park City in his son's dark Jeep Cherokee. Brian Rader was away in Connecticut serving in the military and had left the truck behind for his parents' use. His father liked to ride around town in the pickup when trolling for new projects, parking in front of women's homes and watching his targets or shooting pictures, but tonight he was on a different mission. He rode south to Highway 96 and took it east toward Wichita, exiting a mile later and pulling into the parking lot of a Home Depot. Because of the darkness and the weather, the lot was mostly empty. After circling for a while, he found an isolated pickup and slipped in next to it, carrying with him "Communication #7." Getting out of the Jeep, he examined the pickup before laying a Special K cereal box down on its open metal bed (he'd chosen this box because he was a "serial killer" and thought his wordplay was clever). The pickup's owner, Edgar Bishop, worked at

Home Depot, and within the next twenty-four hours he noticed the Special K box in his vehicle but thought it was trash and tossed it into a wastebasket at his house. Days went by, and after he forgot to take out the garbage, the woman he lived with, Kelly Paul, found the box and saw something handwritten on it: "BTK" and "bomb." Looking inside, she saw a blue-beaded necklace and computer paper, but more time passed before this information reached the police.

Rader hadn't counted on the delay in the box making its way to the authorities. He was also unaware that his hulking figure, wrapped in a winter coat, had been captured on the video surveillance equipment operating round the clock at Home Depot. So had his son's truck. For the first time ever, he'd given the WPD an image of himself, even though it was blurred, but enough of the Cherokee was visible to identify the make and size of the ground clearance and wheelbase. In late January, after retrieving the Special K box and its contents, the police asked Home Depot for the past ninety days' worth of surveillance, focusing on the tapes made earlier in the month. They watched it scores of times, hundreds of times over and over, as if they couldn't quite believe they were finally looking at the killer. He wasn't a myth or a phantom but a normal-looking man in an average-looking truck. Then they began the difficult and time-consuming work of figuring how many middle-aged, white men in the Wichita area owned dark-colored Cherokees (about twenty-five hundred such trucks were registered in Sedgwick County). They were looking for a 1999 or newer model and searched through recent traffic tickets to see if any relatively new Cherokees with white male owners came up in this database, but nothing leaped out at them.

January 15, 2005, marked the thirty-first anniversary of the Otero murders and was another bitter-cold night. Investigators staked out the former Otero residence; watched the drop box at the downtown public library; observed the street signs at First and Kansas, Second and Kansas, and Third and Kansas; and carried out surveillance at Murdock Park, but saw nothing unusual. As they focused on these locations, Rader was at home putting together another package, angry that he'd gotten no response to the one left at Home Depot. Ever since then, he'd sat at work and scanned the paper or kept an eye on the TV or an ear on the radio, following media reports to see or hear something about his latest effort, but apparently the police never found the box. It must have fallen off the truck bed or the WPD was just pretending they didn't have it. The lack of feedback was aggravating, but made him determined to reach out again soon. As BTK, he was always lonely and Lieutenant Landwehr, with his friendly manner and measured voice, had tapped into that loneliness.

Since March 2004, Rader had grown dependent on hearing from the lieutenant or seeing a reaction from law enforcement each time he'd made a move. It wasn't enough to have walked away from every crime without the slightest consequence to himself or his family, not enough to have fooled everyone for three decades and documented all his work with newspaper articles and his own creative horde of materials. He wanted something more—credit and recognition for a lifetime of planning and executing these projects, even if nobody actually knew who he was. He wanted attention and a response from Lieutenant Landwehr because he'd come to feel they had things in common and were more or less in the same business. While he was always hunting for another victim, Landwehr was constantly searching for him. Rader had always respected people in law enforcement and he liked the lieutenant and felt a connection to him.

The bonding process the police and the FBI had been hoping to establish with BTK, almost a year before, had subtly worked. Rader had always needed to see and feel that he was having an effect on the world, and when Landwehr had directed comments at him during those press conferences, he knew he was having an impact. It felt terrible now not to have a response from the WPD about "Communication #7." In his mind, he and Landwehr had been building a relationship, even a kind of trust, but maybe he'd been wrong. He didn't like being ignored—seven days without hearing anything from the cops. The next time he sent them something it needed to be strong and disturbing enough to force them to react.

On January 17, he left a Post Toasties box on North Seneca near Sixty-ninth Street, a rural location not far from Park City. He'd circled the letter *T* in *Toasties* and written the letter *B* above it and *K* below. Red crepe paper, which he'd stuffed inside, poured over the lip of the box. A few days later, while carrying out her duties as an animal control officer and colleague of Rader's, Cindy Plant took a drive on North Seneca, a deep-ditched, sandy road running through the middle of fallow wheat fields. As part of her job, she kept an eye out for litter and took note of the cereal box propped up against a road sign alerting drivers of an upcoming curve, but she didn't think too much about it. It may have been trash but not the kind you worried about or had to pick up, such as abandoned furniture or tires. The colorful box with the big red letters didn't really look like trash, anyway. It hadn't been idly tossed out the window like a piece of junk, but carefully positioned to lean against the post. She couldn't see this from the road, but the box had, in fact, been weighted down with a brick. Plant drove by it several times and always glanced at it but never stopped to take a closer look.

After placing the box by the sign, Rader sent a postcard to KAKE, with a return address of S Killett at 803 North Edgemoor—the Oteros' address back in 1974. The postcard told the TV station where to find "Communication #8," and KAKE soon alerted the police. Detective Otis went to the TV station and met with manager Glen Horn and news anchor Larry Hatteberg. On the back of the postcard, Rader had described the Post Toasties box and its location, adding, "Let me know some how if you or Wichita PD received this. Also let me know if you or PD received #7 . . . 1-8-05."

KAKE had already sent a crew to North Seneca and found the cereal box on the side of the road. Detectives Otis, Tim Relph, and Dana Gouge immediately drove to the area and took possession of the evidence. Inside the box were jewelry, more BTK writings, entitled "CHAPTER 9 HITS: PJ—LITTLE MEX—01-15-1974," and a doll with rope wrapped around its neck and tied to a curved piece of plastic pipe. The doll clearly signified Josephine Otero, who'd been bound and hung from a sewer pipe in her basement. A phrase in the "PJ—LITTLE MEX" document also showed that the author was familiar with the profiling lingo that had developed out of the FBI's Behavioral Science Unit in Quantico, Virginia, in the 1970s. Serial killer experts divided murderers into two categories: organized and disorganized.

"An Organized Sexual Killer did the Murders," Rader wrote in "Communication #8." "It is the true Sadistic Sexual Killer profile that happens here."

In late January, almost three weeks after Rader had dropped off "Communication #7" at the Home Depot, Edgar Bishop and Kelly Paul turned the Special K box over to Detective Otis. It contained a blue-beaded necklace and writing that described BTK's home (he called it his "lair") as a three-story house with an elevator. It had a bondage room, and in the basement he'd planted a bomb to go off if the police came to this residence. This last piece of information seemed false and misleading, but the WPD couldn't ignore it. Through more legwork, detectives learned that Wichita had hundreds of homes with elevators and started doing background checks on them. If BTK could be connected to one of these addresses and the police closed in for the arrest, they'd flood the basement to disable the explosive. Because of the potential bomb threat, the WPD contacted the Bureau of Alcohol, Tobacco and Firearms, and the federal agency joined the investigation.

The Special K box had one other thing inside: a simple question for the police from Rex.

"Can I communicate with Floppy," the author wrote, "and not be traced to a computer. Be honest . . ."

Rex wanted to know if he spoke to the WPD through a computer diskette, could it be connected to an identifiable terminal? If he erased everything from the diskette except the message for the police, would all the other deleted material really be gone? It was an amazing inquiry, and because he'd misled the authorities so many times before, they couldn't be certain that he was really posing such a naive question, but they could only hope he was. For the past decade, American law enforcement had been fighting cyber-crime from one end of the country to the other, gradually growing more and more sophisticated in its ability to track down information generated on computers and then apparently erased. Files "deleted" from hard drives or diskettes usually did not disappear until they had specifically been overwritten. That process could take as long as five or six years, and even writing over something might not erase it for good. Once created and stored electronically, data was far harder to get rid of than most people realized.

The police were eager to tell BTK that such information couldn't be traced, but didn't want to be too obvious or say anything to reveal their strategy. If the media publicized this development, the WPD might have blown a better opportunity than trying to find the Jeep Cherokee. Running down all twenty-five hundred trucks and owners in Sedgwick County was going to take a long time, and what if BTK had borrowed that vehicle and it belonged to someone else?

In "Communication #7," Rader told the police to answer his computer question by running an advertisement in the classified section of the *Eagle* and using his code name. It wasn't the first time the newspaper had become part of the investigation. Back in 1974, law enforcement had placed an ad in the paper in the hope of flushing out BTK, but that hadn't worked. With the approval of then police chief Richard LaMunyon, the WPD had tried running a subliminal ad on television, flashing a message across the screen designed to reach the killer's subconscious, but it had produced no results. In late January 2005, the authorities concluded they had nothing to lose by placing another ad now; it was one more way of expanding the dialogue with the suspect, yet they had to be careful. Without telling the *Eagle* their plan, the police enlisted the services of a well-dressed woman calling herself Cyndi Johnson, who showed up one day at the classified ad department. She refused to give out an address or phone number and wanted to pay in cash. After some discussion, the paper agreed to her terms. She claimed that her cryptic ad was intended to promote an "adult talk" Web site, and it would run from January 28 through February 3. The *Eagle* was concerned that she was soliciting prostitution.

The ad read, "Rex, it will be ok. Contact me PO Box 1st four ref. Numbers at 67202."

Rader was an obsessive newspaper reader, especially on work breaks, and had been scouring the paper looking for a message like this. When he found it in the last week of January, he instantly knew what it meant.

By February 2, he'd prepared another postcard, mailed it off to KAKE, and the station received it the following day. It thanked KAKE for its response on "Communication #7" and "#8" and expressed gratitude to the news team.

It read, "Business Issues: Tell WPD that I receive the Newspaper Tip for a go. Test run soon. Thanks."

KAKE, at the request of the police, did not reveal this communication to its viewers.

Lieutenant Landwehr wondered what kind of game the killer was playing with them now, but Rader's question about the diskette had been sincere. His entire life had been lived as if he could erase the crimes he'd committed as easily as one could delete files from a computer screen. Once something or someone had been eliminated from sight, no matter how much suffering this brought to others, it was forever gone and he was free to plan the next project. The lieutenant had no idea how important his responses had become to the suspect. For the first time ever, BTK was reaching out for a trusted human connection to a living person—and that someone was a homicide detective.

XXVII

As church president, Rader led the council meetings; he kept a log of what had taken place at the last one and set the agenda for the upcoming monthly session. His penchant for organization and detail was as strong at Christ Lutheran as at his office, where everything had to be done precisely the right way. When he took over his new position at the church, his computer printer at home was broken and he hadn't bothered getting it fixed.

One January day he and Pastor Clark met at a fast-food restaurant in Park City to discuss the next council meeting. The men enjoyed each other's company and seemed quite compatible. To Rader, the minister looked like the kind of guy you could tell things to: he was open-minded and curious, wasn't judgmental, and could joke about almost anything. Not many preachers in rural Kansas dressed up like a clown and did whatever it took to get a laugh out of adults or children. Not many spoke their mind as easily as Pastor Clark did. Sometimes Rader wished he had a lighter personality and didn't take things so seriously, but he'd never really been that way. To the pastor, the new president was the sort of man you could depend on. Like most people who ran organizations, the minister wanted to work with those who solved problems instead of creating them. Dennis got things done, whether it was scrubbing the church windows or staying on top of paperwork. You never had to ask him to do anything twice.

They were Midwestern men approaching sixty with similar backgrounds who shared the same faith. They were married with children and had jobs in official capacities. Both had the flat voices of the

Plains and were unpretentious in their clothes, manners, and how they carried themselves. Both wore glasses, were going bald, and had put on weight around the middle in recent years. Physically, there wasn't much to distinguish one from the other, but one man had chosen to humble himself before the source of his anger and fear. He'd made a conscious decision to go toward the pain instead of running away from it and had spoken the deepest truth he knew to another human being. When confessing that he had had a crippling rage at his father, he'd trusted that the person hearing this would know how to respond, and he did.

The minister had decided to go through the suffering instead of around it, and since then he hadn't had to keep repeating his experiences over and over. Until he'd known and admitted what was controlling him, he couldn't go forward. At forty, he left childhood behind and stepped over a new threshold. He was no longer just his father's son, even though his father had abandoned him nearly four decades earlier. Now he could choose his own life instead of wearing someone else's like an impossibly heavy but invisible cloak. It was as if Pastor Clark sensed that at some point—or points—in his future, he was going to need be stronger, and if he didn't lay the foundation for that strength in seminary, he wouldn't be able to do his job.

Both the minister and Rader had used the creativity God had given them, one to pray for others and to ease their burden and to make them laugh, the other to torture and kill and taunt, so he could satisfy the cruel child who'd never made any separation from his parents, but kept returning to their basement to dress up as a woman and stage his own death. Both were Christians, but without some self-awareness and inner ethical participation, the belief system held no meaning. Faith hadn't stopped Rader, nor had singing hymns or quoting Scripture or confessing sins in church or taking Communion on his knees.

The strangest thing was that one man's footsteps seemed to be guided in the right direction, because the preacher just had a knack for stumbling toward the light.

*   *   *

During lunch, Rader made notes about their discussion, and when they were finished, he set them aside on the table. The preacher glanced at them; the new president did so much for Christ Lutheran that the minister now wanted to help him.

"I'll be happy," Pastor Clark said, "to take those back to the church with me and have my secretary type them up."

Rader thought about the offer.

"They'll be done by Sunday," the minister said, "and I can distribute them at church to the council members."

"That's all right," Rader replied. "I can do it myself. I'll use my computer at home."

Pastor Clark decided to let it go, but then Rader mentioned that even though he could type up the notes, his printer was broken.

The preacher had just the solution. "Go on home, write them up, and put them on a floppy disk," he said. "I'll meet you at the church on Saturday morning. Bring the floppy and we'll copy everything out on our system."

"Okay."

On Saturday at ten o'clock sharp, Rader came to Christ Lutheran and Pastor Clark hooked him up with the church computer. Within minutes, the chore was completed and Rader put the purple diskette into his pocket and returned home.

The minister didn't think much about all this but had been struck by the man's lack of computer expertise. Twenty-five years earlier, Rader had employed a Xerox machine at Wichita State University when making duplicates of the letters he was writing to the police or the media, before sending out a third- or fourth-generation copy that was much harder to trace than the original. That had worked out fine, but today's technology required a little more knowledge if you wanted to understand its secrets.

Since the police hadn't heard anything from BTK after his latest postcard to KAKE, they told undercover officer Cyndi Johnson to return to the paper and place another ad, but the *Eagle* no longer wanted to do business with this shady character. Soon afterward, an undercover male officer informed the classified staff that he represented REX Productions; for vague reasons he'd had to fire Cyndi and was now handling this transaction himself, which also smelled funny to the *Eagle*. Without telling the police what it was doing, the paper assigned a reporter to check out the legitimacy of REX Productions.

Then KAKE, also without informing the WPD, decided to send its own message to BTK in response to his recent postcards. News anchor Larry Hatteberg had been covering the murders for decades and had become the media's primary face in the investigation. KAKE and Hatteberg, in directing their on-air words to the killer, stated that they were aware BTK watched televised news reports about the case and added, "Let the record show the message has been received and passed on. Our job, as always, is to be the eyes and ears for the public. As good journalists, we are here, and we are listening and communicating."

While both the police and KAKE were anxious that BTK not go into retreat, he'd been busy with another package. On Tuesday, February 15, Rader dropped "Communication #11" in the mail (numbers 9 and 10 were the two recent postcards sent to KAKE). The new one went to KSAS, the Fox-TV outlet in Wichita, and the next day the station opened the small, reinforced manila envelope and found a pendant necklace, three index cards, and a photocopy of the cover of a 1989 mystery novel, *Rules of Prey*, written by "John Sandford." Sandford's real name was John Camp, and the book's main character was a serial killer called "mad dog." One other item was in the envelope: the purple diskette Rader had taken into Christ Lutheran to print out his church notes. An index card explained the diskette and offered instructions for future contact through a newspaper ad. After examining the contents of the package, KSAS called the police, and Detective Gouge retrieved "Communication #11." When the authorities asked the station not to reveal everything found in the envelope, KSAS agreed.

On Thursday, February 17, Lieutenant Landwehr read a statement aloud to the press, his first public pronouncement in weeks:

"The Behavioral Analysis Unit of the FBI has confirmed two letters as authentic communications from BTK. The letter that was

In January 1974, Joseph Otero, Julie Otero, Josephine Otero,
and Joseph Otero Jr. were BTK's first four victims.
(Courtesy of the Wichita Police Department)

Kathryn Bright, BTK's fifth victim, killed in April 1974;
Shirley Vian, killed in March 1977; Nancy Fox, killed in December 1977;
Vicki Wegerle, killed in September 1986.
(Courtesy of the Wichita Police Department)

Marine Hedge, killed by BTK in
1985, lived just a few doors down
from him in Park City, Kansas.
(Courtesy of the Sedgwick County
District Attorney's Office)

BTK's last known victim, Dolores
Davis, killed just outside of Rader's
hometown north of Wichita in 1991.
(Courtesy of the Sedgwick County
District Attorney's Office)

Dennis Rader was a family man, the father of two children, a Boy Scout leader, and the president of his church. (Courtesy of the Sedgwick County District Attorney's Office)

Dennis Rader's mug shot, taken shortly after his arrest on February 25, 2005. (Courtesy of the Sedgwick County District Attorney's Office)

Park City's City Hall where Rader worked as a compliance officer and kept his "Mother Lode" of incriminating evidence. (Courtesy of the author)

Dennis Rader's modest Park City home. (Courtesy of the author)

Christ Lutheran Church, outside of Park City, Kansas, where Rader was
president of the congregation. (Courtesy of the author)

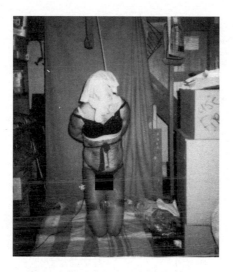

Dennis Rader's photo of himself in bondage, simulating
a hanging in his parents' basement. (Courtesy of the
Sedgwick County District Attorney's Office)

Dennis Rader's masked self-portrait, staring into the
camera in his parents' basement. (Courtesy of the
Sedgwick County District Attorney's Office)

Lt. Ken Landwehr became the official voice and face of the BTK investigation that caught the serial killer after a thirty-one-year hunt. (Courtesy of the Wichita Police Department)

The BTK task force, made up of Wichita Police Department and Kansas Bureau of Investigation officers, arresting Dennis Rader a block from his home on February 25, 2005. (Courtesy of the Wichita Police Department)

Dennis Rader was interviewed for thirty-two hours following his arrest and confessed to ten murders. (Courtesy of the Sedgwick County District Attorney's Office)

The Epic Center in downtown Wichita where, following his arrest, Rader confessed to police for thirty-two hours. (Courtesy of the author)

District Attorney Nola Foulston led the prosecution team that presented evidence resulting in BTK receiving a 175-year sentence. (Courtesy of the Sedgwick County District Attorney's Office)

Steve Osburn, Rader's lead defense attorney, after his client was sentenced to life in prison. (Courtesy of the author)

Date: _Sat, June 11, 2005_

To: _Stephen Singular_

Dear _Mr. Singular_,

Thank you for the letter or correspondence received on ___6-9-05___. To receive any correspondence is always a welcome message to an inmate within SCDF and a highlight or perk for the day.

non at this time

I apologize for the delay in corresponding or getting back to you. Many factors contribute to this problem, many which include the overall Judicial System, timely mailings within SCDF, my main project or interests, inmate requirements or duties, family, close friends and other established pen-pal correspondence. Currently, return correspondence is running about ___2 - 5___ days behind. _normally_

According to your correspondence, you wished for or asked for:

1. A letter back in reference to myself and some possible answers, and/or
2. To establish a possible pen-pal correspondence relationship, and/or
3. Other correspondence and/or reflections from me.

In any case, I sincerely apologize, but I cannot talk about aspects of the "accused" at this time or anything considered protected under the attorney/client privilege.

Thank you for this interest. The spiritual side is very Christian. With Trial date set 6-27-05, and other issues going on, I would like to leave the "Topic", open.

I realize book and such have to get started at some point. But informations at this point in time is limited.

I will leave our correspondence open, and not burn any bridge

(See back side for more correspondence.) _behind me. Thank for interest._

Sincerely,

D.L. Rader   6-11-05
AKA. "The Suspect"
_or_
"Radar"
_or_
"Pod Father"

Dennis L. Rader

Poo
Frog

Page 1

dropped in a UPS box at Second and Kansas streets in October 2004 has been authenticated. This communication contained information about BTK that was subsequently released to the public on November thirtieth, 2004. The FBI can confirm that it's a BTK communication, but cannot confirm the accuracy of the information he wrote about himself in the letter.

"The other communication that the FBI has confirmed is from BTK is the package that was located in December by a Wichita resident in Murdock Park. This package contained the driver's license belonging to Nancy Fox, which BTK took with him from the crime scene.

"Recent communications from BTK have included several items of jewelry. There was jewelry in the Post Toasties box that was left on North Seneca Street, as well as in communication number seven and in the package received yesterday by KSAS, Fox 24. The contents of yesterday's KSAS-Fox 24 communication have been sent to the FBI. We are in the process of determining whether or not any of this jewelry belonged to our victims."

Looking up from the text, Landwehr stared into the assembled cameras, as if making eye contact with a single individual. When he spoke again, his tone was less official: "I have said before . . . that the BTK investigation is the most challenging case I have ever worked on, and that BTK would be very interesting to talk with. I still contend that this is our most challenging case, but I am very pleased with the ongoing dialogue through these letters."

That same day, February 17, the *Eagle* ran a second ad that the police had secretly placed in the paper. It read, "XXX ADULT TALK XXX *www.xxxadulttalk.com* Only read message about card PO is your first four ref. Numbers 67202"

When Rader spotted this in the classified section, he understood the meaning of the strange language and felt good about this response. Like Landwehr, he too was pleased about his ongoing dialogue with the authorities. The game he was playing with them was more intricate and challenging and fun than it had ever been, and in Lieutenant Landwehr, he'd found someone worthy of his intelligence and cunning. At work and in the evenings when he could get away from Paula and go back to his office, he began putting together a new package for law enforcement. This one would be all about Shirley Vian and shaped like a bomb.

In mid-February, many people were closely observing the activities of the WPD, but no one more keenly than the longtime Sedgwick County district attorney, Nola Foulston. Short, feisty, well-dressed, and well-coiffed, she didn't so much stroll through the courthouse in downtown Wichita as strut. She relished prosecuting the biggest cases and taking on the defendants charged with the most heinous offenses. Her most memorable courtroom appearance until now was in the *State of Kansas v. Leroy Hendricks*. A self-confessed sexual predator, Hendricks was the first person to be confined under Kansas's 1994 Sexually Violent Predator Act, not because of a specific crime but because he had mental problems that predisposed him "to commit sexually violent offenses." The case went all the way to the U.S. Supreme Court, and the DA won a precedent-setting victory. In 2003, she was selected the state's Prosecutor of the Year.

"I'm an Italian from New York," Foulston liked telling people when describing her background.

Her father, Dominick "Teddy" Tedesco, was one of seven children of immigrant parents from southern Italy, where his father had been a housepainter and his mother had worked in a lace factory. Born in the United States, Teddy was restless, adventurous, and ambitious. In the 1930s, he left New York's Manhattan College to enroll at Fort Hays State College in Hays, Kansas, where he could be closer to an older brother attending medical school in Omaha. A couple of Teddy's friends followed him out to Fort Hays State, one of them an aspiring young writer named Mickey Spillane. Years later, Spillane gained international literary fame as the creator of the legendary fictional character Mike Hammer, and also wrote about a colorful character named Teddy the Pilot, based on Teddy Tedesco.

Both Tedesco and Spillane were taken with the open spaces of western Kansas and the local brand of chili. Teddy would always come back for more. After returning to New York, marrying a dance artist, and having children, he insisted on herding his family out to Kansas for summer vacations, regaling his kids with stories about Midwestern values and virtues. All three of his children got their undergraduate education at Fort Hays State, and Nola went on to attend Topeka's Washburn University School of Law, receiving her degree in 1975. A year later, she was hired as an assistant district attorney in Kansas's Eighteenth Judicial District, which includes Wichita and Sedgwick County, and in 1988 she became the DA. The Eighteenth Judicial District has the state's largest local prosecutor's office, and Foulston was especially interested in reducing violent crime and crimes against women and children. She was the kind of DA who took the law personally and led the prosecution in thousands of cases.

After taking office in the Eighteenth Judicial District, she maintained her ties with her father's past by getting Mickey Spillane to come to Kansas and give the keynote address at the Wichita Crime Commission. In 1989, Foulston was diagnosed with multiple sclerosis, but this had no effect on her ability to function as district attorney or the fire she brought to the job. If anything, it seemed to make her more determined to go after violent offenders. Nola didn't like people who broke the law, didn't try to hide that, and enjoyed watching defendants squirm. She was drawn to the media glare (too much so, her critics said) and didn't suffer fools lightly, and in the coming months, she'd make all this perfectly clear.

XXVIII

UNLIKE THE POLICE department, the Wichita office of the FBI does not operate out of City Hall. As if to underscore their more prestigious position on the law enforcement ladder, the feds work on the fourth floor of the Epic Center, the downtown's most modern-looking and stylish building. Rising like a monolith from Wichita's flat floor, the structure has three sides, with two of them coming to a point in the sky. In the lobby are marble walls, a glass wall, and colorful works of contemporary art, while a spacious atrium gives the impression that the center is much larger than it is. The elevators feature wooden paneling, the halls are covered with handsome zigzag-patterned carpet, and the entire building has the kind of elegance rarely associated with law and order. The FBI foyer is tiny—no one gets through it without the doors being unlocked to buzz you in—and staring back at you from the wall is a picture of Osama bin Laden and a couple of the world's other most wanted fugitives.

A week before the WPD received the diskette from Rader, the BTK task force began shifting its operation from the sixth floor of City Hall to the fourth floor of the Epic Center. If nothing else, this was a morale booster for the investigators, who'd been working the case for nearly a year, and lately in icy weather, without much progress. Transferring into these upscale surroundings and sitting in on meetings with the police, the KBI, and the FBI gave the lower-level members of the task force a lift, and there were more practical reasons to move everything into the Epic Center: the FBI offices were secured by motion sensors and alarms. Because the media were chronicling every police move, it was easier for law enforcement to come and go from this location without being noticed.

After getting the diskette, Detective Gouge turned it over to Detective Randy Stone, who was trained in computer forensics. As he was getting ready to examine the diskette, a group of officers huddled over his shoulder. Stone was prepared for a long search that might reveal little, but when he inserted the floppy into his computer, only one valid file came up. Called "Test A. RTF," it read, "This is a test. See 3x5 Card for details on Communication with me in the newspaper." The detective entered a command taking him into the "Properties" segment of the diskette, and moments later he saw the names "Christ Lutheran Church" and "Dennis." Another piece of information revealed that the diskette had been used at the Park City Public Library. The officers who'd been standing around Stone's desk stared at the handful of words, talking and pointing at the screen, their excitement growing. Within minutes, Stone had Googled the two names in front of him and discovered that Dennis Rader was president of Christ Lutheran Church, just outside Park City. Less than two hours after getting his hands on the diskette, Stone reported his findings back to his superiors, who just as quickly determined that Rader was a compliance officer for Park City and lived at 6220 Independence Street.

Could this be the man they'd been hunting for? Or were they being deliberately misled?

On one of the index cards that had arrived in the package with the diskette, BTK had written, "Any communications will have a # assigned from now on, encase one is lost or not found." The word *encase* made Detective Stone skeptical about concluding that Dennis Rader was BTK. *EnCase* was the name of a sophisticated computer software program employed by the police and FBI to conduct forensic exams. Surely, the killer must have known that. Wasn't he using this word just to mock the authorities and to hint that all the data on the diskette was false? When Stone called the FBI's regional computer forensic lab in Kansas City, they told him that his instincts about being cautious were right: the WPD was definitely being set up by BTK.

No one yet understood that the word *encase* didn't mean anything and Rader just couldn't spell.

Two task force members—Clint Synder and Tim Relph—drove to Park City to check out Rader's workplace and residence. During the past year, a local man had been swabbed in the village, but that was as close as the investigation had come to the town. The detectives pulled up in front of Rader's home, staring in amazement: 6220 Independence sat on a winding street just south of Sixty-first Street North and was stunningly modest, a little white bungalow with an aging red awning hanging over the front window. A bird feeder hung from a tree limb, and shrubs filled the front yard, keeping some of the house from view even in the dead of winter. The difference between this address and BTK's reputation and aura was jarring. It didn't seem possible that someone who'd put the largest city in Kansas in a state of fear for three decades, someone who'd eluded and tormented the police during all that time, could live *here*. It was so quiet and peaceful and nondescript, so far removed from the nightmares Wichita had known for a generation, so distant from the world's other historically notorious serial killers, wasn't it? Everything was too small and too average, including the town itself, little more than an intersection of two highways filled with gas stations, fast-food joints, and Protestant churches. But this had to be the person they were looking for. In Rader's driveway was a dark Jeep Grand Cherokee, which the police quickly traced to his son, Brian, the same vehicle captured on the Home Depot surveillance tape the month before. The detectives were so excited they could barely contain themselves. If Rader wasn't inside the house, he had to be working no more than five minutes away. They wanted to go arrest him but knew they had to call Lieutenant Landwehr first. The lieutenant told them to come back downtown and they followed orders, but it was the longest ride of their lives.

At the Epic Center they reported their findings, igniting another round of debate. Was this the suspect or not? How many people in Wichita had lately phoned in tips insisting they knew who BTK was and where to find him? Remember last December 1, when a caller had been positive that the man living near the railroad tracks was a serial murderer. That was a bad lead ending in a lawsuit. Despite what the WPD had just learned, it had to be extremely careful and couldn't afford any more public blunders. If this was BTK, only DNA could prove that. Until the task force could come up with a genetic sample from Rader matching the ones collected and preserved from the Otero, Fox, or Wegerle crime scenes, they didn't have anything solid. Uncovering the names of the church and the man had sent a rush of exhilaration and celebration through the handful of task force members aware of this development on February 16, but the case wasn't solved and Lieutenant Landwehr urged restraint. Every mistake from now on could be fatal to a future prosecution. No more arrests would be made until law enforcement had something that would stick; it was a time for absolute silence and more legwork.

The task force put Rader under twenty-four-hour surveillance and noted his habits—when he went to work, when and where he ate lunch, what he did at night. In unmarked cars, they followed him to the compliance office at Park City's City Hall, to Christ Lutheran Church, to his home, his mother's home, and to Leeker's grocery store, where Paula Rader had worked and where the white plastic bag found in Murdock Park last December had come from. From telephone poles, the police studied the neighborhood, also looking at a house in Wichita where Brian Rader had once lived. They tracked Kerri Rader, following her movements after graduating from high school and leaving Park City. She'd gone to Kansas State University in Manhattan and was now married and lived in Michigan. They watched what Paula Rader did throughout the day and everyone Rader had regular contact with was now part of the investigation.

The task force was facing a troubling dilemma: How could they get a DNA sample from the suspect or one of his children without tipping anyone off? In the past, they'd taken mouth swabs from men whom they'd been prepared to arrest on minor violations of the law, so they could get them into custody before a DNA report came back from the lab. But Rader didn't have any legal violations; he appeared to have obeyed every law stringently. The police thought about approaching one of his brothers for a swab, but that was too risky. If Rader had any inkling that he was under surveillance, he'd probably flee Kansas and everything could become a public mess. What could they do? Jokes were flying inside the police department that one of the younger, better-looking task force members should fly up to Michigan, seduce Kerri Rader, and bring back a sample of her DNA.

Days passed and the surveillance continued, with investigators discovering that Rader was definitely a creature of habit. He went to work the same time each morning, meticulously carried out his rounds in his white Park City vehicle, and drove home for lunch—just a few minutes away from his office—at precisely 12:15 p.m. When he arrived at the house, he expected that his wife would have left her job as a bookkeeper sometime earlier, so she could come home before him, prepare his lunch, and have it ready at 12:17 p.m. With limited time to eat, he wanted the food on the table when he hit the front door. There was nothing suspicious about any of his external activities, but the police didn't see Rader in his house or office at night, creating his latest drop-off communication about Shirley Vian. Nearly a week had passed since Detective Stone had uncovered the names on the diskette, and some task force members were getting itchy, edgy, weary of all the speeches about more legwork and staying patient. What if Rader found out he was being watched and bolted? When could they move on this guy? What if he was planning another murder?

The DNA issue was unresolved, but someone had finally posed the right questions. Did Kerri Rader have medical records on file at Kansas State that would include a sample of her genetic material and could they get at them through a search warrant? Almost a year earlier at the Sedgwick County Regional Forensic Science Center, a biology/DNA lab manager, Shelly Steadman, had conducted a polymerase-chain-reaction DNA analysis on Nancy Fox's blue robe.

"The DNA profiles," Steadman had written in April 2004, "obtained from the sperm cell and non-sperm cell fractions of the cutting from the blue robe . . . are consistent with the profile of a common unknown male individual. This individual cannot be excluded as the major contributor to the profile obtained from the left hand fingernail scrapings of Vicki Wegerle."

In the spring of 2004, another DNA analyst, Daniel Fahnestock, performed PCR testing on a swab taken from the Oteros' basement and concluded that the Fox, Wegerle, and Otero murders were all connected through genetic markers.

By the week of Monday, February 21, the task force had gotten a search warrant for Kerri's records at Kansas State. On Tuesday, the KBI's Senior Special Agent Ray Lundin obtained her Pap smear and gave it to the KBI Forensic Lab in Topeka. Rader's name was now circulating throughout the entire task force, and everyone had become aware of the latest developments. By Wednesday, all the investigators were talking about the DNA test and waiting for the results of this exam. If there was no match, the WPD would have to conclude that Rader was being set up and they were still looking for another middle-aged, white man. If a match was made, they'd need to act quickly but quietly. During the testing, Kerri's sample was compared with the DNA found in the basement of the Otero home, where Josephine had been strangled. As the fourth floor of the Epic Center whirred with speculation and anticipation, Lieutenant Landwehr reemphasized that nobody should get excited just yet.

On Wednesday evening, Dennis and Paula had been invited to a meal at the church but had a prior commitment and couldn't make it. Before going to their other engagement, they dropped off a salad and spaghetti sauce in a Crock-Pot at Christ Lutheran, saying hello to a number of fellow worshippers. Since he'd taken over as president and overseen the first two council meetings of 2005, Dennis's stature at the church had grown and people were approaching him with ideas about church business. He really liked having this new authority and the recognition it brought him and was looking forward to the rest of his term.

That Wednesday night, the detectives working at the Epic Center weren't the only ones thinking about BTK. The game the killer had been playing with the police throughout the past eleven months was by far the biggest media story in Wichita, filling the pages of the *Eagle* and the airwaves of all the local TV stations. One couldn't live in the city or surrounding region without knowing something about the WPD's futile investigative efforts and BTK's incredible ability to avoid detection. Some people were more fascinated by this saga than others, and without even thinking about it they found themselves absorbing details of the case from news reports. Dennis and Paula had watched these reports along with everyone else, and in the past couple of days, she'd glanced at something Dennis had scribbled and noticed for the hundredth or thousandth time during their thirty-three-year marriage that he had difficulty with the written word.

"You spell just like BTK," she told her husband.

He didn't say anything.

Lately, Paula had been expressing a lot of fear about their home being attacked by BTK because the killer had recently left a couple of packages near Park City, and everyone in town was talking about it. Rader told her to take some extra precautions to feel safer, such as locking the doors and all the windows, but as for himself, he wasn't all that worried about it.

XXIX

THURSDAY WAS EXTREMELY long and nerve-racking at the Epic Center. Everyone on the task force went about his work and stayed busy doing surveillance in Park City or running down information about the Raders, but all were distracted awaiting the test results. By late afternoon each phone call coming into the center brought a sense of gathering tension. Police officers kept phoning the fourth floor or walking into and out of the building looking for updates, while their bosses were assembling groups of law enforcement personnel. A bomb squad and a SWAT team had been put on alert, an evidence response unit was being prepared, and officials of the Bureau of Alcohol, Tobacco and Firearms were in place. The WPD, the FBI, the KBI, and the Sedgwick County Sheriff's Department were gearing up, but one suburban police department hadn't been told about any of these developments. The Park City PD worked out of City Hall, on the opposite end of the small building holding the compliance office, and the task force feared that if any local cops got wind of the investigation, they might tip Rader off.

All afternoon and early evening, investigators waited for the call to come into the Epic Center from the lab. The deadline was supposed to be 7 p.m., but it came and went. While the police hung near the phones, Rader was in his compliance office preparing a doll, a poem, and a new chapter of his book for the Shirley Vian package. He hoped the "Shirley doll," wired to resemble an explosive, would stymie the cops and frighten them so much they wouldn't touch it. As he tinkered with the doll, he was unaware of the surveillance equipment installed near his house or the detectives roaming in his neighborhood, but as always, he was paying close attention to the clock. He could only spend a couple of nighttime hours at the office before his wife started to expect him home.

By 7:15, many task force members had drifted back to the Epic Center, unable to stay away any longer. Whether the investigation into Rader was going forward or going nowhere, they wanted to know tonight. A full eight days had passed since Detective Stone had found the names on the diskette, and the speculation was getting stale and the waiting unbearable.

At 7:30, a cell phone rang and a KBI agent answered it.

The others moved toward him, straining to listen and trying to read his expression. The agent was nodding and saying little.

He hung up and glanced around. Looking at the task force, he said simply, "We have a match."

The room exploded into cheering and handshakes, into backslaps and high fives, with adults jumping up and down like children.

"The feeling inside that FBI office at that moment," said an officer who'd been on the task force for almost a year, "was absolutely electrifying."

When the first blast of noise subsided, somebody asked the agent what the lab had told him. He gave the shortest and clearest answer he could think of: the "unknown male individual" who'd left semen in the Otero basement was Kerri's father. To put the most cautious spin possible on all this, Dennis Rader may not have been Kerri's father, but Kerri's father was BTK.

Once the cheering had stopped, everyone looked to Lieutenant Landwehr for the next step in the investigation. How much longer did they have to wait?

Not long, was the answer.

The news instantly spread to other task force members who began arriving at the Epic Center to get their instructions for tomorrow. Every time someone new came into the FBI office, there were more handshakes and congratulations. By 10:30 p.m., Lieutenant Landwehr was telling his people to go home and get some rest because they were going to need it in the morning. Nearly seventy people would be dispatched for the next assignment, as search warrants were being prepared for execution at Rader's home, his office, his mother's house, the Park City Public Library, and Christ Lutheran Church. Some of the police officers who normally wore street clothes on the job were told to put on their uniforms tomorrow and to look their best.

The task force tried to follow Landwehr's last order, but that was tough. Everyone was jacked up with visions of what was coming, and while some investigators were in bed before 11:30 p.m., they couldn't fall asleep. The night ticked away with an endless set of scenarios unfolding in their imaginations. When they did manage to doze off at 2 or 3 a.m., they kept waking up in the darkness and wondering if they'd have to shoot BTK in a few hours or if he'd shoot them first. Or would he kill himself? Would he surrender quietly or would they be involved in a high-speed chase? What would the monster be like up close? If they didn't get back to sleep, their reflexes wouldn't be as sharp as they should be, and that could be dangerous.

What if that bomb inside his house went off?

XXX

Friday morning was quite warm for late February, with a slight breeze and the sun casting shadows all across Wichita. Rader had arisen early, as was his custom, eaten breakfast, and put on his compliance uniform, a tan outfit that made him look like more of an authority figure. He gave his name badge the once-over, making sure it was clean, and was ready for work. He liked dressing up in an official outfit, just as he liked having a long-barreled shotgun in his truck. You never knew when it might come in handy. He and Paula said good-bye for the day and he drove to City Hall. After taking care of a few details at the office, he left to make some rounds in his truck, checking in with the rest of the law enforcement community by tuning in his police radio. Nothing much was happening, it seemed, but then a report said the FBI was coming to Park City this morning, which gave him pause.

What would the feds be doing in his hometown? He wasn't aware of any recent local criminal activity or major ongoing investigations. Could they be looking for him?

He considered this, but tried to dismiss the thought. If they did want to talk with him, it was too late to run. But if that was the case, he'd have heard about it by now, as he kept a close ear on this radio. Somebody inside City Hall would have gotten wind of this and let him know.

He went about his job this morning with the same dedication and seriousness he'd shown for the past fourteen years, looking at people's yards and watching out for stray cats or dogs. If citizens in Park City were in violation of any ordinances, they were in big trouble with him.

* * *

The task force had gathered downtown early to cover last-minute details, before moving en masse toward Park City. No one inside the investigation had leaked anything about recent developments, so the police were able to drive north without any interruptions or distractions from the media or anybody else. By 11 a.m., a few unmarked cars, filled with officers in dark suits, had arrived on Rader's block. Half an hour later, the bomb squad showed up. A lab truck came next along with the ATF, as a helicopter whirred overhead, monitoring everything on Independence Street and the surrounding area. Yellow police tape was going up at the ends of the block, shutting down traffic, and neighbors were coming outside and looking at the sky, asking each other what was going on. Police officers moved door-to-door but offered no explanation for their presence, telling people they should be prepared to evacuate the street. Gossip was spreading to other parts of Park City that something important was up, but nobody knew what it was. Folks on Rader's block were standing on their lawns, carrying cameras and starting to snap pictures. By noon, the task force was in place and ready to strike.

At exactly 12:15, Rader left work and got into his truck for the short ride home, where lunch was waiting. Pulling out of the City Hall parking lot, he took a right and drove up to the stoplight on Sixty-first Street North, running through the heart of Park City. Turning left, he slowly made his way toward Independence, which was set back from the highway and curved so he could not yet see any of the activity on his own block. Taking a right onto the access road leading to his house, he glanced in his rearview mirror.

A police car, a Chevy Impala, had moved in behind him, its red light flashing. Rader looked confused; he hadn't been speeding and had used his signal when exiting Sixty-first, the way he always did. He steered the truck to the side of the road and came to a stop, killing the engine. Before the officers behind him could step from their vehicle, he'd pulled open the door and gotten out. Other cars were coming toward him, pinning in him and his vehicle.

Six members of the task force—Detectives Clint Snyder, Dana

Gouge, Kelly Otis, and Tim Relph, plus officers Scott Moon and Dan Harty—charged toward the stunned-looking man, aiming handguns, rifles, and shotguns.

"Hit the ground!" one said.

"Now!"

Rader offered no resistance, going down on all fours and then onto his belly on the cold asphalt. Two FBI agents, John Sullivan and Chuck Pritchett, and two KBI agents, Ray Lundin and Larry Thomas, came forward. Lundin grabbed Rader's right arm and Sullivan his left.

Nobody announced he was under arrest and the suspect didn't say a word.

Detective Gouge handcuffed Rader and asked if he was carrying any weapons.

"A knife," he mumbled, and one officer reached into his pocket and disarmed him.

Rader, who was still on the pavement, glanced up at the policemen and gave a strange little smile, as if acknowledging that law enforcement had finally done its job and he'd been caught.

"He was very compliant," one officer later said.

Detective Relph took Rader to the transport car, where Lieutenant Landwehr was waiting in the backseat. KBI agent Larry Thomas opened the back door, while overhead the helicopter hovered, capturing the arrest using still photography.

With Rader safely tucked into the rear seat, the car pulled away from the access road and got onto Sixty-first Street, heading downtown.

"Hello, Mr. Landwehr," the handcuffed man said in a calm, friendly tone, showing the same little smile.

For the past several minutes, the lieutenant had been nervously watching the arrest from inside the vehicle. The takedown had been so unsettling that Landwehr was having trouble catching his breath.

After gulping once or twice and composing himself, he said, "Hello, Mr. Rader." The men eyed each other almost as if they'd met before.

"Do you know why you're going downtown?" the lieutenant asked.

"I have a pretty good idea."

XXXI

B Y 12:18, Rader was in custody and search warrants were start-ing to be served. Police had already arrived at both the local City Hall, where they were about to confiscate Rader's work papers, and at his home, informing his shocked wife of the arrest and begin-ning to look for evidence. The bomb squad was hunting for explo-sives, the lab truck hovered nearby, the ATF looked on, and the SWAT team wasn't quite ready to stand down. As the task force lead-ers had repeatedly made clear, everything law enforcement did today had to be executed within the confines of due process and the Fourth Amendment rules of search and seizure of private property. The FBI and WPD anticipated a long and costly legal battle against Rader; it was critical that no minor procedural errors committed today be turned against the district attorney's office when it was prosecuting the defendant in court a year or two from now. While the authorities felt certain they had the right man and his DNA from the crime scenes, they couldn't assume this piece of evidence alone would be enough to convict him and possibly bring a death sentence (FBI agents were making plans to fly to Michigan to obtain a current DNA sample from Rader's daughter). The trial would be high profile, and Rader would surely be represented by a number of excellent private lawyers or public defenders. The DA's office would need everything they could muster to win.

As the activity increased around the Rader home, with police swarming everywhere and barking orders, more neighbors came out-side with their pets and stared at 6220 Independence. Some brought out lawn chairs, unfolded them, sat down in the warm, late-February sunshine, and settled in to watch. Motorists on Sixty-first Street and the streets adjacent to Independence were slowing their cars and rubbernecking so much that the officers began handing out tickets. Word of the arrest was spreading through Park City, and people were getting their first taste of what was to come. This was obviously no minor bust, but might have something to do with the BTK case, which many locals were already concerned about. Two of the killer's recent communications had been found not far from Park City, at the Home Depot on Highway 96 and on North Seneca Street. Rumors were now flying up and down Independence Street and beyond, which caused more people to show up and more cars to slow down.

At 12:20, the police came to the Park City Public Library, just off the highway and a couple hundred yards from the arrest. The building was supposed to open at noon on Fridays, and the girl whose job was to unlock the doors had come to work more or less on time but forgotten her key. Now she was being confronted in front of the library by detectives who had a search warrant. Discombobulated, she called the woman who ran the library, Dawn Pilcher, and in a rattled voice said that police officers were gathered outside the building and wanted to go inside and look for evidence. When Dawn asked what they were doing at the library, she was told they had a search warrant and she needed to get down there right away. A short time later, Dawn ushered the police into the library, which seemed designed for children, with its open front room and kids' artwork hanging from the ceiling.

"I didn't let those police in until they showed me that warrant," the librarian says. "Believe me, I wouldn't let just anybody come in and do what they did. You gotta be very careful these days. When they told me why they were here, I didn't know what to think. I didn't know that man—Dennis Rader—had never met him in my life, but the police thought he might have come into this library to do some writing. Boy, was there a lot of activity going on around Park City and inside this building that day. They came in here and checked out our computers, and I guess he'd been on one of them without us even knowing it."

By now the media had been alerted to what was unfolding in Park

City, and a pack of journalists was heading north to Rader's hometown, where they would follow the police to every location. Later in
the day, when reporters tried to get Dawn to come out of the library
and give them an interview, she refused.

"We had to shut down the rest of that afternoon," she says, "and
the police stayed here five hours looking at our computers. They
searched everything. I couldn't go anywhere and it was just very, very
stressful. The most amazing thing was that he lived and worked right
here among us—right up the street! That's what I can't stop thinking
about. I don't look at people the same way anymore. The other
evening a man came to the front door of the library and it was one
minute before closing time and I just didn't feel comfortable with
him. Before all this happened, I'd have let him in, but I went to the
door and locked it for the day and that was that.

"Back in the 1990s, I worked at the *Eagle* and people there talked
about the BTK case all the time and traded stories about the terrible
things he'd done. They were still traumatized by all this, even though
the killing had apparently stopped. People never did stop talking
about it, and it had lately been all over the paper. You know that
Dennis Rader and his wife must have sat on their couch and watched
the ten o'clock news about this case, just like everyone else had been
doing. Can you imagine that? What about his wife? What was she
thinking all that time? If my husband ever did anything like he did,
I'd be in jail for murder."

Pastor Clark had just finished writing his sermon at the church and
was starting out the front door for lunch when he saw four men on the
other side of the glass and thought they wanted to sell him something.
Minutes later, Lieutenant Thomas Bridges was sitting in the minister's
chair in his office reading from a search warrant and explaining that
Christ Lutheran's president had just been arrested in the BTK investigation. After half an hour of listening to Lieutenant Bridges in a state
of disbelief, the preacher began making phone calls. He reached the
Lutheran Synod in Chicago and got through to their crisis-management office, quickly laying out the situation and asking for help. The

shock waves beginning to rumble through Park City were going to hit
the church much harder, and the pastor was thinking not only about
what this would mean for the Rader family, but for his entire congregation. The man in charge of the crisis-management office, Bishop
Gerald Mansholt, was making plane reservations for Wichita and
would be at Christ Lutheran within twenty-four hours.

Through the detectives, the minister learned that Rader had asked
to see him, and when he was able to leave the church that afternoon,
he didn't hesitate to drive downtown to visit the jail or wherever the
man was being held. At the police department at City Hall, he was
told Rader wasn't there and the authorities wouldn't assist him in
getting to the church president. For now the suspect was off-limits to
everyone, and in the future Pastor Clark would need to show them
his papers of ordination, proving he was a minister, before he could
speak to the prisoner. Returning to Park City, the preacher made
plans to meet with Rader's wife and mother, who were totally bewil-
dered. By late afternoon others in the congregation were starting to
hear the news.

In years past, Christ Lutheran had put on a seder for Maundy
Thursday, which fell three days before Easter and commemorated
Jesus' Last Supper. As a youngster, Brian Rader had played one of the
twelve disciples who'd sat at the table with Jesus. During the Christmas season, the church was turned into Bethlehem, and both Brian
and Dennis had lent their hands to building this set, while Paula sang
Christmas carols in the choir. Through all these activities, Donn
Bischoff, an ex-president of Christ Lutheran, had gotten to know the
Rader family. Like Dennis, he was a rock among the worshippers,
someone you could turn to for anything and always count on to make
things better. He and his wife, Deborah, had the same kind of relationship with Paula and Dennis as many others in the congregation.
They were friendly with the couple, but didn't really socialize with
them. A humble-looking man with an open and sincere manner,
Donn had admired the Raders for decades.

He lived outside Wichita and worked for the Kaneb Pipeline Company. On February 25, he came home about four-thirty and went for
a bike ride. When he got back forty-five minutes later, his wife told

him that something was happening with the BTK case in Park City, but she wasn't sure what. Another church member had called their house and asked her a lot of questions.

"The story was all over the news and my wife was in an excited state," Donn says. "I was getting ready to take a shower, and details were coming out about the arrest on the news. They mentioned Independence Street. Deborah and I looked at each other and said that's where Dennis lives and near Paula's mother. They were showing this area on TV, and I thought, 'Man, that's getting close to home!' They said the suspect was a compliance officer in Park City. There were only two of those and one was a woman.

"The phone rang and Channel 12 asked me if I knew Dennis Rader. Things were starting to click and I thought, 'Oops! This is the "person of interest" they're talking about in the media.' The reporter asked me about Dennis, but I didn't say a lot. Pretty soon, they realized they wouldn't get any more news out of me."

When he asked the reporter how she'd gotten his name, she said it was from the church's Web site, where, as the head of the men's breakfast outings at Christ Lutheran, Donn was listed. After hanging up, he immediately got busy trying to cut off outside access to this Web address. All evening his phone kept ringing, with calls from other churchgoers and from another TV station wanting to come to his home and do an interview, but he and Deborah said no. Church members had decided among themselves to offer the media as little as possible, at least for now, because they really didn't know how to respond.

"From that point on," Donn says, "we were in wonderment and shock. Deborah and I thought about going down to the church that evening, but decided to stay home."

The next morning, they drove to Christ Lutheran and threw themselves into tidying up the building and other housekeeping chores. If the church was going to be on television, they wanted it to look good. The media were camped out in the parking lot asking for interviews, and the Bischoffs were the first to show up, but again they brushed them off. By now not just local press were covering the church angle, but national outlets as well.

"For the rest of the day," Donn says, "the national news kept showing a picture of our church with one car in the parking lot, and that car was ours. As the morning went on, more people in the congregation arrived and we all sat around and offered each other support and surmised what might happen next. Deborah and I had intended to go home and watch the press conference about the arrest, but Pastor Clark came to the church so we decided to stay. We had one TV set, and six of us crowded around it. We didn't let the media come inside but some of them tried to. Those people are aggressive.

"Everybody inside that church was just stunned. *Betrayal* was one of the words people were using the most. Some felt deeply betrayed. Some were angry. The big feeling was grief for his family."

XXXII

B<small>Y TWELVE-THIRTY</small> on Friday afternoon, the transport vehicle carrying Rader and Lieutenant Landwehr had reached downtown Wichita, and press reports were erupting about a huge police move against somebody in a northern suburb. Details were fuzzy, but a large story was breaking and the authorities knew they had limited time in which to avoid the coming media onslaught. They'd carefully planned their next piece of strategy. Normally, high-profile criminal suspects were driven into a tunnel below City Hall, discharged from a police car, and taken into custody upstairs, but the task force had feared that today reporters might already be waiting for them at the tunnel entrance. Instead of going to City Hall, they quietly hustled Rader into the Epic Center, which had been chosen for several reasons.

The first was that nobody was expecting them to do this. Second, it was the most impressive structure in Wichita—the most attractive and expensive-looking—with its marble lobby and sweeping atrium. Finally, it housed the local FBI headquarters, where Lieutenant Landwehr and his federal counterpart, behavioral analyst Special Agent Bob Morton, would conduct the initial interview with Rader. The Epic Center's handsome surroundings were meant to convey to the suspect that both he and his case were extremely important and that the authorities had taken him to the highest level of law enforcement. They hoped to appeal to his ego, so he would relax and perhaps open up. Nobody could predict what a suspect might do right after being arrested, so the task force was prepared for silence from Rader or his requesting a lawyer or a long wait before he said anything of substance.

By 12:35 p.m., Landwehr and Morton had taken him to the fourth floor of the Epic Center, where he was swabbed for DNA.

Rader was aware of how many middle-aged, white males in the metropolitan area had been swabbed since the investigation had restarted last March and attempted to joke about this with the men.

"I make four thousand and one," he said, but they didn't respond.

Landwehr read him his Miranda rights, which provided him the opportunity to have an attorney present, but he didn't ask for one. The lieutenant announced that the conversation would be video-taped, and they began. For the next three hours, Landwehr and Morton played a verbal game with the suspect, gradually letting him know that they had his daughter's DNA and were going to compare the genetic material from his own mouth swab with the DNA found at the Otero, Fox, and Wegerle crime scenes. The goal was simply to get a discussion flowing and keep him talking. Landwehr went about this calmly and patiently, his manner unforced. Rader didn't seem to feel threatened and, to the lieutenant's surprise, hadn't even asked why they were interrogating him about the BTK case. After three hours, the questions suddenly became more pointed.

"Have you been following the investigation?" Landwehr said.

"Yeah," Rader replied. "I've been a BTK fan for years—watching it."

"What will happen," Morton said, "if your DNA matches the crime scene DNA?"

"I guess that might be it, then."

What, Landwehr asked, did he remember about the Otero murders?

"Four—well, whatever was in the paper," Rader said. "Four members were killed. A man and a wife, two kids. And the way the paper dictated—it was pretty—pretty brutal. Yeah. You spent quite a bit of time looking for the guy."

"Why were the Oteros murdered?" the lieutenant pressed.

"Well, if you take that murder and some of the others, I would say you've got a serial killer loose." Rader paused. "When was the last one? What year was that?"

Landwehr and Morton weren't sure what he was asking.

Before they could respond, he brought up the year 1986 and muttered, "Oh, Vicki."

Why, Landwehr wanted to know, did he refer to the victim by her first name?

"You got to remember," Rader said, "I've read quite a bit about the cases."

The two men sensed he might be ready to say more and didn't interrupt him.

"It's always intrigued me," he said. "I assume this person left something at the crime scene that you guys could match up with DNA. But after all of these years, they still have that stuff?"

They nodded in unison, thinking he might go on, but he didn't. It was time to play their biggest card.

Landwehr showed Rader the diskette he'd mailed to KSAS, just to see what kind of reaction it produced. For years, FBI profilers had been placing pieces of evidence in front of homicide suspects during interviews, as a way to rattle them or cause a change in their body language. The lieutenant set the flat purple object on the table near Rader.

He couldn't stop looking at the floppy, but didn't speak for a while, as if his mind was making the connections behind his arrest.

"There's no way," he finally said, "I can weasel out of that. Or lie."

They both shook their heads, as though this were a gesture of sympathy or at least understanding.

Rader was silent, but when he began talking again, his tone had shifted and he sounded worried, the floppy clearly upsetting him. He asked about the current status of the death penalty in Kansas (in 1994, the state had instituted lethal injection of convicted murderers).

BTK, he said, might have trouble if he went to prison because he'd killed children. The worst offenders in the eyes of an incarcerated population were those who'd sexually assaulted or taken the lives of kids.

The men nodded again, determined not to say anything until they were certain he was finished. Rader had begun scratching himself.

"You guys have got me," he announced. "How can I get out of it? Isn't any way you can get out of the DNA, right?"

Three hours and fifteen minutes into the interview, Rader glanced at Morton with an expression of vulnerability, giving the FBI agent the opportunity he'd been looking for.

"Say," Morton asked, "who are you?"

Rader didn't respond.

"Say it," Morton said. "Say it."

Rader blurted out, "I'm BTK."

It was the second time in his life he'd said this to another human being, having whispered the words in Nancy Fox's ear as she was dying.

Still, the men did not interrupt him, but let the admission hang in the air.

"I'll tell you the story," Rader said, "but it will take a while. We can start with one and work the others."

As they were agreeing to this, he asked what kind of accommodations he could expect from now on.

"Am I going to be in a special section of the jail," he said, "or am I going to be thrown in with a bunch of the loonies?"

Landwehr assured him that he'd be treated like everyone else taken into custody and held at the Sedgwick County Detention Facility next to the courthouse.

Rader mentioned the messages he'd been sending to the police and press since early 2004.

"Once the media thing started going," he said, "I had to feed the media. The media is like your fan club."

He looked at the diskette again and then at the lieutenant, and in a tone filled with surprise, disappointment, and anger, he said, "How come you lied to me, Ken? How come you lied to me?"

The question stunned Landwehr. It had been incredibly naive of Rader to ask the police if they could trace apparently deleted information on a diskette, but this remark was even more baffling. It was beginning to hit the lieutenant just how deeply this bizarre serial killer had bonded with him, and how much he'd enjoyed their game of hide-and-seek. The man sounded genuinely hurt.

"Because I was trying to catch you," the lieutenant replied.

For the first time that afternoon, Rader became indignant, dis-

mayed that the police, who were sworn to uphold the law, had deliberately misled him.

"Why did you lie to me, Ken?" he said again. "We had such a
good thing going. We had such a rapport."

The men traded startled glances and let him ramble on until he
changed gears again, bringing up the Vian killing and staring down
at the disk. He'd been certain that it was blank except for his own
message to the WPD.

"You guys had to do something else," he complained to Morton.
"I talked to some other people about it and they said, 'Floppies can't
be traced. Floppies can't be traced.' And I thought, 'Should I take a
gamble?' And I knew I was taking a big gamble. And I really thought,
'I know Ken's trying to catch me, but I really thought he was honest
when he gave me the signal: it can't be traced.' I really thought that."

A sigh escaped from Rader and he looked deflated. "The floppy
did me in."

Landwehr and Morton said they were taking a break, but Rader
would not be left alone. As they were going, KBI's Special Agent in
Charge Larry Thomas walked into the room and sat down across
from him.

"Well," Rader said, "you guys got the evidence. There's no way I
can get out of it or beat around the bush. Whether it's a day or two
or a week, you're going to find it, so I might as well just fess up.
They'll probably be things that I've even forgot about. A lot of that
is gone after thirty-one years."

Eyeing Thomas, he said, "You're going to be talking to a guy
that's really weird and has these dreams. . . ."

Sometime later, Landwehr came back in and said that individual
task force members, who'd each been assigned to investigate one of
the BTK murder cases, were ready to interrogate him about specific
crimes.

Rader seemed eager to help them and offered to draw them some
maps.

"I'm going to need some calendars," he said. "You got a simple
pencil or something? I can't work without a pencil. Okay, where do
you want to start?"

XXXIII

NINE HOURS AFTER the interview began, Rader's DNA test came back from the lab and was consistent with genetic markers left behind in the semen at the Otero, Fox, and Wegerle crime scenes. It was now official: he was BTK.

Once the KBI's Larry Thomas had left Rader, a new round of detectives began asking him about the eight murders they were certain he'd committed, plus the deaths of Marine Hedge and Dolores Davis, who'd been killed either in or just outside of Park City. Landwehr and Morton had softened Rader up for these men, and he'd bounced back from the disappointment he'd felt several hours earlier over Landwehr's lying to him about the diskette. By sundown, something extremely unusual was unfolding in the interview room at the Epic Center. Word was filtering out and reaching other task force members on the fourth floor that Rader had started to talk and wouldn't stop. Since admitting that he was BTK in late afternoon, he'd begun to gush out a confession, a stream of language pouring from him, a river of memories and details, as if all this had been pent up for too many decades and could no longer be contained. The bonding set in motion through the communications between Rader and Lieutenant Landwehr eleven months earlier was reaching a climactic crescendo.

On this Friday evening and long into the night, Rader finally found some people he could speak to honestly and openly—just twelve days short of his sixtieth birthday—and he was elated. He didn't have to hide anything anymore. These were the kind of guys he'd always wanted to be around, he felt a natural connection with them because of their work in law enforcement, and they were good listeners. He didn't need to feel so isolated anymore, so cut off from others, and the detectives were leading him toward a psychological breakthrough: he really *had* had an effect on the world, after all. He could see that in the astonished eyes of the men questioning him. Rader had never shown this side of himself to any living person, and the gushing performance was awkward and painful, grotesque and shameless, in its neediness and vanity. His ego was stoked, the police knew exactly how to flatter him into revealing more and more. Everything he'd done since 1974, from naming his projects to imitating James Bond or John Wayne during an assault, had been carried out as if it were part of one large, never-ending movie, and now surrounded by cops who were hanging on his every word and taking notes, he was at long last the star of his own film. Now that he had an audience, he wouldn't shut up, even admitting to the Hedge and Davis murders. The detectives sat back in amazement and let him spew. It was clear that for decades he'd craved someone to speak to, someone to know his secrets, and just as clear that he couldn't feel any of what he'd done to dead or living strangers.

As the hours slipped away, he didn't express any remorse for his victims or their families, but wondered aloud how all this might affect his family and church. He mentioned his vast collection of writings, drawings, and the thousands of slick ads of girls or women, some of them celebrities, that he'd snipped from magazines and pasted onto three-by-five-inch cards. If he got bored sitting at his desk or riding around Park City looking for code violations, he pulled from his wallet pictures of females and imagined what he would do with them. Sex and violence were his constant companions at work or home. Not the act of sex itself—but the consuming thought of it, the longing for sexual release and escape from wherever he was and whatever he was doing. He was interested in all forms of sex all the time, a condition psychologists refer to as paraphilia.

"There was a cup with a girl on it," he said. "I can pick that up and visualize how she would be tied up or something. . . . That's what I did with the slick-ad models. I would visualize how they would be in my fantasy death-to-pretty-girl room or torture room."

If he went to prison, he admitted, he might take up homosexuality in "the big house."

He described the Mother Lode, a jammed-full bottom drawer of a cream-colored metal filing cabinet. It held floppy disks, many drawings of women tied to torture mechanisms, and a three-ring binder entitled "Newspaper Clippings," containing the original articles and national magazine stories about the BTK killings. A maroon binder was for the chapter headings and edited chapters of his book about himself. A white binder cataloged all the messages he'd sent to the police and the media since 1974 and in the cabinet were souvenirs of his crimes, including a gold ring, some poetry he'd written, and the original WPD "wanted poster" from the Otero murders.

Talking like this felt so good that he just kept going, spilling out his fantasies and obsessions. Since childhood he'd known that he was different from other boys and had always wanted someone to notice this and do something about it. In grade school, he'd believed that a grown-up might see him staring at pictures of tied-up women and ask him about this hobby, but no one did. As an adolescent, he'd thought that somebody would catch him strangling a cat or discover his secret desires for Annette Funicello, but that hadn't happened either. In adulthood, he'd modeled his criminal career on a figure from the 1950s—the decade in which Rader's identity had been formed and frozen. Harvey Glatman was a serial killer who'd photographed women in bondage, then tortured and killed them. From Glatman's influence, Rader had conceived his own homicides and the name BTK. Until this evening, no one had ever observed anything important about him or taken seriously what he did inside his private universe or ever stopped him from doing anything, but these police officers were different and more like him.

They *wanted* to hear about trolling and stalking a victim, about bondage and torture and killing with a belt or panty hose or his bare hands. He'd never been able to talk about strangling another person before, but these guys weren't judgmental or putting him down, so he told them that over the years he'd had scores of projects, hundreds of them, outlining a few that hadn't come to fruition. He hadn't ever stopped trolling, but years had passed between some of the murders because he never went forward until he was satisfied with all the details of his planning and organization.

This wasn't at all what he'd expected getting arrested to be like. It was liberating and he was as astonished by what he was doing as everyone else in the room. Rader felt so comfortable with his interrogators that he laughed and joked and told one to write "BTK" on the lid of the cup he'd been drinking from before putting it back in the refrigerator.

He told them where to find the spillover from the Mother Lode, including his Hit Kit, inside his house in a large basket. In some hidden drawers were cheap Barbie doll look-alikes, and in his car was a shotgun. It was important to him that when the detectives recovered all these things from his home, they not disturb his domestic environment too much or create a big mess, because that would upset Paula and he'd spent decades trying to maintain marital calm. Being married wasn't easy for a man like him, he explained, because he always had to manage his time carefully and constantly be aware of his spouse's schedule.

"I have real good sex with my wife but it would be more fun if it was different," he said. "Personally, I would like to live by myself, be a lone wolf completely."

The entire interview lasted thirty-two hours and filled seventeen DVDs. The written material generated from the arrest would come to nearly three thousand pages.

Toward the end, he said that he was never really after a specific victim, but always chasing "a dream."

"Normally, I'm a pretty nice guy," he told the investigators. "I'm sorry, but I am. I've raised kids, I had a wife, president of the church, been in Scouts. It goes on and on and on, but I have a mean streak in me and it occasionally flares up."

Did he ever, Detective Gouge asked, tell anyone about his life as BTK?

"Oh, no. Not a soul. Been extremely hard mentally. It's kind of like a spy thing."

His last act as the criminal persona he'd created was going to be a "final curtain call. I was basically going to do this like a play production. I was going to write a list of the characters and down at the bottom 'BTK Productions' or some wild thing like that. It was going to have all you guys [in it]. . . . Your name was going to show up in there and what you did. Like Ken, the main BTK investigator. All the way back—boom."

While one set of officers was listening to Rader, another spoke with his wife and mother, and another called his son in Connecticut and daughter in Michigan to inform them of the arrest. If the task force was thrilled with taking the man into custody and his nonstop babble during the interview, none of the detectives had looked forward to conveying news of his arrest to his family members. As Rader was enjoying himself at the Epic Center with his tales of nocturnal adventures, his closest relatives were going through the first stages of devastation. His mother was seventy-nine and had difficulty comprehending what the police had told her. His children were staggered and his wife was reeling. Once the first wave of denial had started to fade and the officers had repeated their message enough times for it to begin to sink in, they were met with overwhelming disbelief and sadness. For the police, it was the toughest part of the day.

Another set of officers had driven across town to the plumbing business where one of Rader's younger brothers, Jeff, worked. They wanted to question him about Dennis and his parents and siblings. Like many in Wichita, Jeff hadn't paid a lot of attention to the BTK case, but everyone had heard something about the killer and the WPD's thwarted thirty-one-year effort to find him. When the detectives showed up, he couldn't imagine why they wanted to speak to him; he hadn't broken any laws and neither had anyone else he knew. They drove him to City Hall and put him inside a small room with task force members and an FBI agent, refusing to tell him anything except that he was now part of a criminal investigation. A big man with a large, graying mustache and a prominent belly that stuck out through the bib overalls he liked to wear, he would tell the *Eagle* that in his earlier days he'd been a "hell-raiser." Dennis agreed. When being questioned by the police, he let them know that his younger brother had been the troublemaker in the family when they were growing up, not him. He was never a problem for either of his parents.

When the officers asked Jeff about his grandparents, parents, and three brothers, he answered as best he could. Then they zeroed in on one family member. Did Dennis have a fascination with trains?

"Not that I know of," Jeff said, adding that as a kid he'd loved trains and had played in a nearby train yard.

He kept wondering why they wanted to talk with him, and they kept brushing aside his question and diverting his attention, but then one of the detectives could no longer hold back.

"Your brother is BTK," he said.

Jeff looked at him and began to laugh. "No way! You got the wrong guy."

They all shook their heads and one said, "We're sure."

The FBI agent asked Jeff if he or any of his brothers had ever been sexually abused or abused in other ways by their father. Jeff adamantly denied this and would do so again in the newspaper. His parents were religious and loving people, he explained to everyone who posed this question, and had taught all their children the difference between right and wrong.

On Friday evening, Pastor Clark was able to contact Paula Rader and some of her in-laws.

"Paula was in shock," the minister says. "Just total shock. Like anyone who'd been married to somebody for thirty-three years and then you learn your husband is arrested for killing all these people over so many years. Bewilderment. Anger. Denial. Hurt. Confusion. We all felt betrayed. This was a breach of trust beyond description. The people in our church had prayed with Dennis and knelt beside him on Sunday mornings during Communion. I'd given him the bread and wine."

Pastor Clark had arranged for a social worker in the congregation to come to Christ Lutheran over the weekend with a crisis intervention team and offer counseling to anyone who wanted it. About fifty people would show up to talk and cry and grieve.

Rader had spent his life trying to protect his loved ones from himself, but by Friday night all that had been shattered forever. They weren't suffering just because of his arrest; their identities as his wife and children were under assault, as they were now being publically identified as "relatives of BTK." If their first reaction was revulsion that a husband or father had committed a series of unfathomable crimes, the second sliced much closer to the bone. He'd fooled them for decades, just as he'd fooled the police and the media and his church and his victims when he was lying his way into their homes. If his family hadn't had a clue about the person they'd lived with for twenty or thirty years, or couldn't recognize a monstrosity when they saw one, what else were they missing? If evil could fit in this easily and go unnoticed, where else was it thriving?

XXXIV

LATE FRIDAY, the WPD called Wichita's mayor, Carlos Mayans, and told him that the DNA in storage since 1974 matched that of the suspect arrested earlier in the day: BTK had been caught. Mayans was ecstatic, as were other officials in the city, including District Attorney Nola Foulston, who'd watched some of Rader's confession from behind a glass window. Despite the frenetic media coverage of police activity during the second half of Friday, reporters weren't entirely certain what had happened and unaware of the matching DNA. Sneaking Rader into the Epic Center had been a coup. The authorities didn't want to say anything to the world until they were ready to make a major announcement, and they just about were. The WPD, the KBI, the FBI, and other legal personnel were planning a press conference for Saturday at 10 a.m. inside the council chambers at City Hall. Invitations were going out all night long, and a crowd of two hundred was expected. Following the arrest, the police had taken on the second-hardest task of the day, after confronting Rader's kin. They'd begun notifying the victims' relatives about the Saturday-morning event, should they want to come. *Disbelief* was again the term used to describe the response of this group of people, many of whom had thought they wouldn't live long enough to hear this news. Some did want to attend, and the police said they would brief them privately before 10 a.m. so they would know what to expect. Officers would accompany them to the council chambers and watch over them during what was sure to be an emotional time.

The media were alerted, but told neither the specific reason for the press conference nor the name of the suspect. Both local and national organizations planned to cover it, including CNN, MSNBC, and Fox News. CNN was moving aside every other story on Saturday morning and making Wichita the focal point for the hottest news item in the world. A sense of drama permeated downtown, which was filling up with press vehicles, satellite dishes, and a tangible buzz. By dawn Saturday, the excitement had reached that critical mass that comes when the collective media focus their attention on one place or person.

As the press conference began, the focus quickly dwindled away, with the event becoming odd or incomprehensible and upsetting a number of people. Tuning in from a distant town or another nation, you'd have thought you were watching a political fund-raiser or something designed to boost civic pride, like the opening of new mall. On the City Hall dais were Mayor Mayans, DA Foulston, and representatives of the major agencies involved in the investigation, led by Lieutenant Landwehr, KBI head Larry Welch, Police Chief Norman Williams, and Representative Todd Tiahrt, the Republican congressman who had last July obtained $1 million in federal funding to expand the hunt for BTK.

Chief Williams kicked off the morning by stepping to the mike and saying, "Bottom line: BTK is arrested."

The crowd unleashed wild applause and high-fiving; people jumped out of their seats, tears flowed, and hugs were exchanged. When the cheering ended, everyone thought Williams would announce the killer's name and release his photo and the details of the arrest, but proceedings came to a sudden halt. Various speakers spent the next forty-two minutes thanking one other for their excellent work in catching the most notorious criminal in the region's history, the event detouring into what many would label "a pep rally." In television time, forty-two minutes is beyond eternity, and the national press could not abide this delay. Before the speeches stopped, all the major networks had cut away to other, more pressing business and missed the coming news. They also missed the heart of the story.

The maddening frustration and fear Wichita had experienced during the past three decades was perfectly reflected in those forty-two minutes of the government slapping itself on the back. BTK's savagery, the randomness of his attacks, the ongoing pain he'd inflicted, his mocking of the WPD in his communications, and his ability to elude the police had hurt and embarrassed the city for a generation. If the self-congratulating went on far too long, and if the killer had given the authorities a huge assist by sending them a diskette with his name on it, this was no time to quibble. The event wasn't being held for the convenience of the mass media or for outside observers. The moment had arrived when law enforcement could at last tell the victims' relatives that the beast who'd ravaged their families so many years before had finally been found. The devil was in custody, less than a block away, and it was time to celebrate. If the police and politicians wanted to spread some love for themselves and their city, the hell with CNN and everybody else. A new sign on a store in Wichita said it all: "Even the dogs feel safer now."

The speeches eventually ended and Lieutenant Landwehr stepped forward and identified the individual being charged with ten murders in the BTK case as Dennis Rader of Park City. TV producers were aggravated by forty-two minutes of waiting for the meat of the press conference, but the handful of people watching this at Christ Lutheran Church were downright angry. They didn't know anything about what had taken place at the Epic Center since yesterday afternoon and hadn't accepted that their president was BTK, and not the most decent and reliable member of the congregation. He'd only been charged with these crimes, not tried or convicted. What about the presumption of innocence and objectivity in the media? What about the jury that would hear his case? Rader had just been declared guilty in the press, and this was going to be broadcast throughout Wichita and Kansas, across the nation and around the globe. How could he possibly get a fair shake in the courtroom?

"The press conference was a fiasco," says Donn Bischoff, who viewed it at the church with his wife, Pastor Clark, and a few others, while the media milled outside in the parking lot. "They took sixty minutes to do a two-minute announcement. All circus and no substance. People in general were disgusted."

*   *   *

Following Lieutenant Landwehr's announcement, the police released a photo of Rader taken after he'd put on the standard orange jumpsuit given to those being booked into jails. Broadcast everywhere, it captured one of the most disturbing expressions ever seen on someone who'd just been busted. For decades, Rader had contended that when he was in the mood to kill, Dennis stood aside and BTK or Factor X or a demon named Rex took over his mind and his body and came in for the strangulation. In this photograph, Rader's always-combed hair was mussed, his eyes enraged or deranged, and his entire appearance deeply ugly, but in ways that went beyond the physical. The force behind his eyes looked possessed of an iron will and a blind selfishness, prepared to destroy anything that got in its way—man, woman, child, or animal. You couldn't escape the thought that this was how he appeared when murdering someone. The nasty-looking frog he'd been imagining inside himself and nurturing all those years had leaped out from his bones and taken over his features. The mess he'd always been afraid of creating was all over his face. For someone so concerned with neatness and control, Rader had to be mortified by the picture, which was how he was introduced to the world. Much worse exposure was to come.

Shortly after the arrest, the comic host of HBO's *Real Time with Bill Maher* brought up the picture in connection with the tightwad character George Costanza, played by Jason Alexander on the popular sitcom *Seinfeld*.

"BTK looked just like Jason Alexander," Maher said, "after being told he wouldn't receive any residuals for *Seinfeld*."

It got a big laugh.

XXXV

B Y SATURDAY AFTERNOON, Park City was flooded with sight-seers and tourists visiting Wichita who couldn't resist driving up to the small town that had spawned BTK. Out-of-staters were taking snapshots of the house on Independence Street as locals yelled at them to move on. Journalists were canvassing every place Rader had worked since 1971 and talking with his neighbors, digging up as many stories about the good things he'd done in Park City as about his mean-spirited behavior on the job. His arrest set loose the chilling idea of sadistic evil living right next door, but struck at something else just as unsettling. Most people want to believe they can't easily be misled by appearances and to think well of others. An *Eagle* reporter interviewed George Martin, a scoutmaster and Rader friend who'd watched him teach Boy Scouts about knot tying, overnight campouts, and other outdoor skills. While recounting what a wonderful teacher and presence Rader had been for these youngsters, Martin broke down and wept.

Pranksters in Wichita had found the number for Rader's mother and begun making crank calls to her home. She'd stopped answering the phone, while Paula had gone underground and would stay there for months; Pastor Clark said she'd left the state. Rader's children also tried to escape media scrutiny, but not everything journalists did over the weekend added to the confusion and pain. On several occasions, Pastor Clark had come out from Christ Lutheran to speak to the press, and a brother whom he'd been estranged from for years saw one these televised news clips, gave the minister a call, and they had a heartfelt reunion.

On Sunday morning as worshippers arrived at the church, the media remained camped outside. Pastor Clark had been concerned that the congregation might stay away because of the publicity surrounding the president of Christ Lutheran, but the opposite happened, although no one from Rader's family made an appearance.

"Both services were huge," says Donn Bischoff. "The media crush was here but people walked right by the reporters in the parking lot without saying much to them and flocked into the sanctuary. We're such a family of friends and nearly everyone who's a member came that day. People talked about Dennis and the arrest and there was a lot of co-support and co-griefing. A lot of hugging and a lot of tears. People were comparing it to a death in the family or a really tough divorce. Except in a divorce the other person is still there, but Dennis was gone. That was the strangest part. We were so used to seeing him there, but he was absent and that was starting to hit us and it just kept hitting us throughout the day."

As the early service got under way, Pastor Clark and Bishop Mansholt from Chicago stood together at the head of the sanctuary. The minister shared some of the thoughts and prayers already pouring in from other Lutheran churches around the country, a process that would continue for weeks and bring in hundreds of messages of hope and love and healing, which the minister would tack to a bulletin board in the lobby.

"This is a very difficult time for you as a congregation," the bishop said. "Not only are our hearts heavy, but we grieve with you. The very foundations of our faith are shaken."

He asked worshippers to remember the families of BTK's victims and the family of Dennis Rader. For now, Christ Lutheran had taken no action to remove the arrested man as its president.

"We are not here to judge him," Pastor Clark said of Rader, "but to support him as a brother of Christ."

When the time came to gather the young children around him by the altar, the minister called the boys and girls up and sat down beside them. Smiling at their innocent faces, he cradled a stuffed bear and a yellow toy taxicab, saying these were some of his favorite toys. The children smiled back.

"Has anyone ever taken one of your favorite toys?" he asked.

A couple of kids nodded and he said, "You want to stay angry, but Jesus wants us to let go and forgive."

They listened quietly, but adults up and down the pews were sobbing, which continued during the service. The invisible web of relationships Rader had built all around him for decades was being broken, one by one, throughout the sanctuary.

Pastor Clark's sermon that morning was printed out and given to the media for distribution. At the start, his voice wavered a bit and so did his thoughts, but then he seemed to steady himself and find his way, just as he had his entire life. Rader had always been drawn to language, even as he mangled it in his writings, and now words were being used to try to make sense of the wounds that had opened up inside of Christ Lutheran Church:

"The events that have unfolded the past forty-eight hours have the power to destroy, to devastate us as a body of Christ, or these events can bring us together and strengthen us as a faith community in a way that will never be the same. These events have the power and energy to be a wedge that drives us apart, or they can be a force that will hold us together in these trying times.

" 'It makes no sense!' 'What is it all about?' 'What has just happened?' 'I just don't understand.'

"A sense of relief for some, a feeling of confusion for others! Where is the justice? Where is God? Why us, God? It can't be my son! It isn't my father! I just don't believe it! This is where many of us are in these troubled times. How can it be?

"And there are many others who cry out, 'Finally! It's over! What a relief! There is a God!' Or, 'Thank God!'

"There is such a tension between what is going on and what is real. Our understandings are mixed. Our views are varied. Our minds are troubled. Our hearts are heavy. We turn to God in confusion.

"We are in the midst of the Lenten season. We are in one of those dark valleys in our life journeys, both individually and as a body of Christ here at Christ Lutheran Church. We are in the midst of the Lenten season where we turn to the pain-filled, bled-on cross that held our lord and savior, Jesus Christ. We reflect on the pain and suffering our lord experienced and endured as he hung on the cross for each and every one of us.

"I had my sermon for today prepared and comfortably tucked away for one final once-over. Then on Friday afternoon of this past week a police officer came to the door of our church with papers in hand, and it changed everything. The name Dennis Rader was spoken softly but firmly. I was told Dennis had been arrested as a suspect in the BTK murders. I was told that many believed that Dennis Rader was very possibly the BTK murderer. I was told they had the authority to search the church premises for evidence pertaining to this arrest.

"The world changed that very moment. Nothing would ever be the same. Nothing would ever be able to restore life and its meaning back to what it was just a few short moments before that day. Whether the allegations were true or whether there was a misunderstanding, things had changed in a moment's notice. And yet, I can truly say, there was one thing that did not and had not changed that February day in 2005.

"As I began to think about what was happening, what was unfolding before my very eyes, I found myself listening to the final words of the Gospel of Matthew: 'And remember, I am with you always, to the end of the age' (Matthew 28:20b). 'I will always be with you to the end of the age.'

"Jesus has just given his disciples a very challenging task. He had presented each and every one of them with a task that had the potential of being life-threatening. Go and teach, to baptize and make disciples. That was quite a challenge, quite a demand, especially in those times. Their leader had just been crucified on a cross. They, the disciples, were frightened! Who would protect them? Who would keep them safe from those who disliked them, those who objected to what they had to say? Jesus assures them no matter what happens, he would walk with them, be with them to eternity.

"Sometimes, when we are in the valleys of life, we cannot see the presence of God in our life. Sometimes, the experiences are so dark that we cannot see through the muck and mire. And in those times we can lose hope. We lost sight of the light of Christ in our life and the darkness seems to overtake us. And yet, when we listen to the words of the Gospel writer John, in the first chapter of John, we hear words of hope, of light, of assurance.

"John 1:1, 3b–5: 'In the beginning was the word, and the word was with God. He was in the beginning with God. . . . What has come into being in him was life, and life was the light of all the people. The light shines in the darkness, and the darkness did not overcome it.'

"Christ is the light for all people. Christ's light shines in the darkness, and darkness cannot overcome the light. Christ will be with us through all the ages, in the dark times as well as in the light times. We have been challenged this week. And we are not sure what to do with it.

"One thing's sure—Christ is with us. The light of Christ continues to shine and lead us in the paths of darkness. As we continue forward to seek the truth that Christ wants us to know, we are to continue to pray for all concerned. We are to pray for the peace and comfort for those victims and family members of the BTK murderer. We must lift them up and ask God for continued strength in the days ahead. We must pray for healing of heart and soul for those who have been victimized in this tragic series of murders.

"We are to pray for all law enforcement people for the time and energy they have committed to the task of solving this problem. As we continue on as a body of Christ, it is important that we show compassion and love towards Dennis. If what is claimed is true, we should be about the business of asking for God's help in healing of heart and soul. As we travel from this day forward, we should pray for all of Dennis Rader's family members. Bring them peace and comfort as they too wonder what each new day brings.

"As a body of Christ, we can let the power of these events that come before us either destroy us, to overcome us, or these events can bind us up to a stronger body, to a stronger community in Christ. We have that choice. I propose that we choose to let this be a time of strengthening, of renewing and healing. As we continue to let Christ's light shine in our world, let us become the stronger in faith, in love, and in hope.

" 'The light shines in the darkness, and the darkness did not overcome it.'

"Jesus tells us that if we continue in his Word, we will know the truth and the truth will make us free. The truth from God will free us from the anger, the pain, the bitterness, the hardened heart, the release from being lost and confused. As a body of Christ, we are to continue to search for the truth that Christ brings us on the cross. As we look forward to the Lord's empty tomb and the hope of new life, may Christ's light continually shine in your darkness.

"Amen."

Following the service, two men stood outside and watched their young boys playing together on the swing set next to the church, the children swaying back and forth in the chilly late February wind, their hair flying up and down. Behind them was a half circle of tall pines separating Christ Lutheran's property from the fields that had been sown with winter wheat, a crop brought into the Midwest from Russia more than a century ago, so that the land could stay productive during the long cold months. Once the wheat had been harvested in June, the same fields could be planted again with beans or turned into pasture for grazing during the summer. The year-round growing of crops was a useful and practical concept in a place and among a people known for their practicality.

The boys kept swinging, laughing and calling out to one another in high, happy voices, while the men exchanged remembrances of their youth in Wichita and being terrified of BTK, especially at night, thinking their house would be the next one he broke into. They spoke of his grisly crimes and of how diligently Dennis Rader had washed the windows at the church, painted white stripes on the parking lot, maintained the sound system, and handed out crayons to their own kids before the services began. One man hunched his shoulders and kicked at the cold ground with the toes of his shoes and glanced over at the boys, turning his back on the other man and wiping at his eyes.

XXXVI

THAT SUNDAY, the police finally stopped questioning Rader and left him locked up, completely alone for the first time since his arrest. On Friday and Saturday, they'd tried to give him a break from the interrogation so he could get some sleep, but he'd refused their offer. He wanted to keep talking, so they let him, for thirty-two hours straight, but now the process was over. Having drained him of information while giving him their complete attention, they quickly abandoned him, no one coming round even to say hello. He couldn't have visitors yet and spent all day Sunday with nothing to do but think about the events since noon Friday. His bond had been set at $10 million, making it impossible for him to be released for any reason. He'd heard nothing from his wife or children, his minister or brothers or mother. During the church services, he kept thinking about Christ Lutheran and what Pastor Clark was saying to the worshippers and if they were talking about him. He missed his dog, Dudley, terribly.

Months later, he'd look back on this last Sunday in February, his first hours of solitary incarceration, and call it the lowest day of his life. He'd wanted to keep talking to the police and had been surprised when they wrapped up the interrogation. The relief he'd felt on Friday and Saturday, from being able to open up to the detectives, came crashing to an end. The police had heard enough and didn't want to hear any more; like others who'd investigated the case since 1974, some would have trouble dismissing or forgetting parts of what he'd told them, and the jaunty way he'd laid out his life. It hadn't seemed human. These men weren't his friends or colleagues in law enforcement, but as manipulative as Lieutenant Landwehr had been with the diskette. They didn't need him anymore and there was no one left to talk to. The confinement and the silence and the end-of-February weather, often tinged with dullness and depression, filled the cell and made him stir-crazy with questions he couldn't answer.

Where was Paula? Why hadn't Pastor Clark come to see him? Shouldn't he have asked for a lawyer before telling the police everything?

XXXVII

THE LOCAL AND NATIONAL media had descended on Christ Lutheran and wouldn't easily give up their interview requests. One out-of-town journalist tried to barge her way into the church by carrying an arrangement of fruit for the minister. The *Oprah Winfrey Show* sent a bouquet of flowers in the hope of nailing down a chat with a leading player in the drama (everyone wanted Paula, but the congregation had closed ranks around her, no one breathing a word about where she'd gone or if she'd ever come back). *Good Morning America* jumped into the fray, along with *People* magazine and many newspaper reporters. Everybody wanted to know the same things: Hadn't anyone ever noticed that he or she was living or working or praying next to a serial killer? Why couldn't the police find this guy? Had every single person in the case been in utter denial?

At the church, Pastor Clark set out a basket in the lobby for collecting cards for the Rader family, which he gave to Paula and her children. Worshippers made care packages—bright yellow gift bags filled with devotional books, snacks, and boxes of Kleenex—for Paula and Rader's mother. The minister continued sticking pushpins into a map on the bulletin board to illustrate where supportive e-mails to Christ Lutheran had originated, and it was an impressive sight. Tacked to the top of the board was a sign proclaiming: GOD'S GRACE AND LOVE ABOUNDS.

"We here at Riverview [a Baptist church in Wichita]," read one message, "want you and your congregation to know we are praying for you in this difficult time. We are also praying for the Rader family.

What heartache and pain they surely are going through as well as your whole church."

A letter from the First Lutheran Church in Akeley, Minnesota, said, "We are aware of the extreme shock, pain and anguish that you are experiencing as fellow members of the body of Christ."

A Michigan congregation mailed in a teddy bear, an Illinois preacher sent in colorful prayer birds made of ribbon, and somebody gave the church a check for $250. Little flags on the map denoted places mailing in multiple messages. On Sunday, March 6, Christ Lutheran ushers gave e-mail prayers and cards to everyone entering the sanctuary. A few negative e-mails had come in, which the minister kept in a special pile, and one day he intended to gather all these and burn them as part of a purging ritual.

In recent years, the United States had become a country where tragedies sprang up instantly and left behind huge memorials to the dead: the Oklahoma City bombing; Columbine High School; other schools or office buildings where enraged employees had opened fire and left bodies scattered on the floor; the hole in the ground where the World Trade Center had once stood in New York City; and many other places. Now it was Christ Lutheran's turn, and the number of heartfelt messages it received from strangers showed the widespread thoughts and feelings the arrest had unleashed.

The shock following all these tragedies wasn't just because so many had died in an apparently random or meaningless way, and it filtered into the words of the survivors or those who tried to explain the violence. People had expected to be protected by something—their government or religion or family or job or money—and had imagined themselves immune to such chaos and grief. Now they felt not just hurt, but betrayed. The bloodshed emerging from coast to coast hinted at the terrible secret that there was no such protection and nobody was safe from the horrors that would surely come again, but who knew when or where? A way of looking at life securely intact just a few days before had been destroyed, no longer adequate in the face of this harsh American reality. A new definition of evil, as Pastor Clark had once put it, seemed necessary, following a rash of murders driven by pure rage.

Just weeks after Rader's arrest, Christ Lutheran would be sending its own messages of support and prayer northward to people on Minnesota's Red Lake Indian Reservation. Sixteen-year-old Jeff Weise had shot his grandfather and a woman to death, then opened fire at his high school killing five students, a teacher, and an unarmed guard, before taking his own life.

FINAL
CURTAIN CALL

———

Cut off even in the blossoms of my sin,
Unhousel'd, disappointed, unanel'd,
No reckoning made, but sent to my account
With all my imperfections on my head.

— WILLIAM SHAKESPEARE, *Hamlet*

XXXVIII

RIGHT AFTER RADER'S arrest, the prison chaplain at the Sedgwick County Detention Facility gave the new inmate a Bible, which he devoutly read. On Tuesday, March 1, Pastor Clark showed his ordination papers at the jail and began driving there twice a week to visit his former assistant. He was separated from Rader by a thick pane of glass and they spoke on the phone for about forty-five minutes each session. The men didn't discuss the case, the crimes, or legal strategy, and the minister always let the incarcerated man set the agenda, while the preacher gave him updates on Paula and his children. They focused on spiritual issues—God and sin, forgiveness and salvation—closing their eyes and praying together on the phone. Pastor Clark wanted to give him Communion, but SCDF denied this request. The minister was the only person who regularly came to visit Rader, and his attitude toward the inmate never wavered.

When Pastor Clark was a boy, his mother had become upset with him and said that even though she didn't like something he'd done, she still loved him. Each time he entered the jail, these words reverberated through him and helped clarify his commitment to the prisoner. He and Dennis were both sinners and children of God, and the preacher's mission remained what it had always been: taking care of the soul of each worshipper at his church. How could Rader make this right before the Lord? What needed to be done for the inmate to find eternal life in heaven? Pastor Clark wasn't a judge or a jury or a cop or a lawyer or a media pundit. He had a specific job to do with a hurting parishioner, and he was going to do it.

When it became known through the press that the minister was supporting Rader at the jail, ugly phone calls and pieces of hate mail and e-mail began arriving at Christ Lutheran for Pastor Clark, some of it from outraged Christians. Why wasn't the preacher doing the same thing for the victims' families? Why was he trying to help this monster? Did he really think that someone like Rader could be saved? The stronger the criticism, the more resolute the pastor became. He was angry at how the WPD, the media, and District Attorney Foulston had tried and convicted Rader at that Saturday the twenty-sixth press conference, which left the minister more determined to stand by the abandoned prisoner.

In March, this became even more difficult after Rader told Pastor Clark and Donn Bischoff, who'd replaced him as the new church president, that he was in fact BTK and had killed ten people. All the allegations against him were true. Until now, only the police and DA's office had known the full extent of his confession, and the authorities had kept this information to themselves so it would not adversely affect their courtroom case. If Rader's arrest had put Christ Lutheran in a terribly difficult position, his admitting this to Pastor Clark and Bischoff made their situation even more challenging. In the coming months, both men would be interviewed by journalists and have to pretend that Rader might be innocent. Both played their parts well and kept their secrets quiet, but it wasn't like either of them to fudge the truth in public. Now they were, however inadvertently, part of Dennis Rader's life of deception. Despite what the inmate had told them, neither they nor anyone else knew how the case would turn out legally, because Rader hadn't yet decided what he intended to do in court. He could still go to trial and fight the charges or plead not guilty by reason of insanity.

Pastor Clark was fiercely protective of what went on between Rader and himself at the jail, but gradually revealed that the prisoner talked about being possessed by a demon. It was the same thing Rader had been saying to the media and the police since the 1970s: an outside force had the power to take over his mind and body and make him do despicable things. The minister wasn't sure what to make of this, but couldn't easily dismiss it; the idea of demonic possession stimulated him spiritually and intellectually, and he returned to cer-

tain biblical passages, looking at them in a new way. He began reading about demons, seeking out people who'd examined the subject,
and started thinking about exorcism, eager to learn more about it.

Going to the Sedgwick County Detention Facility became a part
of his new work routine, and the more he went, the more heat he felt.
He was under attack not just from those who believed he shouldn't
support Rader, but the Wichita branch of the nationwide antiabortion
group Operation Rescue, which would soon blast Christ Lutheran for
not publicly denouncing the jailed man. Jan Clark, the minister's wife,
was concerned about her husband's safety, but he refused to worry
much about this. He'd been called to the pulpit to serve people who
needed him, and no one had ever needed him more than Rader did
now. What good was all that talk on Sunday morning about the infi-
nite power and hope of God's love and mercy if you withheld the
promise of that from those who'd sinned the deepest? Grace and salvation were not idle goals, but eternal questions that everyone had to
face. Nobody could expect this kind of work to be clear of potholes or
sudden twists of fortune or mysterious ravines. Pastor Clark listened
to his wife and began taking more precautions now, locking the doors
on his truck and making sure the windows at his home were shut tight,
but what else could he do? If people wanted to do him harm, he
couldn't stop them. If he let fear define or control him, or refused to
reach out to a man at the lowest moment of his existence, what kind
of a minister was he?

The pastor tried to facilitate communication between Rader and
his family, but there wasn't much to do on that front. His wife and
children stayed away, but Kerri, who'd grown up adoring her father,
wrote him a sharp letter saying that he'd ruined all their lives, her
message reducing her father to tears. Only one of Rader's younger
brothers, who'd been serving in wartime Iraq but came home after
the arrest, went to the jail with the minister. It was Pastor Clark who
stayed faithful to the inmate every Tuesday and Thursday, going to
the detention facility and passing through the security measures to
get inside. Privately, after being told that Rader was BTK, the minister began praying that the man would plead guilty and be done
with this charade. The sooner his courtroom battles were over and

he'd accepted responsibility for his crimes in front of society, the quicker he could focus on coming to terms with God.

The hole that Rader's absence had left at Christ Lutheran was tangible. Following the arrest, people didn't merely talk about missing him at the services or the church dinners or the monthly council meetings. For months afterward, congregants spoke of seeing or sensing his lingering presence in the hallways or the sanctuary. He'd been there so much in recent years that it was as if a part of him were still around. One Sunday morning in mid-March, right before the late service began, Pastor Clark caught himself as he was about to call over his shoulder to ask Dennis to go up to the altar and light the candles.

Then he realized the man was never coming back.

XXXIX

W HEN HE WAS TAKEN into custody, Rader's income was between
$2,000 and $3,000 a month, which his wife supplemented
with income from her bookkeeping duties. With the loss of his paycheck, he couldn't afford the kind of legal help necessary to defend
himself against ten first-degree-murder charges. He was appointed
two public defenders, Steve Osburn and Sarah McKinnon, who
began trying to fashion a legal strategy out of nearly impossible circumstances: he'd spent thirty-two videotaped hours bragging about
his crimes to the police. All the murders he'd confessed to had
occurred between 1974 and 1991, when Kansas did not have the
death penalty in effect. It was reinstated in 1994, but Rader claimed
that he hadn't killed anyone after this date—a sore issue inside the
district attorney's office. As soon as the arrest was announced, media
rumors began flying that Rader had admitted to more than ten homicides, but Nola Foulston adamantly denied this. The DA, who might
have been looking at spending years and millions of dollars to pros-
ecute Rader successfully, didn't want her case muddied by such questions. The official story was that he absolutely hadn't murdered
anybody after 1991, but not everyone accepted it. Commentators
around the nation enjoyed speculating on television that BTK had
strangled far more than ten victims, and whenever they did this, Foulston grew more indignant.

Most serial killers don't just stop killing, and Rader had told
investigators that he'd continued to stalk victims and even picked out
the day for his latest attack—October 22, 2004—but this project
hadn't come to fruition. As a compliance officer, he'd traveled around

Kansas looking for criminal opportunities, seeking out targets, and breaking into homes. If he'd committed homicides beyond Wichita and Sedgwick County following the reinstatement of the death penalty, confessing to them could lead to death by lethal injection. Rader closely monitored developments in law enforcement, including advances in DNA research, and by the mid-1990s he knew that if he left behind any genetic material at a crime scene, the authorities could much more easily tie it to an individual suspect. That may have been reason enough to quit.

Under these legal conditions, the worst punishment he could receive was ten consecutive life sentences—unless he could come up with an explanation for his actions that included mental illness; then he might be committed to a psychiatric institution. His defense team began exploring this option and brought in five mental health experts to examine the defendant. It's difficult to get five psychiatrists to agree on anything, let alone something as complex as one's motives for killing ten people. With little hesitation, all five said the same thing. Rader was stone-cold sane in legal terms: he knew the difference between right and wrong when taking someone's life.

In its final report on the case, the district attorney's office would reiterate this finding:

"Dennis Rader did not suffer from any mental disease or defect."

XL

NEITHER RADER'S ARREST nor his prison confession to Pastor Clark had shaken the minister's faith in God, just as his son's accident hadn't in 1998, but they had thrown a kink in his theology. The State of Kansas may have decided that BTK was perfectly sane after killing ten people, but that explanation didn't satisfy the minister. Until February 25, 2005, six decades of living and forty years of thinking about issues like good and evil had convinced him that he could put these questions to bed, but his complacency had just been shattered. If he and the rest of the world could this easily be deceived by someone he greatly respected and admired, something more must be going on. He didn't know what it was or if finding any answers was possible, but that didn't matter. When your perceptions and belief system had been jarred to their foundation, that was a sign for you to do something bold. You had an obligation to reopen your investigation into the truth.

As Pastor Clark liked to say, "If God wants me to know more about something, He'll point me in the right direction. All this may be a dead end, but I'm open to where it may lead."

The minister was going in search of a new definition of evil, and he was hardly alone. He was about to start knocking into people, ideas, and social forces that drove the cultural and spiritual war that had permeated the United States since the 1960s and had given rise to modern evangelism. In the 1980s, the emerging Christian right had established two hundred TV stations, a thousand radio stations, and ten thousand elementary schools throughout America, while demanding that one of every four government employees share their faith. By

2005, these expectations seemed too modest. Born-again fundamentalists now occupied critical positions in the U.S. Congress, on the Supreme Court, and in the White House. Evangelical Christianity had swept through not just religion but every aspect of contemporary life: the media, education, the military, entertainment, politics, and was making headway in the teaching of science.

Many Christians believed that our nation was engaged in a bitter spiritual war, with evil struggling against good on every side and the Apocalypse approaching fast. Other realities were interacting with our normal one, and the results were wicked. As mainstream a minister as Billy Graham, when announcing his retirement from a New York City pulpit in June 2005, spoke openly of Satan and said the End Times were near. As the last days of earth arrived and the spiritual war intensified, the Devil himself would become much more clever, devious, and destructive—entering churches, Christian homes, and worshippers themselves, stopping at nothing to win. Variations on this message were constantly broadcast not just over radio and television; tens of millions of books had been sold around this theme: when Satan stooped this low, demons would take the form of human beings and the Final Days were at hand.

This kind of thinking had reached into many corners of America, including the prison system. In county jails and state or federal penal facilities from coast to coast, accused or convicted felons were coming forward and talking about demonic possession or otherworldly forces at work on them. They had blanked out when killing or raping or attacking a victim—something foreign had taken over their mind and body so they weren't fully responsible for what they'd done.

On July 16, 2005, *Time* magazine reported that Joseph Edward Duncan, suspected of killing three people in the Northwest, had written this on his blog before the murders: "God has shown me the right choice, but my demons have me tied to a spit and the fire has already been lit." In Denver, a serial rapist, Brent J. Brents, testified that he hadn't been present during the rapes but had fallen into unconscious darkness, where something else was committing his offenses. In Las Vegas, a California man, Stephen Michael Ressa, went on a homicidal spree in his car and later said that demons were standing on the sidewalk pointing at him and needed to be run over. Jailhouse preachers and prison chaplains often agreed with these views of inmate crimes and used Scripture to back them up. They said that "demonic invasions" and "dark principalities" were at loose throughout the land and fighting for every soul they could win.

This phenomenon wasn't occurring only in prisons. So many Catholics had been coming forward and asking for help with demons—Italy alone was reporting half a million annual cases of possession—that the Vatican officially sanctioned teaching a course about exorcism and revised its exorcism guidelines for the first time since 1614. Rome's leading exorcist, Father Gabriele Amorth, was averaging ten attempts a day to rid people of demons (some tormented Christians had reputedly spit nails at the priest). It wasn't just Catholics who were experiencing the paranormal. Since the turn of the new millennium, Protestants and evangelicals in particular had been seeking out hundreds and thousands of exorcisms from pastors armed with Bibles and the demand that the demon come forward, speak its name out loud, and depart the body of the possessed.

On another side of this debate stood science. Medical experts could now study the human brain in ways never before available, using MRIs and PET (positron-emission tomography) scans to locate and map any differences between the criminal mind and the brains of people who obeyed the law. Scientists hoped to discover if aberrant behavior could be tied to chemical imbalances, genetic defects, hyperactivity or lack of activity in certain areas of the brain. Was crime a mental health problem instead of a moral failing or character disorder? If that was true, would it be possible to identify at-risk young people before they ended up inside the criminal justice system? Some of the most advanced research into this subject was taking place at universities, but this was not an academic issue. At the start of the twenty-first century, America had 2 million people in prisons, more than any other country on earth, and the social cost of all this crime was incalculable.

Certain acts of violence were clouded by greed or intimate passions between the killer and the victim, but others seemed to be about nothing more than pure evil—the human penchant for destruction—

and Rader's fell into that category. He'd gained nothing by murdering ten people, except to relieve his anxiety and later express his feelings when writing about or drawing pictures of the deaths. Since his arrest, he'd made no serious attempt to explain the killings, other than a few casual remarks delivered to the police or other interviewers. He claimed that as a child he'd been dropped on his head and this might have caused brain damage and destroyed his moral sense (or he may have read in Peter Vronsky's *Serial Killers* that some *other* serial murderers said they'd been dropped on their heads as youngsters, so he decided to use this excuse for himself). No medical evidence supported that he had brain damage, but he hadn't been tested in the kind of depth provided by MRIs and PET scans. His other explanation was that a demonic force had taken hold of him decades ago and never let go. He'd been possessed by Rex or a perverse-looking force that from time to time had silently and invisibly entered him, turning him into a killing machine. When Rex wasn't present, he was free to be a decent and loving husband, a good father, steady employee, and faithful president of Christ Lutheran Church.

While many segments of evangelism had embraced the notion of demonic possession, Pastor Clark had long resisted the more extreme aspects of fundamentalism, by nature tolerant and accepting of his flaws and other people's. He didn't talk much about the hot-button Christian-right political issues, such as abortion, and spoke proudly of the fact that gay people worshipped at his church (Lutherans had taken no official position on the subject of homosexual marriage). When it came to his faith, he'd tried to hold on to a lighter touch.

"Take your work seriously," he liked to say, "but not yourself."

And, "If you don't think God has a sense of humor, look at how He created me."

Until the spring of 2005, the preacher hadn't worried much about the Apocalypse or demons invading his sanctuary and kneeling at the altar to receive Communion. He'd stood aside from the more divisive elements of his faith, but now he didn't know what to believe. Maybe he hadn't given the devil his due.

"I don't have all the answers now," he said a few months after the arrest, "but I've come to realize that we look at evil things in the world from the psychological model and try to understand the human mind and how it makes a person do what they do. Sally did something bad because she was abused as a child or the environment shaped her to commit a crime. Johnny did something bad because as a boy he was dropped on his head or he's chemically imbalanced. After Easter of this year, I began visiting with many people and came to realize there's another model out there for understanding evil. We haven't really considered the possibility of Satan working actively in the world, but I've been talking with people with years of experience in this area. They've seen very strange things, like objects flying across rooms, which is so un-Lutheran. In our faith, we don't really deal with evil in this way.

"In a passage about Maundy Thursday, Jesus announces his betrayer and washes Judas' feet and offers the Passover meal to his disciples. He says, 'The one who dips his bread in this dish is his betrayer.' Then Christ announces, 'Satan enters into him.' Is Jesus saying that Satan is real and actually does enter into people and take them over? Is he saying that he could see this? All that's happened with Dennis makes me read Scripture differently now, and this has opened up new realms for me in terms of understanding the world. I'm rethinking my theology.

"I don't know if Dennis was one hundred percent in control of his choices or if a demonic power was working through him, but I'm becoming more and more open to that possibility. I have so many questions. How do these dark forces take charge of a mind or heart or soul? How do you get rid of them? What if psychologists can't explain everything? Why did my faith work in my life but his didn't? How could he be two completely different people? When he was here at the church, he was sincere in what he said and did, so this is very hard to understand. I've had a glimpse of something with him and had an experience that other people haven't. In my biweekly conversations with him at the jail, I've watched him very closely. I see emotions rising in him over all the pain and suffering he's caused others, but I see something pushing them down, not letting them out. I see this physically, like something's holding him back. I can see the good Dennis Rader struggling against the bad one.

"I keep thinking about Job in the Bible. Satan took everything from him but his life, but Job remained faithful to God. If there's a parallel here, Satan has taken everything away from Dennis but his life. He has nothing—no job, no family, no friends, no future. He's a shell now, sitting there in prison, but God is still there for him. Question is, can he remain faithful to God and make things right with the situation he's in?"

In speaking to others about his new spiritual search, the minister kept hearing about a book published in the 1940s, *The Screwtape Letters,* by C. S. Lewis. Pastor Clark was unfamiliar with the fictional work, which Lewis had written when London was under siege during World War II. An English Christian intellectual, the author had imagined that one of the more experienced devils in Hades, named Screwtape, was writing to his nephew, a younger devil named Wormwood, about the finer points of capturing souls for Satan. The younger devil was just learning the ropes of evil while the older one tried patiently, and sometimes not so patiently, to instruct him on closing these deals. The book is clever and highly sophisticated—its central message that Satan is constantly striving in subtle and devious ways to undermine human goodness. People selling religion or politicians peddling democracy or patriotism can be dangerous. Anyone not on guard against his or her own weaknesses can give in to temptation without even recognizing this and gradually slide into the pit of damnation. The small lapses and mistakes made by individuals as they go about their daily lives or chase the distractions of love and sex can result in tragedies as large as the Second World War. Satan and his minions never rest, Lewis tells the reader, and they're ingeniously intelligent.

The book staked out territory in the cultural war coming to America—three or four decades before it arrived. Unknown forces and dimensions are working against mankind, using techniques that can't be seen or understood, but are countered by humbly trusting in Jesus, holding on to a belief in God, and having a constant awareness of where one can go astray. The enemy is always pounding at the gate, sin is our natural state, and we're forever on the verge of sliding into it. Once a soul is lost, it cannot be reclaimed from the consuming fires. At the end of the story, Wormwood fails to bring the soul of the man they've been working on to Satan, but it remains a horrible tale of human frailty, written at one of the bleakest hours of European history.

By early spring, you could almost hear Pastor Clark's mind churning with the thoughts the book had stirred inside him.

"Reading *The Screwtape Letters* has definitely affected my thinking," he said, "and made me wonder if Satan really is an active force in turning people away from God. For me, sin is all about a broken relationship with God, instead of paying attention to what He wants us to do. I like to discuss this with my wife, Jan, who works in the field of psychology in prison, but we don't always agree. Sometimes we argue about it. She knows a lot about the psychological model for evil, but it's the spiritual model that we as a society don't really want to look at because it raises difficult questions. It says, at least for some Christians, that we're not totally responsible for our actions and can blame our behavior on Satan. We have to be very careful not to make this option a cop-out, but who's to say that this couldn't have happened to Dennis?"

The preacher hadn't yet revealed that Rader had confessed to him at the jail, and he didn't seem comfortable being in this position.

"Let's say Dennis is guilty," he said. "Look at what he's done to the families of the victims he killed. In some cases, people were driven away from their faith by these murders and have concluded there is no God. Then the devil has won. The ripple effect of all this has hurt people in ways we can't imagine. I've got to sort all this out so I can help our congregation as we go though this experience together. Dennis is making us deal head-on with the big questions of the law and of grace and of sin. If he's responsible for these deaths, he has to pay the consequences. If he claims his crimes to society and to God, he'll be forgiven and he'll be a free man, even if he's in prison. He'll have the capacity of serving God in ways we can't begin to comprehend, but only Dennis knows how to do this.

"The fine line here is trying to decide what part of this story fits into our faith journey. Fundamentalists are constantly doing battle with Satan, which is one extreme, but the other is not to recognize

Satan at all. Nothing in seminary prepared me for what's happened since last February twenty-fifth."

While searching for a new definition of evil, Pastor Clark hadn't lost his sense of humor or his penchant for silliness. Seven years earlier, following his son's accident, he'd gone to a bona fide clown school in La Crosse, Wisconsin, for times like these.

"At clown school, I learned how to juggle three balls at the same time," he says. "After Dennis ended up in jail, believe me, I had a lot more than that to juggle. My job, Dennis's needs, his family members, the media, my family members, the bad stuff coming at our church, and the congregation."

That spring, the minister put on his clown suit, made jokes every chance he got, and used laughter to escape the depravity of Rader's crimes and the gravity of going to the jail twice a week. When visitors came to his church office, he spoke about the toy frog he kept perched on a shelf—there to remind him of the magical possibilities of life, even when things seemed grim. Pastor Clark didn't really like performing as a clown at birthday parties "unless the celebrant was at least ninety years old," but preferred working nursing homes, grief seminars, or anywhere he could do tricks, tie balloons into animal-like shapes, or just get crazy in public. Whenever he went on a long road trip, he took along his polka-dot outfit, yellow mop wig, and big red nose.

"You never know when someone is going to need a clown," he says. "I love making people laugh, because that engenders endorphins inside of them and it's very healing. Getting goofy helps you relax and is good for you. Trust me, I can be real goofy and do things as a clown I couldn't get away with otherwise. The Lutheran thing is that you don't laugh in church. It's supposed to be pious and serious. I'm still breakin' the ice on this."

In large part because of the minister's attitude and actions following the arrest, the publicity surrounding Rader did not hurt Christ Lutheran, as its leaders had feared it might. Attendance at the Sunday-morning services actually began to grow, the congregation coming together around the crisis and sending out weekly prayers to Paula, Dennis, their family, and the victims' relatives. The little church had been staggered but was moving forward.

"Pastor Clark played a mighty big role in keeping us together after this BTK thing blew up in our face," says one longtime worshipper. "People here were reeling and didn't know what to think. It was just an unbelievable event. For months, Pastor had to take care of everything and everybody, and he knew exactly what to do. The load was on his shoulders and he carried it for all of us."

XLI

On another side of the debate about the nature of evil stood the discipline of human psychology. Just off Harry Street in east Wichita, Dr. Howard Brodsky worked in a small office located behind an auto parts store and a Church's Chicken. The building looked funky and Dr. Brodsky's front window held a sign reading PSYCHOLOGICAL SERVICES—ADDICTION SERVICES CLINIC. In the lobby, classic rock filled the room, and a receptionist with brilliant metallic red hair greeted visitors from behind a chaotically crowded desk. The houseplants scattered in the corners looked as if they hadn't been watered for three months and were tilting toward the floor. The coffeepot was severely stained, and nothing inside these walls matched one's expectations. The whole place felt jumpy and alive and refreshing, which was similar to the feeling of meeting Dr. Brodsky. Tall and bony, with unruly gray hair and a graying mustache, he didn't sit on a chair but spread out all over it. Usually, a little smile was forming at the sides of his mouth and you didn't know if he was grinning at you or thinking about something funny. When he wasn't smiling at you or your comments, he might suddenly start to laugh, which could be disconcerting. You got the feeling that he'd begun psychoanalyzing you the moment he'd shaken your hand.

A native of St. Paul, Minnesota, from a family rooted in progressive politics, Dr. Brodsky had taken a degree in psychology from the University of Minnesota in 1967, a master's in psychology from the University of Wisconsin–Milwaukee in 1969, and then served an internship at Children's Hospital of Los Angeles. By the mid-1970s, he'd earned a Ph.D. from the University of Wisconsin–Milwaukee and pursued postdoctoral training in forensic psychology at the California School of Professional Psychology at Berkeley, before gravitating back to the Midwest. In 1975, he moved to Wichita and for the next decade was chief psychologist for Sedgwick County Mental Health, before going into private practice. With a special interest in forensics, Dr. Brodsky had been an expert witness at legal proceedings throughout Kansas and done his share of courtroom testifying about defendants' competency to stand trial. He did not have a high opinion of either state or federal criminal profilers, who'd become much more prominent in both law enforcement and the media since the 1970s.

"The press loves to talk to profilers, but I'm not a profiler," he says. "Profiling means that someone who doesn't have a degree in something serious thinks he can solve crimes."

Years ago, he'd had the opportunity to look at pieces of evidence in the BTK case.

"I saw some written stuff and some pencil line drawings of a crime scene," he says. "I came away thinking that this man was very, very unhappy inside his own head. He had an ugly, nasty attitude— barbarically antifemale. I thought that his attitude would have to be picked up by others and make him stand out in the community. Serial killers can blend in, but he was so negative toward women that I felt he had to be a recluse. If he wasn't a recluse, he must have been around people who were very naive or sought out victims who were also that way."

Dr. Brodsky was incisive, outspoken, and had earned a reputation in Wichita, through professional work and media appearances, as not believing in stating and restating the obvious.

"For a long time," he points out, "I've been the go-to guy in town for analyzing all the weird and disgusting stuff that people do."

He liked to say challenging things in public, and that kind of behavior was bound to annoy some. On April 1, 2004, after the WPD had reopened the BTK investigation, two plainclothes officers showed up at his clinic without an appointment.

"Everyone in the state of Kansas was looking over his shoulder at every white guy who was around sixty," he says. "I was a white guy around that age. These officers came in and wanted to talk with me. I thought they wanted to consult with me on a technical legal issue about a case, but they were here to swab me for DNA. When I asked if they were kidding, they said, 'No, we aren't. This isn't an April fool's joke.' Somebody had turned me in as a BTK suspect. That's when you know you're having an impact on things."

Several months later, two more strangers arrived at his doorstep, but this time they'd come to his home.

"They were," he says, "attractive female officers who were looking for another swab. I'd been named as a suspect *again*. I told them that I'd already been done at the office and my DNA had been cleared."

On February 26, 2005, when the Wichita authorities held their press conference announcing the capture of BTK, Dr. Brodsky was quite nervous for the city where he'd lived for the past three decades.

"Before arresting Rader," he says, "the police had made a huge assumption that this man had actually sired his daughter. His wife could have had an affair. Or his daughter could have been adopted or started with other seed. They took a chance on this and we'd already seen what had happened when they'd taken other chances. Remember the Hispanic man they'd taken into custody last December? Well, I knew they were wrong on that one. In a big Hispanic family like that, everyone knows what everyone else is doing and everybody talks about it with everyone else. He'd never have been able to sneak around and get away with all those crimes for all those years. As soon as I heard about him, I thought the police were in trouble.

"When Dennis Rader was arrested, everyone I talked to was very reserved about this. It was, 'Okay, let's just hope we don't embarrass ourselves again.' I felt uncomfortable because we'd been led astray before and we had a shared humiliation with the local police. Then they had their press conference and it turned into a lovefest and then that was embarrassing. They seemed awfully sure of themselves that day, almost too sure, and that raised other questions. Psychologists know that whenever you put an observer in the mix, it changes how people behave. When the police were interviewing Rader right after arresting him, did he start making things up to impress them? But this time, I think they got it right."

Because of his expertise in forensic psychology and because he enjoyed interacting with the media, Dr. Brodsky provided commentary on the case for KAKE-TV. During courtroom proceedings, he often appeared on the air and offered his views, one of the few public interpreters of the BTK phenomenon who tried to put the defendant into the fuller context of his background.

"Dennis Rader," Dr. Brodsky says, "is cut off from his real motivations, as are many offenders. After they've been caught breaking the law, they frequently say things like 'The criminal side of me is a separate part of myself which I have no control over.' You can call it a demon or whatever you want. It's just a way to avoid trying to learn anything about yourself or finding any answers. Rader was exposed to religion as a child, and he embraced that religion as an adult. These kinds of conservative faiths don't comfortably allow for a person to have any feelings of deviance. He had deep needs to be deviant and to be shocking, but he could never go to anybody and say this. He had to hide it so he shoved it all aside into what he eventually called a 'demon personality.' We all have demons."

Dr. Brodsky likes to mention that he'd overcome one of his own personal demons—an awkward shyness about public speaking—and turned himself into a local and national commentator on the BTK case.

"A more liberal theology," he says, "allows for people to be more at ease with their baser instincts. Men have these instincts, whether people like to admit that or not, especially when it comes to sex and aggression. We're guilty until proven innocent, and we have to be socialized appropriately to separate ourselves from these things. That's part of the process males experience when becoming healthy adults. The baser instincts need a way to surface enough to be worked through, but Rader had no place to put them and couldn't talk about them or let anyone see his darker side. His need to be seen as good was overwhelming, which was why he was so active in his church and his family and in the Cub Scouts. He was nice to some people right up until the time he killed them.

"He always had to be the gentleman in public—so polite and neat and organized and in control of things—but he was faking all of these roles in the community. We saw his real face in that disheveled photograph somebody took of him right after his arrest. The widespread exposure of that picture must have been worse for him than losing his freedom. He looked liked Saddam Hussein—right after Saddam was arrested. The uncontrollable, unacceptable part of Rader had finally come out for the whole world to see. The demon he talks about is the opposite of the very conservative environment he grew up in, where he couldn't let anything get messy. It wasn't a demon that was controlling him, but an inward demand for perfection combined with no outward release of his real needs. The murders were an escape into a fantasy life, but he had so many other alternatives.

"He could have gone out and looked at porn. He might have gotten divorced or had extramarital affairs. There are people who like being tied up but not hurt, and he could have sought them out, but he didn't do any of these things. He was a man with a very limited sexual history and experience. No woman has ever come forward since the BTK case started and said that she was one of his lovers. It never happened. Having an affair would have meant showing his imperfect or bad side to other people—living people. He could only be himself and vent in front of the dead.

"There were creative solutions to his psychological problems, but what he did was the opposite of creative. He read books about other serial killers and decided to copy them. He took a lot of known things about this subject and wove them together into BTK. Instead of finding his own identity, or becoming an original at something, he made himself into a composite of other criminals. He's like the history of serial killing all rolled into one person. In his mind, he said, 'I've got these fantasies and I've gotta act them out and be a sexual killer.'

"There was no other outlet for him because of his religious background. It didn't allow him to be who he was. He couldn't have gone to his minister and said, 'I have these very violent sexual fantasies. I want to do all these things.' That would have made him not okay inside that church forever. Remember, the Lutherans here in Kansas are a lot more conservative than those I grew up around in Minnesota."

What conclusions had Dr. Brodsky reached from observing the thirty-one-year-old case and Dennis Rader?

"He never took any responsibility for his own life," he says. "That's the message behind the murders. You control your destiny, so I don't blame a demon for these tragedies. I blame him. He could have fed the beast in many other ways. Getting honest feedback from others is one of them. Sharing your secrets with someone—anyone, a buddy or a mental health professional—can help you move through things. Reveal your vulnerabilities to someone, your needs. Let others know something about you. Man is a social animal, not made for isolation. He never bounced anything off of anybody so nobody guessed what he was hiding. Thousands of BTK tips came in to the police, but he was never turned in by anyone.

"I was turned in twice. Can you imagine that?"

XLII

By the spring of 2005, the faces of Carmen, Charlie, and Danny Otero; Kevin Bright; Steve Relford; and Jeff Davis, the son of Dolores Davis, had begun appearing on TV screens across the nation. They were often asked to talk about the case or Rader's arrest, so the pain and sorrow ingrained in Charlie's and Steve's features, in particular, came into living rooms everywhere and conveyed more emotion and more residual grief than anything they said. It was Jeff Davis who used language as his primary tool in describing his experience and feelings as a BTK victim. A former police officer, Davis had taken a wrenching downturn following the brutal 1991 death of his mother; he fell into a depression, saw his marriage disintegrate, and struggled with whether he wanted to live. Years passed before he emerged from the trauma unleashed by the murder.

In the mid-1990s, Davis wrote a book about the crime, and after it was published, somebody mailed him a letter speculating about the night his mother was killed. The letter was filled with eerie details about the slaying and may have been written by Rader himself, in a perverse attempt to deepen Jeff's anguish. The author of the letter mentioned that Dolores had reminded him of a long-lost love and raised the notion that some of BTK's unexpressed rage against women may have come from being spurned earlier in his life in romance (the same thing that had driven Ted Bundy to kill young females). If Jeff hadn't been damaged enough by the gruesome way his mother had died, and by the horrific aftermath of the killer taking her into the countryside near Park City and leaving her outside on the frozen winter ground, the letter only made things worse. Once

Rader had been arrested and identified as BTK, the other victims' relatives who spoke in public showed some restraint, but not Jeff. Someone needed to let out what everyone was feeling about the defendant, and Jeff was perfectly suited for that role. His anger was bottomless and his ability to put it into words impressive. As the legal case started to unfold, he would become the poet of contempt and a necessary voice for what lay ahead.

But it wasn't Jeff whom Rader was concerned about. During 2004 and early 2005, when he was creating new communications for the WPD or the media, he'd watched televised interviews with some of the relatives, trying to pick up bits of information to use in his packages. Now that he was behind bars, part of his confession included that he was afraid of Charlie Otero, because of his intense looks and the way he handled himself on the airwaves. In the middle of his police interrogation, Rader said that Charlie was "gonna cut me up and feed me to the sharks. . . . Well, hopefully, he won't find me."

In reality, Charlie Otero acted in public with as much self-control and dignity as the other victims' relatives and seemed to want to get the BTK murders behind him. It was Jeff Davis who wasn't going to let the case go before letting out some of his bile.

As he sharpened his tongue, the wheels of justice began to grind all around Rader. His wife, who'd been slipping into and out of town without anyone except her inner circle knowing her whereabouts, was ready for a quick divorce. She asked a judge to waive the normal waiting period of sixty days and her request was granted. The Rader house, which had a $45,000 mortgage on it, was going up for sale in July, and this was destined to set off a bevy of lawsuits. Should the defendant be found guilty of the ten murders, some of the victims' relatives wanted to sue him in wrongful-death actions and collect damages, yet he had limited assets. The main one was his home, but people close to Paula and many others in Wichita felt she shouldn't be financially punished if her husband turned out to be BTK in a court of law. She ought to be able to unload the house and start a new life with the equity from the sale in her pocket. By late spring, Paula's comings and goings were not quite as mysterious as they'd been since March, but the media were still hounding her for interviews and she basically remained in hiding. She was spending some of her time in the Wichita area at an undisclosed location and had even begun attending a few services at Christ Lutheran.

"Paula has come back to church and people have been very supportive of her," Donn Bischoff said in June. "It's got to be so tough for her to walk in that front door, but she hasn't let that keep her away. She seems to be holding up, but who can imagine what she's going through? When she comes here, we don't ask her questions, but just give her hugs and commiserate with her."

The judge handling the criminal case, the Honorable Gregory Waller, had picked mid-April for Rader's preliminary hearing. The defendant, wearing a blue sport coat, a bulletproof vest, and shackles on his ankles, appeared in court at that time to waive the hearing. In early May, he was scheduled to make another court appearance to enter a plea, and as this date approached, both media and criminal justice circles were abuzz with speculation about what he might do. He could declare his guilt and the only thing left would be for Judge Waller to sentence him; he could plead innocent and the start of his trial would be set on a calendar; or he could stand silent and enter no plea at all. He chose silence, deepening the speculation about how the case might legally be resolved. Judge Waller named June 27 for the opening day of the trial.

The district attorney was ready to go to court. She was armed with ten videotaped murder confessions, while public defenders Steve Osburn and Sarah McKinnon scrambled to find a way to represent Rader against the stupefying charges. McKinnon, who spent up to six hours a day with Rader working on his case, was faced with more than trying to concoct an impossible legal strategy (especially since he'd been found sane by the five psychiatrists). She found it extremely difficult just to be around the man, with his flat manner and his self-involved, inarticulate way of speaking about his actions as BTK. The details of the murders were hugely distressing, and the crime-scene photos were nightmarish, but all of this came with doing her job. Every accused person deserved the best available defense, and she would diligently attempt to give him that. Yet the experience was haunting, in part because Rader was a family man and a self-professed Christian who seemed so average on the surface. Every now and then McKinnon felt that she could see a little piece of the defendant at work inside herself or in other people who were perfectly normal, and this was both maddening and frightening.

After leaving the office at the close of a workday, she often needed to talk about all this with someone, but that was a problem too. She couldn't divulge many things because of the attorney-client privilege. McKinnon spoke about certain aspects of the case at home until she wore out her husband, Reno County district judge Steven Becker, who didn't want any more of Dennis Rader in his house than was absolutely necessary. McKinnon was coping as well as she could, but struggling. Rader didn't look or act like Satan when he was with her, but what he'd done was diabolical, and the lawyer had a hard time reconciling his two sides. Like the seasoned homicide detectives or psychologists who'd studied the BTK evidence over the years and decades, the experience of confronting what Rader had done—and now Rader himself—was debilitating. McKinnon soon lost twenty-five pounds.

Part of the difficulty for his defense team was the uncertainty as to what the defendant planned to do on June 27. He'd been reading the Bible and praying for direction, but hadn't revealed his plans to anyone, including his attorneys. The scuttlebutt around the court-house and Christ Lutheran Church was that Paula had gotten word to Rader in his cell, begging her husband not to go to trial and bring further shame to their family. Pastor Clark was praying for the same outcome, but didn't feel it was his job to give the jailed man legal advice. As late June approached, Rader was again faced with several choices. He could plead guilty and wait to be sentenced by the judge, or he could plead not guilty by reason of insanity and try to find a psychiatrist who would declare him mentally impaired. He could plead innocent and a trial would commence at some future time (by late June, no juror questionnaires for this case had been sent out to the people of Sedgwick County). Or he could enter a plea of no con-test, which meant that he didn't openly admit his guilt but acknowledged there was enough evidence to convict him. If that happened, Judge Waller would decide the next move. By the last week of the month, all these options were still available.

As he sat in jail day after day thinking about what to do, Rader was establishing a new identity. He had a lot of interaction with other inmates, who'd dubbed him The Suspect, or Radar. Because of all the publicity and notoriety surrounding his case, he soon became known as The Podfather (at the Sedgwick County Detention Facility, prisoners lived in different areas called pods). Within a few weeks of arriving at SCDF, he'd figured out what countless other men and women had discovered after being locked up: incarceration was like attending graduate school for criminal behavior. Rader quickly learned how to start fires and rob banks.

For being such a renowned defendant, Rader struck many of the inmates as rather naive and strangely innocent, more like someone in law enforcement than someone who'd been violating the law since his teenage years. But like everybody else, he adapted to the jail's routine, rising at 5:30 a.m. for breakfast, reading the Bible and relentlessly tidying up his cell in the morning, writing poetry and waiting for visitors in the afternoon, an early dinner, lights out at 10:30 p.m., and then using the bulb in his cell to play solitaire until midnight. He tried to stay as busy as possible, repeating to himself the old line of the imprisoned: "Do the time; don't let the time do you." Many hours were spent over Scripture and answering his flood of mail. Instead of being shunned by the world following the arrest, he was overwhelmed by the number of strangers sending him letters, eager to see him in person or probe his mind through an exchange of writing. By midsummer, he'd received 436 pieces of mail and sent out more than 300 himself, to forty-three American cities and one in Holland. Now that he was safely behind bars, several females desired to start a romantic relationship with him, but he was only interested in one.

Not long after he was booked at SCDF, a thirty-eight-year-old married woman from Topeka, Kristin Casarona, began writing him (her interest was not romantic). She'd been surprised from news reports that the BTK suspect was a husband, a father, a man of faith, and president of his church. She too was a Christian and felt that no matter what he may have done in the past, it was never too late to be saved. In her letters, she expressed concern to him about his salvation, and they bonded around their religious beliefs. Over the next few months, she visited him numerous times in jail, and their correspondence ran to five hundred pages, which would eventually be subpoenaed by the DA's office as potential evidence if Rader went to trial. The two of them talked by phone through the pane of glass; they prayed together and he cried in front of her when speaking about his wife and children. She was thinking of writing a book about him, offering a spiritual message to readers, and he was willing to help. His faith appeared to be growing stronger in prison, and when writing to others, he made a point of saying that the BTK story was "very Christian." On some of those letters, he included a small drawing of a frog, but it wasn't the nasty-looking creature named Rex that he'd blamed for the murders. It was a well-proportioned, normal-looking frog and showed that regardless of what people had told him when he was a youngster, he had some artistic skills.

Part of Rader's new identity included an emotional shift, however shallow or hollow it may have been. His daughter's impassioned letter to him about how he'd destroyed their lives had made him weep. He'd displayed his feelings to Pastor Clark, and when talking about his family with Kristin Casarona, he'd broken down on the phone. His tears were mostly about what he'd done to his own relatives or about how much he missed his freedom and previous life, but he did bring up the suffering he'd imposed on his victims and their kin. Not everyone saw these as true expressions of sorrow or remorse, but for a man who'd never been able to feel anything about the murders and had used them to promote himself and mock law enforcement for more than thirty years, they were movement in a different direction.

Confessing to the police had been the start of this process. He'd told interviewers that he'd never realized how afraid the Wichita population had been of him since 1974, yet during all that time he'd lived with a woman who was terrified of BTK. It hadn't registered inside him that what he was doing to Paula, whom he professed to love, was the same thing he was doing to hundreds of thousands of others. A tiny fragment of the dead granite that made up his inner life was showing a fissure, as if he could finally start to sense his effect on other people. Not until he began speaking the truth and embracing his past could he feel a piece of the misery himself. Instead of being alone in his new life, he was surrounded by those who wanted to interact with and know more about him. He'd evolved into the object of local and national media attention, with reporters, network stars, criminologists, and psychological profilers lining up to speak to him. The moment he'd stopped hiding from others, the world took a step toward him, and another truth emerged. He'd always had alternatives, but never given himself the chance to discover whom else he might have become.

In late June, a few days before the scheduled start of his trial, Rader spoke with a Wichita TV station, KSN, Channel 3, talking about life in jail and his unfolding legal situation. By now he was adapting to his new home and starting to sound like a lot of other prisoners, no longer attempting to bend his image to comfort the people he'd always tried to please in the past. The facade was cracking, and his televised appearance came as a shock to some.

"I watched this and had real concerns about Dennis," says Donn Bischoff. "This was not the person we know at Christ Lutheran, and I was worried that prison was changing him in a bad way. Just the tone of his voice and his manner—they were not what we were used to at Sunday-morning services or at church dinners. I pray for him and think of him often.

"If he's guilty, and he really is BTK, I have grave concerns for his soul and its prospects. I pray for that as much as I do for his current situation in the jail. If he killed these people, I hope he can form a relationship with God that gets him forgiveness and salvation in the future. Many in Wichita don't feel this way and I understand that: if you do the deed, don't complain about taking the heat. They want to see him hanged, but I'm concerned with his soul. I still have faith that if Dennis is guilty, God can give him grace. The Bible, if you read it closely, is a pretty gory book. People did murders all over the place, but there was still forgiveness from God.

"As Lutherans, we emphasize the grace and gift of God over the works of man. Our way is to ask God to act and to be gracious and forgiving. We hope Dennis can ask for God's forgiveness and then receive it."

XLIII

O N FATHER'S DAY in Park City, June 19, a young boy sat next
to his bicycle on the grass in the gleaming midday sun. Light fell
across his face and illuminated some nearby pieces of rusting cowboy
sculpture that had been placed around town as a reminder of the
region's history. The smell of just mown clover sweetened the air, and
the streets were quiet and empty, peacefulness everywhere. Right outside the village, big hay bales were lined up in pastures, horses grazed
in open fields, and wildflowers grew in the ditches. Down the road a
mile, the late service was just letting out at Christ Lutheran, and a hot
wind blew through the row of pines encircling the church, the swing
set creaking and going silent as the breeze rose and fell. Birds chirped
softly on the branches and pinecones lay scattered across the crowded
parking lot.

Old and young worshippers walked outside with the modest,
awkward movements of country people everywhere when they have
to do something in public. They shook hands and leaned on their
cars and made small talk, lingering on the asphalt in their casual Sunday clothes, no longer needing to dress up for the Lord. Their parents and grandparents would never have understood this, but now
everyone had agreed that you could pray just as well in shirtsleeves
and open collars as in a dark suit and tie. A black woman emerged
from Christ Lutheran pushing Tim Clark in his wheelchair and
beside them was Tai, a big Labrador wearing a harness, Tim's constant companion and helper. People came up to greet the young man,
touch his shoulder, and wish him well. He stared at them, not quite

comprehending, and the trio made their way to a vehicle where Tim and the dog were placed safely inside and the car backed up and slowly pulled away.

The wind came up again, stronger this time, and the trees kept whispering and the whispering sounded like secrets getting louder each time the breeze returned—almost ready to be revealed.

XLIV

E IGHT DAYS LATER, June 27, saw ninety-nine-degree heat come to Wichita and lie down on the city like a damp cloth. The pavement was scorched and the humidity choking, but Judge Waller's courtroom was air-conditioned and perfectly comfortable. He'd scheduled Rader's court appearance for 9 a.m., but by eight-thirty nobody knew what Rader intended to do. He'd come to his decision alone in his cell but hadn't told it to anyone, his two lawyers as uncertain as the DA herself. Word around the courthouse was that Nola Foulston wanted to go to trial. She'd get a huge amount of face time on TV, win a slam-dunk, extremely high-profile case, further her career, and spend weeks or months watching the defendant squirm through the presentation of some startling evidence (only the police and the prosecutors had yet seen certain images). In a small way, she'd also be able to settle a personal score with Rader. In his extensive collection of three-by-five index cards of imaginary sexual scenarios, one was named Nola. She'd been in the DA's office for almost as many years as BTK had been committing crimes, and their day in court together had finally come.

Courtrooms are rarely, contrary to popular belief, venues for the truth. During the past half century, fictional TV has created the illusion, through witness outbursts and confessions erupting within a thirty- or sixty-minute program (minus time-outs for commercials), that this is how the criminal justice system operates. All of the tedious stuff is left out and all of the drama is heightened. In nonfiction courtrooms, you don't often learn the full reality behind a murder case, let alone why a crime happened, and much of what goes on in front of judges and juries is designed to muddy the facts. Prosecutors are paid to prove one set of charges and to get convictions. Defense lawyers are paid to instill reasonable doubt into jurors. Murder defendants rarely testify, and if they do, they portray themselves as innocently as they can. The law is largely about compromise and trying to process as quickly and efficiently as possible the vast number of criminals our society produces. Up close, the system resembles an assembly line and the huge, costly business it is.

If Rader decided to try to convince a jury that he'd been possessed by a demon since roughly 1960, he was confronted with at least one major hurdle. As millions knew from watching the popular 1970s film *The Exorcist,* people said to be demon-possessed experienced bodily contortions, voice alterations, speaking in strange dialects, and other dramatic changes. They spit out physical objects and often had super-human strength. The defendant had never gone through anything like this, not even a facial contortion. Also, in the general Catholic Church interpretation of demonic possession, those under the control of otherworldly forces engaged in small acts of evil, such as swearing uncontrollably or scratching holes in the walls with their fingernails or breaking dishes. They didn't turn into serial killers.

This morning Rader was wearing a handsome beige suit, a pressed white shirt, and a dark tie. He had a trimmed salt-and-pepper goatee and was clean-shaven. Since February, he'd lost weight. His forehead was flushed, and before long it would turn redder and be dotted with beads of perspiration. Court TV was covering the proceeding live on national television, and its host, Rikki Klieman, along with some other attorneys, had laid out Rader's legal options for the viewing audience. It was entirely possible that nothing much would happen today, or that one group of lawyers or another would ask for a delay or get bogged down in technicalities. As the opening of court got closer, the on-air speculation intensified.

At precisely 9 a.m., Judge Waller, an African-American who was appropriately solemn on the bench, brought his courtroom to order and looked out at the gallery. Lieutenant Landwehr was present as were several BTK task force detectives and victims' relatives, who'd wanted to be witnesses to whatever took place this morning. Pastor

Clark was sitting in the second row behind the defendant, his eyes rarely leaving Rader. On either side of the accused were his attorneys, Sarah McKinnon and Steve Osburn.

Without fanfare, the judge asked the defendant to stand, alongside his counsel.

What plea was he going to enter?

"Guilty, Your Honor," Rader said in the flat Midwestern voice that many people were hearing for the first time.

With these three words, under the U.S. Constitution, he'd just waived his right to a trial by jury. The case was over; he'd spend the rest of his life in prison. Thirty seconds into the session, the drama had ended, or so it seemed.

The judge asked if Rader was satisfied with his decision.

"I'm pretty happy with this," he answered in the same flat tone, sounding thoroughly in control of himself and the situation. "I'm ready to go."

He began thanking his lawyers for their help and made a point of stating that the judge had been "very fair" with him.

A sense of surprise, even shock, was flowing through the courtroom, as if most people had been expecting something much more complex or unclear to come from Rader's mouth. Almost nothing that unfolds in court is simple or straightforward, but this was, and the moment he pled guilty, it was obvious that he'd made the right decision. Sedgwick County and the state had just saved huge amounts of time and money. The DA would not have to put on a lengthy trial that was bound to become a macabre spectacle. The police, Pastor Clark, and Christ Lutheran Church could all stop pretending Rader was innocent. Prayers had been answered and Paula Rader and her family were not going to be subjected to further public shame and humiliation. A huge bubble had just exploded in front of everyone inside the courtroom and those watching on TV. Something strange was afoot, an odd feeling was in the air. In a time when public truth was hard to come by, especially public truth inside the criminal justice system, somebody was stepping forward and at least trying to be honest.

Judge Waller began reading through the ten counts, emphasizing again and again that Rader had "willingly," "maliciously," and "with premeditation" taken the lives of each of these individuals. Throughout this, the defendant dropped his head, but when the judge asked once more for his plea, he raised it and looked right at the man.

"Yes, Your Honor," he said, reaffirming his guilt. "Yes, sir."

Rader's expression was focused and severe—conjuring up Lenin addressing the politburo in the old Soviet Union—but he looked unnaturally calm.

Pastor Clark was watching him from just a few feet away.

"People said Dennis was emotionless or disconnected during his guilty plea," the preacher says, "but that wasn't true. I was right next to him and I can read his mannerisms because of all the time I spent with him in jail. As he stood in front of the judge, emotion was rising in him and wanting to crack him open, but something else was pushing it back down. A physical battle was taking place inside of him. He was struggling right then with his demons, and it was in his body language. He wasn't cold at all, or detached, but that was hard to see on TV. He was really sweating this and it took some courage to do what he did."

When the judge finished going through the charges, he asked for clarification. Rader seemed to be pleading guilty for practical reasons: he wanted to spare everyone a long and grinding legal ordeal. Because the evidence was stacked against him, it was time to cut his losses, but this was not quite the same thing as acknowledging guilt. Was Rader pleading guilty, Judge Waller wanted to know for the record, because he wanted this process to be over or was he doing it because he was truly guilty?

After a moment's hesitation, Rader said, "Because I'm guilty, Your Honor."

With that statement, everything was coming to a swift conclusion. The defendant had taken responsibility for his crimes, there was no cause for further questioning, and the only thing left was for the judge to impose a life sentence, or ten life sentences, but that would probably occur at a later date. The session could be wrapped up soon, but His Honor was not finished.

Whether he wanted a more complete account of Rader's guilt, so the defendant could never successfully appeal his conviction, or whether he intuited that something more needed to be done, Judge Waller did the opposite of what Wichita's officials had fallen into when announcing the BTK arrest. They'd become sidetracked with self-congratulation, but the judge now plunged deeper into the case, as if he knew this was a special opportunity and his job was to bring it to the surface. He was preparing to ask Rader to describe his crimes, and Rader would not balk. A new chapter was about to be written in the history of live television. A serial killer was ready to speak to the court and into the camera, telling America and parts of the world exactly what he'd done to ten homicide victims, while giving the judge and the public a lecture on how people like himself think, plan, troll, stalk, and end lives. He wasn't just a serial killer but a student of serial killing, and his mentality and actions embodied nearly the entire scope of the subject. As he began to talk, one could sense a collective gasp from everyone watching, as if reality was the last thing anyone expected.

"At first, I didn't understand what Judge Waller was doing with Dennis," says Pastor Clark. "I thought he would just plead guilty and the judge would speak and that would be that. When he started asking him in depth about the crimes, and Dennis began giving his answers, I was upset. All this was new stuff to me—I had no idea what he was going to say. We'd never talked about any of it at the jail, and it was shocking. But gradually, I began to understand what the judge was trying to do. I came away thinking he was very wise.

"He was getting all the information he'll need for sentencing without having to hear any more. The district attorney wants to grandstand and have her day in court. She wants to drag all this out and use the case to promote herself, but the judge just wants to get to the sentencing. After this hearing, he can be done with it. I have a lot of admiration for him because he was in charge of that courtroom."

"All morning long," says Dr. Howard Brodsky, who was analyzing the hearing for KAKE, "Judge Waller was buying Dennis Rader's brain. The judge is a very modest man, but he's also very smart and you could see that on display in the courtroom. From the start he engaged Rader in a one-on-one dialogue, using what I call the foot-in-the-door technique. It's an old sales trick you employ with your good, long-term customers. They've already bought things from you in the past, so you have your foot in the door. You start off by getting them to answer the easy questions, as the judge did at first with Rader. Get them to say yes to each one and get them to trust you. Earn their respect and prepare them for the harder questions to come. The judge led Rader gently into the murders and got him to reveal more and more."

Slowly and patiently, with a deep voice and a demeanor that evoked the notion of justice itself, Judge Waller probed for the details behind the murders. He was asking the right person. Nobody had ever been more detail-oriented than the defendant or had a better memory for long-ago, gruesome events, and here was his opportunity to show just how much had stayed in his mind since the mid-1970s. As the judge led Rader toward addressing his first homicides, one of the oldest BTK mysteries emerged once again. How had he been able to break into the Otero home, get rid of an aggressive dog, subdue two adults and two children, all of whom were trained in the martial arts, tie them up one by one, and murder them without firing a gun or getting so much as a scratch on himself? Had he had an accomplice?

The killer was ready to talk again, only this time to an audience of millions. Lieutenant Landwehr, and everyone else, looked on in revulsion and amazement.

Shortly before 9 a.m. on January 15, 1974, Joey Otero emerged through the back door to let out the family dog as Rader overpowered him and charged inside the house, confining the animal in the fenced-in yard. Even though the man appeared menacing holding a gun and wearing a large air force parka, its pockets stuffed with rolls of black tape, plastic bags, wire cutters, rope, and a knife, Joseph Otero saw the stranger standing in his home and thought it was a joke.

"Who sent you over?" he said. "My brother-in-law?"

Rader was surprised by the question and explained that he was a fugitive who was wanted in California. Joseph believed him and didn't resist when the intruder said he just needed to tie all of them up, get some food, money, and their car, and he wouldn't harm them. He backed up his request by brandishing a .22-caliber pistol and showing them the hollow-point bullets inside the loaded gun. The family obediently lay down on the floor in the living room. After more discussion, he led them into the parents' bedroom, set down the pistol, and tied all their hands behind them with adhesive tape and venetian-blind cord. He'd preknotted the bindings and was able to work quickly, but the family was beginning to complain that the cords were too tight. The sound was bothering Rader—he'd always hated loud noise—draining his concentration and aggravating him. He tried to work faster, but his own sweat was soaking his clothing and his hands were shaking.

This was the dream he'd always wanted, but it had already gone wrong. He was supposed to be alone with the females and act out his fantasies, but two other people were in the house. What should he do now? He thought about leaving, going outside and walking back to his car, but all four had seen his face and could identify him. It was their fault for ruining his plan, and the dream needed an ending. Julie Otero was laid out on the bed, next to her daughter, while Joseph and Joey were sprawled on the floor. They were complaining again about the cord hurting their hands and trying to break loose. All were getting louder, grating against his nerves, and he was starting to panic, running into another room and picking up some plastic bags. Heading back in the bedroom, he had to establish control and quiet them down.

He slipped a bag over Joseph's head, grabbed the cord with both hands, and began choking the man. He'd never strangled a human being before and didn't know how much pressure it took so he tightened his grip, and when Joseph stopped moving, Rader thought he was dead. He walked over to Julie, who knew that he was coming to kill her and her children. She screamed and writhed on the bed and he was no longer looking down at a staged photo of a woman in a detective magazine but staring into the living eyes of terror, those of a real woman, a mother whose children were in the room watching her get strangled. Cats and dogs made small sounds as you forced the air from their lungs, but they couldn't speak or put up much fight. Julie was fighting in every way she could, and the children were shrieking and crying and he had to make all of them stop. Julie passed out on the mattress and she too looked dead.

He turned to Josie and began strangling her, but her father had bitten a hole through the bag on his head and was gasping for air. He was struggling to get free—to save himself and his family, but Rader choked him again, harder this time, not letting up until the man fell into a heap on the floor. The children were yelling and sobbing, and Rader took Joey into another room and tied two T-shirts and a bag over his head so he couldn't do what his father had done and chew through them. He strangled the boy until Joey had almost stopped breathing, then pulled back and observed as the youngster battled for air, rolling off the bed and dying.

Julie had regained consciousness and was shouting in the next room, begging for her daughter's life.

"You killed my boy!" she said. "You killed my boy!"

Rader rushed back to her and bent down over Julie on the bed, strangling her again in front of Josephine.

The little girl saw her mother die and could do nothing but watch, tears streaming across her cheeks and cries coming from her lips. When Rader was finished with Julie, he helped the girl stand and walked her out of the bedroom and toward the basement.

He'd always liked basements and thought of them as dungeons for playacting, especially the basement of his parents' home. Down there, he'd change into women's clothing, put on a blond wig, tie himself to a sewer pipe, and fake his own suicide.

On the steps leading downstairs, he asked Josie if she had a camera, which he'd forgotten to bring with him this morning.

She said no and asked what was going to happen to her.

"Well, honey," he replied, "you're going to be in heaven tonight with the rest of your family."

In the basement, he removed pieces of her clothing, pulling her panties down to the dark socks around her ankles and tying her legs with white cotton rope, binding her hands tightly behind her. He looped a cord about her neck and cinched it to a sewer pipe, gradually increasing the pressure on the cord and strangling her as she hung limply against the pipe.

"Mommy!" Josie said, as she was dying. "Mommy! Mommy! Mommy!"

When she'd quit breathing, he masturbated near her body and walked up to the main floor, collecting his gear and straightening up the house. Once everything had been rearranged to his satisfaction, he looked around for something to steal and took automobile keys and a radio, as Perry Smith had done fifteen years earlier at the Clutter home in western Kansas, right before killing a mother, father, and their two children.

Driving the Oteros' car, he passed through the midmorning residential streets and back to the Dillon's parking lot where his own vehicle was parked, his hands aching from the strain of choking four people.

XLV

COURTROOM OBSERVERS later said that as the morning wore on, Rader began most of his sentences with *I* and his testimony revealed a sickening self-absorption and egotism. That was true, but because of Judge Waller a more important game was unfolding—a public purging of the evil Rader had created, the torment and hatefulness he'd imposed on an entire city for more than three decades. BTK had become an urban legend, larger than life, and the community needed to demystify him and cleanse itself of that image before it could leave this tragic episode behind. That process could only happen by learning some of the facts and by seeing who he really was: an inarticulate, bumbling, average-looking man.

Rader went through each of his crimes in a matter-of-fact voice that left people convinced he was either strikingly sane or completely insane; all ten murders were laid out in detail. He talked about his numerous "projects" and how he'd selected his victims, blandly speaking of "putting down" men, women, and children—as if he were ending a cat's life at the vet's. He described strangling to death a boy and a girl as though he were reading from an owner's manual, and in the courtroom, the victims' relatives watched him in disbelief, hugging and clinging to one another for support, weeping into their hands. Until now, many of them had never known how their loved ones had died. The detectives stared up at Rader in humble silence; hearing all this for the second time didn't make it any easier. During the confession, defense lawyers Steve Osburn and Sarah McKinnon stood next to Rader with their heads bowed and shame in their body language. They were probably happy with this development; Rader's outpouring meant that their days of representing him were nearly over.

As he continued talking, parts of the killer slid out of control. His left hand shook, his face turned redder, and he repeatedly wiped at the sweat on his forehead. He drank a lot of water, and toward the end, when explaining how he'd murdered Dolores Davis, he began popping his lips together, an unconscious gesture, a weird and eerie smacking sound that filled the room and passed out through TV screens with a charge. For the first time that morning, the mask had fallen and the chaos he feared so much in the external world had taken over his face, the strange noise hinting at buried impulses of lust and violence. No one, including Rikki Klieman, the veteran anchor of Court TV, had ever seen anything like it. When the cameras cut back to her in the studio, the lawyers' mouths were hanging open.

For those closer to the action, the past hour had brought a palpable sense of tension and horror.

"It was unbearable," Pastor Clark says. "I was in the second row, right behind all the attorneys, and several times I just wanted to get up and leave, but I stayed and listened. The courtroom was in a state of shock. No comments. Nothing. No sounds, except for crying. A stillness and hush I've never heard before. Just below the surface, Dennis was really battling with himself and his emotions, pushing through this, no matter how long it took. I've talked to him three times since he pled guilty, and he was very relieved after all this came out. It was a great weight off of him."

"I was watching the guilty plea," says Dr. Brodsky, "and I was thinking, 'Holy cripes. I never thought I'd live long enough to see this.' It took away my last piece of doubt that the police had arrested the right man and he really was BTK. Here was an honest-to-God serial killer telling us his story in court and on television. He knew who he was long before the rest of us did and had been trying to say these things for decades in his writings and drawings. Now was his chance to be more explicit. He'd gotten this killing bug and couldn't shake it.

"The account of the Otero crimes was just stunning. The crime occurred on a busy street in the middle of the workday morning and they were the most unlikely victims you could imagine. A small house in a crowded neighborhood, with dad and mom and the dog all trained to fight. Nothing sustains bad male behavior like trying to avoid humiliation. By early 1974, Rader had lost his job at Cessna and had to do something now so he no longer felt humiliated. If you recall in *In Cold Blood*, Smith and Hickock went to the Clutter farm looking for a lot of cash. Once they got there and found no money, they couldn't deal with the fact that somebody they'd met back in prison who'd said the cash would be there had lied to them. It was all a fib, but instead of just admitting this and leaving, they killed four people.

"In court, Rader constructed everything so that his actions seemed inevitable, but that's just how he tells the story. Factor X arrived and I had to do all this. He's remembering it this way to let himself off the hook. In watching him plead guilty, I saw an emotional chameleon, which really surprised me. He has no personality of his own and gives people what he thinks they want. Even being a serial killer was just a role for him to play."

Members of the BTK task force who weren't in court that morning gathered around a TV set on the fourth floor of City Hall to watch the proceeding. Those who'd interviewed Rader in late February already knew how he'd strangled Marine Hedge and taken pictures of her inside the church. Once Rader's confession began, they were certain he was going to tell the judge about going to Christ Lutheran and posing her for bondage photographs, and they were right.

"When he began talking about Marine Hedge," says an investigator on the task force, "it got very, very quiet around the office. Even though we knew what was coming, people here were speechless."

When the confession concluded, Judge Waller announced he would set the sentencing for mid-August and court adjourned. Around noon, Lieutenant Landwehr made his way to a local Scotch 'N Sirloin, where he celebrated with a relaxed and very relieved lunch. His part in the BTK saga was all but finished, and he expressed little interest in speaking publicly about his role. The DA, on the contrary, took to the media circuit and appeared live on Court TV in a talkative, combative mood. When a guest lawyer on the show suggested to Foulston that Rader had probably killed more than ten people, Nola blew up, making it clear that the attorney was ignorant of the facts in the case and there were no unsolved murders. The host of the program, Nancy Grace, had made a career out of being abrasive with people on live television and could snipe with the best of them. When she tried to tone down the DA, Nola let *her* have it and Grace got her off the air.

Foulston was clearly determined to present some of her case at the sentencing hearing, which Judge Waller scheduled for August 17. Now that Rader had put his spin on the facts, the district attorney's office and the WPD wanted to do the same, to ensure that Rader would never be eligible for parole. On the first nine murder counts, he could receive a life sentence but come up for parole after fifteen years on each one. On the tenth count—the murder of Dolores Davis—the DA was seeking the "hard forty," meaning that Rader would not be eligible for parole for forty years for this homicide.

Following the guilty plea, there was a lingering sense that he hadn't told the whole truth and secrets still remained.

"During the confession, he left the *T* out of *BTK*," says Tony Ruark, the Wichita psychologist who'd studied the murder photos and Rader's writings and drawings while trying to help the police solve the case in the late 1970s. "He gave us a direct but very sanitized version of the events. He didn't talk about torturing people until they were nearly dead and then torturing them some more. You can see why he needed a Factor X to explain how he was capable of doing these things. That's how he dissociates from his actions, and he was doing something like that in the courtroom."

The district attorney wanted the chance to punish and humiliate Rader further, which may have seemed unnecessary, but Foulston had seen BTK evidence that almost no one else had. Law enforcement believed the crimes still needed to be exposed and purged in the kind of ritual that had not yet occurred, and the DA wouldn't rest until this had been done.

XLVI

Pastor Clark had had no warning about the pictures of Marine Hedge taken at the church, but fortunately he'd scheduled a counseling session at Christ Lutheran for the evening of June 27. Only members were allowed into the session, and thirty people showed up, giving into more anger and tears and their profound sense of betrayal. Christ Lutheran's leadership wasn't unprepared for dealing with human turmoil, because for years, the Stephen Ministries had been helping worshippers suffering emotionally or spiritually, while church elders had laid on hands and prayed for those seeking guidance in confronting pain or loss. The elders occasionally anointed someone with oil, as had been done in the Bible, as a sign of God's healing power of love. In the past, Rader had been a part of the church's prayers for others, but on this night prayers were once again offered for his victims, their relatives, Rader himself, his family, and the Christ Lutheran community. Since being arrested, Rader had written the church and tried to say he was sorry, but many could not accept this as a sincere apology. Like the district attorney, they wanted something more, especially after seeing him tell his story in court.

For months Donn Bischoff, who'd visited Rader in jail in the spring, had known that he was BTK. Still, the man's public confession was a jolt.

"The bit about his bringing the dead woman into our church really disturbed our members," Bischoff said a few days after the guilty plea, while sitting in the library at Christ Lutheran, where Rader had chaired two council meetings. "It gave them the chills. It gave me the chills. It was a direct violation of us, as if he'd gone into

249

our homes and done this. Even after we'd started to accept that Dennis might be BTK, we never imagined that he'd done anything like this."

What did he think of Rader's demeanor in court?

"It gave me great pause," he said, "to see so little emotion flowing through such a detailed and packed description of all his memories of the crimes. I expected a lot more outpouring of feeling, but this was a courtroom and the whole atmosphere was one of stating the facts. Dennis was very lacking in emotion, and that causes people at the church to doubt if he's really remorseful. I know that his greatest remorse is what all this has done to his family and to Christ Lutheran. I've gotten less sense of remorse from him for his victims.

"I'm at a loss how anyone who seemed such an instinctively good person—he'd open doors for you and pick things up for people who dropped them—could be so absolutely cold in committing these acts. It just doesn't fit, so calling it the work of a demon is as good as anything else. Dennis doesn't have a split personality, but one and the same personality did all this."

Bischoff was asked what he'd learned since the arrest. He's a thoughtful man who takes his time before answering any question, and just when you think he's finished speaking, he goes deeper.

"For me," he said, "the lesson is an awakening to looking differently at people who've done very ugly things. Like many others, I'd hear about a serial killer or a dictator or someone who seemed completely evil, and I'd judge that individual quickly and never think too much about it, but now that individual was in our church. We saw someone who acted like a very nice person but was doing these terrible things, so we have to get a new attitude about what constitutes mercy and forgiveness. Prior to this, I'd never have asked God for mercy for the souls of these famous serial killers or dictators, but this put a different light on it. Dennis was one of us at Christ Lutheran, and he still is. I want to ask God to give Dennis forgiveness and mercy so that he can be saved.

"Our role is take care of people. In the Bible, God says to visit people in jail and give comfort, so I hope the congregation can do that with Dennis. They don't have to forgive him or to like him, but at least they can put the judgment in God's hands instead of theirs. Let God be the judge."

As he was speaking, there was a knock at the door and Pastor Clark stepped inside. For months he'd been fielding calls from local and national reporters and TV shows asking to speak either with him or with Paula or with both of them. The confession had set off another frenzy of interview requests.

"*People* magazine is trying to get me to get Paula to talk to them," he told Bischoff, who since March had taken over as church council president. "A woman editor in New York is calling. Not a writer, mind you, but an editor. They're starting to bring out the big guns to see if they can land Paula. The editor offered to fly out here and meet me for a cup of tea and get my view of the situation and see what we could do."

Pastor Clark smiled and said, "It'd take a lot more than a cup of tea to get me interested in something like that."

Bischoff nodded, as if he understood perfectly and agreed with everything the minister was saying. The church had had all the publicity it wanted, from New York or anywhere else.

The pastor turned to go, but stopped at the threshold and whirled around.

"I'm not calling that woman back," he said to Bischoff. "I'm not making any long-distance calls on the church's dime to talk to these people."

"All right," Bischoff said.

"I just want you to know that."

"I do."

"We're not going to pay for that and I give you my word," Pastor Clark said, shutting the door behind him.

XLVII

On June 27 and during the next few days, news clips of Rader admitting his guilt were played across the nation and around the globe. People everywhere were taken aback by his flat delivery, his lack of apology, and the heinous nature of his crimes, which set off discussions about the media paying so much attention to a man who had behaved like a monster. It was an old debate, reaching back to when the first playwrights, had put together stories about ancient tragedies. Why focus on the painful and the grisly when there were so many other, more uplifting things to look at? One answer was that evil, instead of hiding inside institutions or behind huge bureaucracies, occasionally got to wear a specific human face. That face was fairly irresistible to look at, even for those who claimed to be the guardians of public morality, and the Wichita media embodied this contradiction. They couldn't give the case enough coverage—the *Eagle* going so far as to ask readers to tell its staff what else the paper should go out and report on about Dennis Rader—while trying to disdain any real interest in the subject matter. Sex and violence had driven the press for decades, but this was difficult to acknowledge in a place that was supposed to be better than that.

The BTK case was the biggest thing that had happened to Wichita since its prominence as a military aircraft manufacturing center during World War II; the city seemed to revel in and be repelled by the serial killer spotlight. People were captivated by something they probably shouldn't have been, and that was uncomfortable. Rader was not an import to the area who'd come in and done grotesque things to the locals, but a native son, a product of this time and place, which was why he'd never stood out in the community and was so hard to catch. In his desire to be socially useful and almost always pleasant, in his religion, his politics, and his reluctance to look below the surface of his own life, the killer reflected much about his background. That too was uncomfortable. Once he'd admitted his guilt, some parts of the media that had breathlessly been covering the BTK story for years now tried to distance themselves from it, shrugging and labeling him just another serial killer. It was a curious stance. If Rader's life demonstrated anything, it was that denying pain or complexity, shoving down unruly feelings, staying on the surface, and refusing to probe uncomfortable human problems had never solved anything, but only made them worse.

Some people very much wanted to look below the man's surface and examine both his background and his biology. Psychologist Tony Ruark was one and had begun trying to interview Rader following his arrest. He wrote him letters seeking to go in depth with the defendant about his childhood, but Rader was busy fending off media requests, working with his lawyers, and praying on the phone with his minister. Over decades of professional experience, Ruark had examined patients who, like Rader, had become sexually aroused as youngsters when receiving physical punishment, and the psychologist wanted to know how these two things—sexual urges and death—had become so intimately linked inside BTK.

"We're beginning to learn that there may be a strong genetic component for antisocial personalities," Ruark said, following the confession. "A part of his behavior may be driven by that, but for him to torture women in such extreme ways has to be related to things that occurred after he was born. I'd want to know much more about his interaction with his parents and his wife, and his early sexual experience. I'd want to explore his mother spanking him when he was small. Fetishes can get started very young. When one of my patients was only four or five, she got repeatedly spanked until her flesh burned. Then the adult who was sadistically abusing her rubbed her softly on her buttocks and she remembered all this as pleasurable. She developed pathological sexual appetites. I wonder what happened to Rader.

"His background allowed him to pigeonhole his life extremely well. He was brutally murdering people at night and going to church the next morning, but I don't think his religion was a facade. I think he's very sincere about his faith, but has this marvelous capacity to act without a conscience. If these terrible things had happened to his own family, he'd be very upset. He sees himself as two completely different people: Factor X and a practicing Christian."

Joycee Kennedy had worked in the field of mental health in Colorado for thirty years, treating individual patients, running a special high school for teenagers who'd been kicked out of regular schools, and taking in troubled kids because she felt they were better off with her family than in foster care. Her dealings with disturbed adolescents had been as close as in the rooms inside her home. A clinical social worker, Kennedy had been part of a team involved with the National Child Traumatic Stress Network and was coauthor of *Bridging Worlds: Understanding and Facilitating Adolescent Recovery from the Trauma of Abuse.* For much of her career, she'd pushed against the grain, believing that the tremendous emphasis in the psychiatric world on tagging children or adults with specific labels and then treating them based on this diagnosis—whether it was right or wrong—missed the larger point. People with significant emotional problems, no matter what you called them, couldn't *feel* things. They didn't connect their behavior with causing human suffering.

"They're lacking a modem," she says. "That's how I've come think of it. They can physically describe what another person looks like when they're hurting them—and even talk about the fear in someone's eyes when they're being attacked—but they don't have the part inside that allows them to sense and feel another's pain. We try to rationalize our understanding of all this by sticking a name on it, like narcissism or antisocial personality, because we don't want to feel the reality of this either. We label it to make it safer, but that doesn't make it safer. These people don't feel the way we do. They don't sense the needs or even the existence of another person.

"I worked with a teenage boy and tried very hard to bond with him. He had violent impulses, but I thought making a connection with him would make a difference, and he'd feel how invested I was in him getting better. I met his family, took him to lunch, went to sports activities with him, and spent a lot of time with him. He never sensed my caring for him. After all the work I'd done with him for three years, he went out and sexually assaulted a girl. If she hadn't come forward and reported the crime, we'd have never known he'd done it or been able to give him other treatment. All this was terrifying for me. I was like a chair to the boy—he couldn't feel my existence when I was sitting right next to him. I wasn't asking the right questions or grasping who these people are. I'd been a professional in this field for twenty years before realizing that my assessments were wrong."

At that point, the focus of her work changed.

"Our current model for mental health," she says, "doesn't define the problem accurately. We call the at-risk population evildoers or career criminals or bad people. These are just metaphors for a certain type of behavior. The underlying basis for the problems is neurobiological. People like this have impaired sensory-emotional integration. Scientists like Dr. Raine are starting to understand how alterations in the brain and central nervous system contribute to these kinds of impairment."

Dr. Adrian Raine, of the Department of Psychology at the University of Southern California, is one of the leading researchers into the biology of crime and the author of the 1993 study *The Psychopathology of Crime: Criminal Behavior as a Clinical Disorder*. He's tried to isolate why violent offenders lack the inhibitions that keep some people from hurting others. In those who kill, Dr. Raine has found less activity in the part of the brain that regulates and controls emotion and behavior. The gray matter of violent criminals holds 11 percent fewer neurons in the prefrontal cortex than the brains of the rest of the population.

"Violent offenders," Dr. Raine concluded, "just do not have the emergency brakes to stop their runaway aggressive behavior."

In short, bad brains—and not character flaws or moral deficiencies—lead to bad behavior.

In December 2004, Dr. Raine appeared on a British Broadcasting Corporation program entitled "Unlocking Crime: The Biological Key."

"One of the reasons we have repeatedly failed to stop crime," he said, "is because we have systematically ignored the biological and genetic contributions to crime causation."

"In America," says Joycee Kennedy, "we look at the whole reality of violence as a criminal justice problem. That's just another faulty label. We don't have a criminal justice problem. We have a mental health crisis because of how dangerous some people are and how much harm they inflict on society. They *are* sick. They *are* mentally ill, no matter how the legal system defines them. The idea of legal sanity or insanity is archaic. It doesn't mean anything. Many, many murderers are intelligent and can rationalize what they do, so they appear sane, whether they happen to be individual killers or leaders of societies that have become violent. You can't kill five or ten or fifteen human beings and be normal and sane. These are very damaged human beings because their neurobiological system is impaired. They can't control themselves because they can't input the sensory data where it belongs and don't feel what they are doing to someone else.

"Something useful should be done with BTK. He should be studied in depth. You can do this nonintrusively with MRIs and PET scans and other medical techniques. Take pictures of his brain and central nervous system. Watch his heart-rate variability. Maybe he really was dropped on his head and does have an injury there. We have a great opportunity here to take someone who is terribly impaired and try to understand from a biological perspective why he did what he did. He's a horrifically scary person. When he talks about demons, he's trying to say something important about himself and using the word *demon* is the best he can do. There's something wrong with him and he doesn't understand what it is. Unfortunately, he never took the next step of getting help.

"Because he was bright, he learned how to be a husband and a father and could function in an intellectual capacity in those roles. Going to church was the same thing, but no modem was connecting this with his actions as BTK. When he told the police after his arrest that he didn't understand that people in Wichita were afraid of him, he was telling the truth. He can't feel what they're feeling.

"Maybe if we can start to comprehend more about someone like him, we can begin to identify potential offenders before they become violent. We're very, very good at locking people up, but not so good at identifying at-risk people before they do something bad. Perhaps we can isolate their problems and foster more capacity inside of them to integrate feeling and emotion. We need to study this guy. I've never seen a better candidate for this kind of investigation and research. We need a new paradigm for understanding violence, and he and people like him could help create it. If we can identify the roots of the problem, we can make huge strides against it and ultimately prevent some of it."

"The good that can come from this case," says Dr. Brodsky, "is in helping our children, and especially our boys, understand and express their own eccentricities and impulses better, and not experience so much shame and humiliation. Boys go through very painful times taming their impulses to become helpful to society, and if they don't, we can all see what can happen."

For Rader, the humiliation was soon to deepen.

XLVIII

O N Sunday, July 10, the *Eagle* ran a huge front-page story on the BTK confession as members of Christ Lutheran gathered for their regular services. Pastor Clark and the congregation once more prayed for Paula and her "new life," which seemed about to include the sale of the Rader home. On July 11 another spectacle would come to Park City when Michelle Borin, the owner of one of the better-known exotic-dance clubs in the area, Michelle's Beach House, offered $90,000 for the residence at auction. This was $33,000 more than the appraised value and easily beat all the other bids. Women everywhere had expressed sympathy for Paula, and Borin made such a generous offer because she wanted to help BTK's ex-wife try to recover, at least financially, from the recent events. The auction took place in the Raders' backyard and drew about as much attention as his arrest. The media was all over town, fast-food joints were jammed, Independence Street was again blocked off to sight-seers, and police were ticketing anyone who got out of line. Initially, the sale looked like a windfall for Paula, but the money soon became entangled in the wrongful-death claims filed by the victims' relatives, and the sale fell through.

When the second service ended on July 10, shortly before noon, worshippers milled in the lobby, pumping the minister's hand, speaking among themselves or eating cookies and sipping coffee in the dining area. Christ Lutheran never seemed so much like a community as when the parishioners were chatting after church, while their kids ran around the building or went outside and played in the yard or on the swings. As the adults began filtering toward the parking lot, one aging man lingered in the foyer and brought up the BTK case without being prompted. People at the church still needed to talk about it.

"BTK stood right here and shook our hands," he said. "He took up the collection. We're still trying to believe what happened. I'll never believe it. It'll never make any sense. After he confessed last month, the women here got even more frightened than they were. They were a lot more frightened than the men because he was killing women right over in Park City—the last two victims. He knew the routines of the women in this church and was probably watching some of them during the services. Knew where they lived and if they were married or alone. They could have been targets. This has been really hard on them."

Once the other members had left Christ Lutheran, Pastor Clark and his wife sat down in the dining room, ready to eat. Jan Clark had prepared a cold meal and spread it out in front of them. At a nearby table, a young African man and Wichita State student named Joseph was feeding Tim, while Tai lay on the floor and watched over them, the dog rarely taking its eyes off the young man in the wheelchair. From time to time, the parents glanced over at their son to make sure he was all right. Jan wore a flowery dress and had short, graying hair and glasses. Like her husband, she was Midwestern in appearance, but not as outgoing or irreverent as Pastor Clark, at least not with strangers. One could not quite imagine her ever donning a clown outfit.

Pastor Clark had once thought about becoming a prison warden, but it was his wife who'd pursued a career inside the penal system. In 1987, with a master's degree in psychology from Pittsburg (Kansas) State University, she'd begun working with teenage boys who'd committed crimes. Six years later, when her husband was transferred to Beloit, Kansas, she treated girls, and when the minister came to Christ Lutheran in early 2001, she took a job with the El Dorado Correctional Facility, just up the road from Wichita. At El Dorado, she did psychological evaluations of incoming adult male prisoners who were sex offenders or suffering from mental illness. El Dorado housed some of Kansas's most notorious criminals, including death-row inmates. After Rader was sentenced on August 17, his first stop (and perhaps his last) would be El Dorado, where he would be tested by a variety of medical and psychological experts, but Jan was not expected to participate in that evaluation.

Unlike her husband, she did not talk easily about the BTK case. While it had propelled Pastor Clark on an outward journey and an inward redefinition of his view of evil, she seemed to have withdrawn into her church, her friends, and herself to deal with the event. She conveyed a ferociously protective quality, especially when asked about people she truly cared for, and that quality spread out around her like a big, invisible fan that she was going to retreat behind at any moment. Jan seemed deeply hurt by Dennis Rader and gave the impression that what he'd done was not only beyond shameful, but that dwelling on it now was not productive. This wasn't just about deviant sex and murder, but deviant sex and murder that had lived and breathed right inside the church. When she spoke of BTK, one could still feel the shudder his revelations had sent through Christ Lutheran. One could sense the lingering hint of evil within these walls, and the depths of his deception. Jan may have had every bit as much to say on the subject as her husband did, but talking about it in depth was clearly not comfortable. Giving the devil too much attention could be a sin.

Shortly after the police had arrived at the church last February 25 to inform Pastor Clark that Rader had been taken into custody, the minister had called his wife with the news. Jan had spent nearly two decades dealing with a criminal population and listening to them talk about themselves and their offenses. One of the first things she told her husband on the twenty-fifth was that he should be prepared for Rader to say that he'd already repented for all his sins and had made things right with God.

"As much of a shock as the arrest was to Mike and me," Jan said at lunch, "my first reaction was that we now had a whole new layer of victims—all the people who'd trusted and loved Dennis and felt they knew him. They felt completely abused."

She took a bite of salad and glanced at her son.

"Our experience with Tim has helped in many ways," she said, "because we knew from that that everyone handles these kinds of things differently. Mike and I are his parents, but we still experienced this horrible accident in different ways. We had to come to terms with that fact that because our backgrounds, our personalities, and our places in our individual journeys were different, we weren't going to respond the same. Hundreds of people knew Dennis and Paula, and each one had a unique relationship with them and was going to grieve differently. Some will get a lot angrier than others. Some won't get angry at all or say anything. You need a variety of ways to minister to them to get through this.

"Some people have told Paula to come forward and tell her side of the story. I don't believe in that. I'd teach her communication skills and just to say 'No comment' to everyone. Maybe five or ten years from now, after she's gone through a long healing process, it will be different, but no good can come from her speaking right now. People will want to know the details of her marriage and her intimate life and there's no need to tell anyone about that. I'd like to meet with the women here and listen to what they have to say about all this. They need to be gentle with each other. Everyone will deal with it differently, and some won't deal with it at all or show a lot of feelings and we shouldn't force them to."

Jan had visited Rader at the jail. Like everyone else at the church, she'd never had any reason to suspect him of criminal behavior, but after his guilty plea she was presented with an array of offenses that were extreme—even by the standards of her work. As a psychologist, she seemed challenged by understanding him, but as a Christian she didn't want to get too close to all this. Her feelings toward Rader were perhaps more complicated than her husband's, because she was a woman and he'd stalked and killed primarily women, and because she evaluated antisocial personalities for a living.

"I think Dennis was mocking everyone at our church," she said, laying down her fork, her tone more forceful. "I think he was fooling us with his Christianity and feeling superior to us."

Her husband stared at her but didn't interrupt.

"Dennis had a lot of compulsive-obsessive traits," she said. "When you're like that, you want to be in control of your life. I saw him one time in jail and he told me things I won't tell you. At eight or nine, he realized he was not thinking right and was interested in things his friends weren't. He already recognized that in himself, in the realm of sexual fantasy. He was exposed to some things his friends weren't, and other kids might have forgotten about them, but he didn't. I worked with a thirteen-year-old girl who was a violent offender. Her father was a drug addict and her mother an alcoholic. She became addicted to the adrenaline rush of her crimes. Each crime she committed had to be more risky than the one before for her to get that same rush of adrenaline. I believe that what Dennis experienced as a child got that kind of process going for him. And what you go through as a young child influences how your brain develops."

When it appeared she was going to delve further into his psychological profile, she pulled back.

"What I'm most interested in," she said, "is that the outcome of Dennis's story, whatever it is, must be for the glory of God. It will get people's attention, but we must learn to provide the right kind of nurturing environment for children, and you must give them the spiritual background for handling these problems."

Picking up her fork, she again glanced at her son.

"Dennis," the pastor said, "has been trying to understand his own behavior for years. He somehow allowed a demonic power or force to enter his heart and soul and it took charge. Not every day, not all the time, but it uses him for evil purposes and he believes he has no control over it. I don't know if he can ever get control of it through faith. He never talked about any of this to me or at the church and I can't deal with an issue like this until someone comes to me and speaks the truth. You have to be ready in your heart to talk about your problems. I can't be the one to do it for you."

Jan was asked if she'd had experience working with people who claimed to be possessed by demons.

"The scary thing," she said, "is that since Dennis was arrested, three inmates have come to me and talked about demonic forces. That had never happened before. The first one was just six days after the arrest. A man came to me who'd been having hallucinations. People at my job had tried to put him on medication, but he said he didn't need it. I agreed with him and asked what was going on. He said, 'I can handle it.' I sat there and was quiet. I didn't ask him any leading questions and I try never to impose my beliefs on others. I want them to tell me about their own experiences and where they get their strength. He said, 'If you promise not to put me on medication, I'll tell you some things.' "

She agreed with his request.

"He told me," Jan said, "about a dark, black, floating figure that had been inside the prison. It had no eyes, but was looking down at him. He also said that when he was sleeping, something kept waking him up. This had happened several times and it was like he was struggling with it, trying to push it away, or it would do something bad to him. He said that something was trying to engage him in a physical battle and take over his body. The only way he could make it leave was that he'd memorized Bible verses and if he would think them and concentrate very hard on them, it would go away. He told me about being in the county jail and he looked up one day and saw a black image with no arms or legs. It was about a person's height and had no eyes, but it looked directly at him. He was with a friend, but tried not to react to the image because he didn't want anyone to think he was crazy. His friend looked at him and said, 'I saw it too.' "

She paused and added, "I pray for this man and so far he isn't on medication."

Jan looked around the church, as if remembering where she was, then pushed away from the table.

"I will only devote so much of my life to talking about Dennis Rader," she said, "and I'm about done for today."

Did she believe that Rader had truly repented his crimes?

"Oh, no," she said. "He hasn't repented at all. Look at all the attention he's getting from this."

She stood and began clearing the dishes.

"Dennis," her husband said, "has acknowledged his crimes to the secular world and will accept his punishment, but that's just a part of it. He's still salvageable if he makes things right with God. A year ago, he was stalking his eleventh victim, so that can only reflect a broken relationship with God. It's up to him to heal that. The things I've done in my life are not as ugly and horrendous as what Dennis has done, but I still have to deal with my own sins. And I sin. There but for the grace of God go I. Dennis is a work in progress, like all of us."

The pastor got up, helped his wife put away the food, and they both went over to check on Tim, who'd finished his meal. They said goodbye to their son and Joseph wheeled Tim out of the church, as the minister and Jan walked toward the front door. In the parking lot, they stepped into separate vehicles and drove away.

Three days from now, the minister would get in his pickup, with the RUFUS license plate, and head north, taking along with him some reading materials and his clown outfit. Who knew when others along the road might need a few laughs? Some years earlier, Pastor Clark had fallen off a ladder and seriously injured his back; at times, he could only relieve the pain by lying flat on blocks of ice, and driving could exacerbate the problem. He was about to start a trip of more than a thousand miles to consult with an expert on demonic possession and exorcism. Uncharacteristically, he was keeping his plans vague but going somewhere near the top of Minnesota to spend a few days asking questions of a highly knowledgeable Lutheran missionary who'd spent time in Africa and had witnessed paranormal phenomena. The pastor didn't want to learn to perform exorcisms himself, and wasn't sure where any of this was leading him, but felt compelled to make this journey, despite his back pain.

"For a long time," he said before leaving, "my claim to fame was that I was the minister who'd once sold condoms, but I think that's been surpassed. Now I'll be known as the pastor of a famous serial killer. The search I'm on is more than anything I could have ever dreamt of. It might be a dead end or it might not be. Who can say? All I know is, I gotta go."

XLIX

Tuesday, August 16, was cloudy and cooler in Wichita, the air thick with moisture. Media trucks were camped around the courthouse, just as they had been in recent years at other famous trials across the country. Reporters clustered inside roped-off enclosures or moved in and out of white tents representing CNN, Fox TV, MSNBC, Court TV, and local news outlets. All were waiting for tomorrow's sentencing, the final act of the legal drama that had begun with Rader's arrest. Ever since 1974, BTK had controlled the narrative of the story, deciding when to kill, whom to kill, and what version of his crimes he would write to the police. The same pattern had continued when he'd confessed to Lieutenant Landwehr and the other detectives, then repeated itself in court last June 27. Instead of giving the district attorney the chance to put on her case, he'd told the world what had happened and omitted whatever he'd wanted to. On August 17, 2005, for the first time ever, someone else was going to take command of the narrative and force Rader to listen to it, with a national TV camera trained on his face.

"So far, he may think he looks pretty good," said Dr. Brodsky the day before the proceeding. He would be commenting on the sentencing for KAKE. "But he has to know what's coming tomorrow. Humiliation is the key thing he's always tried to avoid, and now he can't escape it. If he could commit suicide between today and in the morning, he might do it. The people at the jail had better place him under a special watch. I think you're going to see him dissolve right in front of your eyes in the courtroom. Public humiliation is his real punishment. In the past, this kind of total exposure in front of others made him kill them."

Representatives of the nationwide antiabortion group Operation Rescue were gathered outside the courthouse and handing out a flyer titled "Churches & Serial Killers." It compared Rader to Wichita abortion doctor George Tiller, a member of the Reformation Lutheran Church. The flyer featured a large colored photo of Rader in his orange prison jumpsuit alongside one of "Tiller the Killer." According to Operation Rescue, Tiller's sins including bragging about his "late-term child killing business," and the flyer also took a swipe at Rader's former house of worship and by implication Pastor Clark and the church council.

"The false gospel in the Church allows Dennis Rader to remain a member at Christ Lutheran Church," read the handout. "He has been removed, not by the church, to their shame, but by the State and is now behind bars."

By the afternoon of August 16, security around the courthouse was extremely tight, with patrol cars cruising up and down the block looking for anything unusual. Anyone stopping to snap a picture of the courthouse or the nearby detention facility where Rader was being held was approached by guards and asked to produce identification. It would be that way all night.

Sentencing was set for nine Wednesday morning, and courtroom seating was limited. By 5:30 a.m., spectators were lined up outside the courthouse waiting for the front doors to open ninety minutes later. By 6 a.m., those on line outnumbered the available seats, and when the front doors were unlocked, there was a mad dash to see who could get through the metal detectors the fastest; a number of people were detained for searches and never made it into the courtroom.

Half an hour before the start of the hearing, the BTK cast was assembling in the lobby. Pastor Clark wore his white clerical collar and moved swiftly through the crowd, brushing off one media request after another. The day before, he'd ducked numerous interview opportunities to be with his congregation and pay another visit to Rader at the jail. The sentencing wasn't the only thing on his mind. His aging mother, who lived several hours away in another part of Kansas, had fallen ill and her son needed to be with her, but that would have to wait until the legal process was concluded. The minister would be in the courtroom for Rader, no matter how long the sentencing took.

Lieutenant Landwehr strolled through the lobby in a dark, dapper suit and a red tie, as polite and as tight-lipped as the preacher. Up on the second floor, DA Foulston was about to leave her elegantly appointed digs for the courtroom. The foyer of her office, with its fresh-cut lilies, beautiful vases, and polished wooden furniture, looked like the award-winning work of an interior designer. A small green statue of Lady Justice, blindfolded and holding out scales in front of her, had to be the image Nola wanted to project of herself. Down in the lobby, the victims' families, led by Charlie Otero, Kevin Bright, and Steve Relford, were streaming in and forming a circular group near the elevators, as the press swarmed around them. On television, Charlie's face came across so powerfully that a viewer was easily convinced he was a large man, but in person he was much smaller. It was the sorrow in his eyes that filled the TV screen. The group was trying to avoid reporters or onlookers, and the atmosphere around them was one of collective determination and mutual support. Listening to a recounting of BTK's crimes would be gut-wrenching all over again, but had to be done for the story to have an ending.

Not everyone agreed with this assessment. Following Rader's confession, many people in Wichita, especially those at Christ Lutheran, felt that more than enough information about the case had already been aired and Judge Waller should simply impose a series of life sentences on the guilty man and be done with it. That would take only a few minutes, and Rader could be driven off to the El Dorado Correctional Facility for good. The metropolitan area had heard plenty about the horrendous nature of the crimes, and anything more was overkill. Even police officers at City Hall had been heard grumbling that the DA wouldn't be content until she got into court for a couple more days, but further testimony really wasn't necessary. Foulston herself felt that a more complete record of the case needed to be made and the judge went along with her. It was the right move, because things were coming that would expand the context of the entire BTK phenomenon, and shine more light into Rader's darkness.

"What will happen starting Wednesday morning is the unfolding of a huge morality play," Dr. Brodsky said on Tuesday afternoon. "Society finally gets its chance to show that good has triumphed over evil."

Society would also get the chance to see a few things that had until now been kept safely out of sight.

By 8:45 a.m. on Wednesday, the courthouse was crackling with energy and movement. All the victims' relatives had been led upstairs to Judge Waller's courtroom and the lawyers had assembled one last time. Outside, TV reporters were scurrying to find leftover interview subjects, while journalists in the media room were seriously discontented. Scribes from all over the country had flown in for the event, setting up their laptops and assorted electronic gadgets in an unused courtroom one floor below the sentencing. As nine o'clock approached, they were on their second or third cups of coffee and in high gear, busting out jokes about crime and punishment and making fun of the district attorney and her perfect hairdo. Everything seemed to be in good shape until they discovered that the public relations arm of Wichita's criminal justice system hadn't provided any large monitors for them to watch the sentencing on. One tiny, fuzzy TV, lost amid a stack of papers and wires, was the only thing the assembled press had to view. The DA had put together a lengthy, impressive, and graphic PowerPoint presentation, but they'd barely be able to see it under these conditions. The *New York Times, People* magazine, *USA Today,* Fox TV, MSNCB-TV, National Public Radio, and assorted other media reps all huddled around the little box shouting insults at Wichita.

Squinting at this dismal excuse for a TV, one reporter cried out, "I forgot my binoculars!"

Somebody left the room to go in search of a better television.

As court came to order, the two seats reserved for Rader's family remained empty. The day would be devoted solely to a recitation of the murders, with one law enforcement officer after another—KBI Agents Ray Lundin and Larry Thomas; WPD detectives Clint Snyder, Dana Gouge, Kelly Otis, and Tim Relph; Sedgwick County's Thomas Lee and Sam Houston—taking the witness stand and giving the most detailed account yet of Rader's criminal history. Accompanying the testimony were a series of pictures of the victims, their facial wounds and hemorrhaging strangulation marks on display for the courtroom and the TV cameras, but their eyes had usually been blocked out. The effect of the choking on the pupils and sockets had been deemed too much for the public to see. The photos often showed the victims bound and partially nude, the final indignity for themselves and their families.

This testimony wasn't wrapped up by the afternoon recess, and the litany of death had gradually laid a pall over both the courtroom and the media room. Inside the latter, the joking had long since stopped, wisecracking totally inappropriate in this setting. One floor up, the victims' relatives leaned on one another for strength throughout the day and shed more tears, while Pastor Clark absorbed the presentation with growing dismay. This was not at all what he'd expected after Judge Waller had nudged Rader toward his confession on June 27.

Not only had BTK brutalized and murdered ten people, the detectives said on August 17, but he'd assigned each of them a role as his sexual slave or personal attendant in the afterlife. Once they were dead, they'd still be forced to try to satisfy his basest needs.

"It was horrendous," the minister said later of the first day of the hearing, "and it was very painful for me personally to sit there and listen. I felt for the victims' families and couldn't fathom what they were thinking during this testimony. If I were one of them, I'd have been extremely upset."

In court Rader looked even thinner and much paler now, less full of the self-assurance he'd shown seven weeks earlier when confessing, his dark sport coat hanging loosely around his shrinking frame. The easier and more sociable parts of his postarrest period were coming to a close. Instead of spending his time as the "Podfather" at the county jail, he was about to enter a new facility where he'd spend all but one hour a day in solitary confinement, at least during his initial evaluation period. If the district attorney had her way, he'd never be allowed to read or watch anything about himself, never have any access to female images he could fantasize over, or be given drawing implements that he could use to create bondage or sexual pictures. Since late June, Rader had seemed to be receding inside his own skin and looked more like a frightened teenager than an adult serial killer. In addition to everything else he was facing, the DA had gone out of her way in the courtroom to portray him as a pedophile, drawing upon Rader's own statements to the police last February 25 and 26, when he'd spoken about the Otero murders and implied that he was attracted to children.

"The only thing," he said, "I ever got close to is Josephine, and I never had sex with any kids or anything like that. But if the opportunity would arise as I got older . . ."

Nola's use of the word *pedophile* was not subtle. She appeared to be sending a message to Rader's future fellow inmates that was intended to mark him as the lowest level of criminal—a child molester—and a potential target. She took great pleasure in pointing out to one of the detectives on the stand that Rader was not a law enforcement officer, like those who'd arrested and interrogated him, but merely a Park City dogcatcher. After all the unspeakably ugly and vicious things BTK had done to the opposite sex over the years, here was one woman who was going to kick his ego in public.

When the session ended on Wednesday, all the reporters and spectators walked out into the warm and sunny late afternoon, loitering on the pavement or the grass in front of the courthouse. While journalists scattered for interviews, turning toward a lawyer in the case or a victim's relative with the same synchronized movement of birds in flight or fish swimming after food, one man stood off by himself on the sidewalk out by the street. He wore an ill-fitting blue police costume and police cap, hugely oversize black shoes, and carried a nightstick that he swung round and round in the air. Real policemen and women were patrolling outside by the courthouse, working security duty, and they were trying hard to ignore him. So were other officers who came and went through the area, as the police department at City Hall was less than a block away. The man was waving at passengers in cars and nodding at pedestrians, yet saying nothing, and it was a quietly outrageous performance.

He was a mime, dressed up like a Keystone Kop, and he was mocking the Wichita Police Department to its face. Five days earlier, NBC television had aired a two-hour special on Rader, and during it he'd likened the WPD when they were hunting for him to the Keystone Kops, the comic law enforcement figures in old silent films. The mime was funny and gave substance to a feeling that had been present in the courtroom all day long, but nobody had voiced it. While the detectives were meticulously describing Rader's behavior from 1974 to 1991, it slowly sunk in that he hadn't been a master criminal, as he'd thought of himself, but a terribly inefficient bungler, breaking into homes in broad daylight, killing people in front of living witnesses while wearing no disguise, leaving DNA samples at three separate locations, and immediately unleashing chaos almost everywhere. On only two occasions—the murders of Nancy Fox and Marine Hedge—had he actually had the time to do what he wanted to do with the victims. Every other crime scene had quickly descended into a homicidal mess. He was a bumbling, sloppy, incompetent killer, yet for more than three decades no one had come close to identifying him as BTK. Whether he meant to or not, the mime had flushed out another secret.

It wasn't just Rader's perversity that was on display in the courtroom, but another mysterious human perversity about how much we want to trust others and for things to be as they seem to be. Rader had shown just how easy it was to mislead people and make them believe that black was white, and vice versa. Unlike fictional TV, which usually resolves everything neatly and quickly, this case unleashed the terrifying unpredictability and murkiness of real life, where little is obvious and we're always working in the dark. If Rader hadn't continued sending in provocative messages to the media and the police, it's unlikely he'd ever have been caught. The devil, even when you were looking right at him, was about as hard to see as C. S. Lewis had indicated he was in *The Screwtape Letters,* especially when he buried his violence under his pious religious convictions.

That evening on CNN, *Larry King Live* featured a panel of commentators who discussed the day's BTK testimony, while Jeff Davis appeared on CNBC's *The Big Idea,* hosted by Donny Deutsch. With Deutsch's encouragement, Davis began a long rant against the man who'd killed his mother, warming up for his chance to speak in court the next day.

L

On Thursday morning a gentle breeze was blowing and the sun was out at dawn, as the participants gathered downtown for the final day of the hearing. Yesterday had been more or less predictable, but that phase of the sentencing was almost over. By now, those watching in court or on TV knew in exhaustive detail what had happened in these crimes, but the why remained elusive. As Captain Sam Houston of the Sedgwick County Sheriff's Department was completing his testimony about the murder of Dolores Davis, he brought out a new series of photographs. These were different from Wednesday's crime-scene pictures, and one depicted the flesh-tone mask Rader had placed over the dead woman's face shortly after the strangling. He'd dabbed rouge on the cheeks and painted the lips to "pretty up" the corpse and make Dolores "more feminine." Then he'd snapped pictures of her lying on the wintry ground, partially nude, her body no longer intact because of the weather and nighttime predators. In the courtroom and the media room, these images were met with silence and something like disbelief, as if people had at last been exposed to the most bizarre elements this case had to offer. They hadn't.

Six months earlier, when talking to detectives about his Mother Lode, Rader had brought up this mask. He hadn't used it just for taking photos of his tenth victim, but for other photos of himself.

"When you find my archives," he said, "you'll find that mask in a lot of pictures. Those are me. Assimilated self-bondage . . . You get a Polaroid with a tripod, and you run like a ten-foot cord with a squeeze bottle, and you stick the squeeze bottle in your hands and take the picture."

The mask was for his "sexual fantasy things, my self-bondage things. I would wear that and I would try to take the pictures so I looked like maybe I was a female or a person in distress. . . . When you're in bondage, it's a sexual fantasy. You can really get high on that kind of stuff. . . . If I ever had to be put away, I wanted to be hung, but I guess they don't do that anymore."

Continuing the PowerPoint presentation, Captain Houston brought out more pictures retrieved from the Mother Lode, images that had been in the cabinet by Rader's office desk for years. They went by quickly, but were on the screen long enough to deliver a growing shock. One showed a blown-up photo of him in a chair wearing panty hose, a heavily rouged female mask, and a curly blond wig, taken in his parents' basement. Rader stared directly into the lens, head cocked, his legs demurely set together, his posture suggesting that he was trying to sit like a woman. In another photo, he was dressed in one of his victim's undergarments with his ankles, knees, and calves bound in black tape, exactly the image he'd created decades earlier as a boy drawing dark lines on female dolls. His face was covered and his hands were tied behind his back. In the next photo, he was in the basement wearing the apparel of a woman he'd killed. In another basement image, he was nude and on his knees with a cord looped around his neck, acting out his own death by hanging, just as he'd done in the Otero home with Josephine.

Still other pictures had been shot outdoors in warm weather, somewhere between Park City and Hutchinson, Kansas. Rader had found a remote area of the countryside, dug a full-length grave with a shovel, spread the dirt out around the hole, tied himself up, covered his head with a female mask, lay down in the grave facing upward, and captured these images using the remote-control camera. In another he was wrapped almost completely in plastic, as if he was suffocating. What he hadn't been able to do with Dolores Davis, he'd done with his own face and body, leaving only his buttocks exposed.

Absolute silence had come over the courtroom and among the reporters. A feeling not present throughout Wednesday or early Thursday was floating into the proceeding and shifting its tone. After one had heard the detectives narrate the crimes for six or seven

straight hours, Rader had seemed nothing more than the embodi-
ment of evil, a human cover over an inhuman beast, someone so
unlike the rest of us that nobody could grasp or sense his reality, but
these photos were revealing more. He hadn't just posed his victims in
revolting and humiliating bondage positions, but done the same thing
to himself. He hadn't just killed them but had staged his own death
under similar circumstances—wearing makeup and women's clothing, hiding in his parents' basement, trapped inside a self he could
only blame on demons, while his mother and father went about their
daily routines with no awareness of the child they'd created. The
images conveyed what he'd never been able to put into words.

Pain and shame and desperation leaked out from these photos
and filtered into the courtroom, the media room, and reached the
TV viewing audience, touching anyone who'd ever struggled with
intolerance over his or her sexual identity, or sexual torment, anyone who'd ever fought the war of self-acceptance and self-love, anyone who'd ever wondered why God had made him as he was. Or
anybody who'd ever angrily asked why he or she had been born into
a particular place with a particular family of strangers. Instead of
making Rader look worse and even more pathetic, the freakish pic
tures rendered him human at last.

The PowerPoint presentation went on and one journalist tapped
another on the shoulder.

"I'm not sure," he whispered, "that Nola knows what she's doing
now. Yesterday's testimony was all about how bad Rader is, and she
should have stopped there. This is about how sick he is and the sick-
ness isn't just his. You can hear the tumblers falling into place for
people as they look at these photographs. This is no longer just about
a serial killer but about a weird small-town guy growing up in
Kansas, surrounded by all the repression and conservatism. It hurts
to look at this."

As the photos rolled by, Rader stared down into the wooden table
in front of him, fiddling with his hands or wiping the sweat from his
forehead. The larger the images became—totally filling up the proceeding—the smaller he looked in his chair. His eyes were dim and
red, starting to tear up, as his real secrets were slipping out into the

open. The inner life he'd hid for the past half century was being broadcast to the nation and the world, the exposure now complete.

"In my thirty-five years of clinical practice, I've dealt with a number of people who were fascinated by fetishes and bizarre sexual stimuli," Tony Ruark later said. "But I'd never seen anything like these pictures or Rader's pansexual interest in every single erotic area. Men, women, children, and all the autoerotic stuff. He lived this every day of his life, and he did it alone. There are groups of people who get together and practice these things, but he could never do that, so he just went further into himself. If I could interview him, I'd want to know about the sex life he had with his wife. Was it once a year? Once a month? Once a week? I can't imagine that anything with her was as satisfying for him as what he did with bondage and sadism and cross-dressing.

"I find myself wondering how he had time for a normal life, with all this fantasizing and cutting out of these advertisements and keeping notebooks on what he did. That takes a lot of effort. Many people have one or two unusual sexual appetites, but he had them all. His sexual fantasies dominated his life and affected his decision-making, which is the definition of mental illness."

Lieutenant Landwehr took the stand and talked about items retrieved from Rader's home, including pornography, and the man's ventures into autoeroticism during Cub Scout camping trips. The lieutenant also offered a few more photographs. All the pictures so far had been somewhat artistic—bringing to mind the work of a demented Diane Arbus—but the final group would deepen this impression. One felt they were meant to represent Rader's masterpiece, his ultimate effort to leave behind aesthetic images of himself and his bottomless self-involvement. Outside in the sunny, wooded landscape of rural Kansas in the spring of 1991, he'd constructed an incredibly elaborate system of ropes and pulleys in a tree, put on women's clothing, tied himself into bondage with strips of black tape, and hung upside down from branches, swinging through the air yet not moving his arms or legs, like a mummy in flight, unable to spread his wings or go anywhere. Another picture showed him with chains and collars wrapped tightly around his neck, torturing himself right up to the edge of death before letting himself have another breath. He'd done what artists everywhere do—found an outward expression for his inner reality— and the photos conjured up the most avante-garde art exhibit you could imagine, one that might find an audience in a sexual subculture in New York or London or San Francisco. That they'd been shot in a Midwestern forest by a man who voted for law-and-order Republicans and was the president of a small, conservative church only heightened their pathos. They inevitably evoked the recent images of American soldiers torturing Iraquis in Abu Ghraib prison west of Baghdad, but Rader had done this to himself.

The tormentor and the tormented came together in these pictures and pushed the message across. If you were human, you'd just seen the source of Rader's crimes—glimpsing into the heart and soul of somebody who actually thought he could get away with denying who he was. The photos screamed out not to judge people harshly for their sexuality.

"In these images," says Joycee Kennedy, "he's punishing his craziness. And he's punishing himself for being ill."

LI

LIEUTENANT LANDWEHR stepped down from the stand and court ended for the morning with a wave of relief. The halls were swarming with talk about the photos, and even veteran crime reporters, convinced they'd known everything about BTK, looked startled. The case had entered new territory, and Thursday's testimony was only half over. That afternoon, after waiting more than three decades in some instances, the victims' relatives would finally get their chance to vent in front of the killer. In recent weeks, Rader had told media representatives that he and others might need a box of Kleenex at the sentencing, but so far he hadn't fully broken down. When court was recalled to order, one after another of the victims walked to the microphone that had been set up in the gallery. Charlie Otero went first and was remarkably soft-spoken and self-contained, given the carnage the fifteen-year-old had witnessed in his home in January 1974.

"I speak for all members of my family, living and dead," he said. "Dennis Rader caused irreparable damage to my blood family. I've never allowed his actions to send me to the dark side. I truly feel the Lord will pass judgment on him. Dennis Rader has failed in his efforts to kill the Oteros."

With that he sat down, and his sister, Carmen Otero Montoya, took his place at the mike.

"You have seen my face before," she said to the defendant, in a voice quaking with emotion. "It is the face of my mother. My mother taught me most of all to face fears. . . . You are such a coward. My father loved my mother with a love you can't imagine. My sister,

Josie, such a sweet girl . . . It's amazing to me you could be so cruel to such a sweet child. . . . You took away the most loving and adorable child in Joey. . . . A man with a gun against a little boy. You are such a coward. In my world, family is everything . . ."

As Carmen continued, Rader bowed his head and wept, unable to look up until she was finished.

"My sister," Kevin Bright said, "lived for five hours after his attack and she lost twenty pints of blood. I wish the gun [Rader was wielding during the crime] would have gone off [into Rader's stomach] and it had ended there. . . . I'm glad I was there that day to stop him from acting out his sexual fantasy on her."

Rader took off his glasses, set them on the defense table, and dabbed at his eyes with a tissue.

Steve Relford went next and could only get out, "I'd like for him to suffer for the rest of his life."

He returned to his seat, and Beverly Plapp, Nancy Fox's sister, came up to the microphone, bitterly chastising Rader for assigning degrading positions to his victims in the afterlife. In one BTK fantasy, spelled out by the prosecution on Wednesday, the dead Nancy was supposed to have been his "primary mistress."

"As far as I'm concerned," Beverly said, trembling at the podium, "Dennis Rader doesn't deserve to live. This man needs to be thrown into a deep, dark hole and left to rot. On the day he dies, Nancy and all his victims will be watching as he burns in hell."

Bill Wegerle, who'd come to the hearing with his daughter, Stephanie Clyne, had spent almost eighteen years under suspicion for the murder of his wife, Vicki. From September 1986 until March 2004, when BTK renewed communication with the media and the police, Bill had lived with both the loss of his spouse and the feeling that people believed he was a killer.

"It's all in the light now," he told the court. "No punishment you can exact upon him will satisfy our needs. We won't have to see him or deal with him or hear from him ever again."

Stephanie followed her father to the mike. She looked strikingly like Vicki had looked in the 1980s, and she pointed out to the judge that her own children would never know their grandmother.

"What did any of us do to deserve this?" she said, nearly too distraught to talk. "I ask you today, Your Honor, to have no remorse for him."

As she walked back to the gallery, Jeff Davis, who had sat patiently through the other statements, came forward. He'd been waiting fourteen years for this moment and had put an extraordinary amount of thought and feeling into what he wanted to say. His voice was strong and clear and he began by employing a rhetorical device used in the first century BC by Cicero when comparing himself favorably to others in the Roman Senate. If I were you, Davis boomed again and again at Rader, and then he finished each remark by underscoring that he could never be anything near this doomed and wretched man.

Like a hellfire-and-brimstone preacher, Davis called the defendant a "walking cesspool . . . social sewage . . . a demon from hell . . . a eunuch and pervert . . . a quagmire of madness . . . a cockroach" who had "profaned Christianity and blasphemed in God's house.

"Your wife has divorced you," the orator said, driving the words into Rader, "and your children have disowned you. You'd still be a free man if you'd kept your mouth shut."

Looking around the courtroom as if the task of condemning BTK had left him spent, Davis added, "Good can triumph over the most hideous forms of evil," and then he was finished.

His words had stopped, but they rang in the air for a while with a cleansing echo. Somebody had needed to be publicly rude to BTK, at least for a few minutes, and Davis had gladly done so.

Before sentencing was passed, Rader's lead attorney, Steve Osburn, asked Judge Waller for leniency for his client, claiming that the killer had "in effect . . . turned himself in. . . . Ninety-five percent of what we heard today came from him. He believes he's possessed by demons . . . since early childhood . . ."

The judge listened respectfully and then asked the defendant if he had anything to say.

As Rader rose from his chair, tears remained on his face, his lower lip quivered, and he looked more shrunken still. The monster everyone had been describing had shriveled into a balding, sad-eyed, sixty-year-old man. It was his last chance to speak in court, and he was going to make the most of it, but before he could start, the victims' relatives, led by Jeff Davis, stood and marched out of the courtroom in protest. Rader looked taken aback by their departure, as if they should have been keenly interested in his final speech. Over six decades, he'd never learned to talk honestly about himself to anyone, and when he tried to that afternoon, the ideas were mangled, the language stunted, and the sentiments often inappropriate. He began by comparing himself to those he'd murdered: he and Joseph Otero had been in the air force; he and Marine Hedge had both loved to garden; and he'd always wanted to play the piano like Vicki Wegerle. Standing at the defense table, he felt compelled to explain to the judge and the victims' families (even though they'd left the courtroom) that parts of his life were similar to the lives of those he'd taken. As he spoke, Lieutenant Landwehr stared on in anger.

"I had a great fondness for animals," Rader said, clearing his throat. "I had pets and . . . I read somewhere that she [Dolores Davis] had her last Christmas with her family, and I did too. . . . I had a lot of memories as a kid with a dog. . . . A boy and a dog is what you have to have when you're a kid."

He took off his glasses, blew his nose, and cried some more.

A sore spot with him was that the WPD had invaded his daughter's privacy and taken Kerri's DNA, as if the detectives should have left his family out of the investigation. He was also irritated that in their PowerPoint presentation, the police had testified about finding a few examples of pornography in his vast collection of BTK material. He wanted to clear up the impression anyone might have gotten that he'd had a lot of porn stashed around the house. Since his arrest nearly six months earlier, he hadn't tried to apologize for murdering ten people, but it was important to him that those watching didn't think that he was drawn to smut.

"The bottom line," he said, "is that I'm very selfish and self-centered. . . . People will say that I'm not a Christian, but I believe that I am. . . . I have to rebuild humility, basically humble myself now."

After rambling for about five minutes, he started to find his composure, speaking of his respect for law enforcement, groping to say he was sorry, critiquing the DA's PowerPoint presentation, and making small corrections in what the investigators had said about his crimes—a detail man to the very end. Then he stunned everyone by commencing a round of thank-yous to the people involved in his arrest and detention during the past few months. This went on and on, as reporters turned to one another and compared it to a Hollywood speech on Oscar night, a fitting close to Rader's criminal career, which he'd always thought of as BTK Productions. He praised Lieutenant Landwehr, the Wichita and Sedgwick County police forces, his defense team, and the pod deputies at the detention facility.

"They finally opened up and became human," he said of the other inmates at the jail.

When he thanked the guard who'd picked out his clothes for court appearances, the district attorney rolled her eyes.

Rader's monologue had gone on for twenty minutes and had long since veered into absurdity, but he now brought it back to something real.

"Pastor Clark," he said, looking at the minister with an expression of genuine gratitude. "He's been my main man, came to see me . . . twice a week. If there was anybody I was dishonest to, it was that man right there . . . and for him to stay with me and be strong, well, he's a good man. . . . Early this week, we went through my confession. I sat down with him, went through each of the people I've killed, confessed on that, and I felt . . . some bonds there in that time with him."

The minister had bowed his head and Rader paused to gather himself.

"Family," he said, stumbling forward with dogged determination, "the last victims. I don't even want to start with them. . . . My wife's gone on, divorced. She's trying to stay out of harm's way . . . my kids . . . are basically supportive."

The judge made a sound from the bench and began fidgeting, his patience nearing its limit, but Rader was not deterred, reading a poem from a Christian book and then quoting John from the New Testament:

"He who follows me shall not walk in darkness but have light of life."

Clearing his throat one more time, Rader said, "Now that I let everybody know what's going on, I expect to be healed and have life, and hope that God will accept me. . . . We speak of a man as an evil man. A dark side is there, but now the light is beginning to shine."

Reluctantly, it seemed, Rader lowered himself into his chair and Judge Waller turned to the district attorney.

"Does the State," he said, "care to be heard?"

Foulston stood and in a withering tone slammed what Rader had just done, mocking his speech as the "Golden Globe Awards" for law enforcement. She was hardly finished, calling him a "wilted flower" and a "crashed meteor" and reemphasizing to the court that he should never be allowed to have drawing tools or pictures of men, women, children, or animals or other potentially erotic material in his cell.

When the DA had concluded with a flourish, the judge let the courtroom settle for a few moments. Then calmly and with no wasted effort whatsoever, he pronounced Rader's sentence: ten consecutive life terms, with the defendant receiving the "hard forty" for the Dolores Davis murder. He would not be eligible for parole for 175 years. Court was suddenly adjourned and the BTK saga was legally resolved, but now the TV commentators opened fire on America's airwaves.

Rader's behavior, both since 1974 and in the courtroom that afternoon, had been so unsettling that the national media interrupted their normal broadcasting to analyze his performance. CNN's Jeff Greenfield, a hard-core political pundit, weighed in with "This fellow is just pure evil," while former FBI profiler Clint Van Zandt declared that society could benefit by studying BTK in prison. Court TV reported that Pastor Clark was worried about Rader's safety, and Jeff Davis continued his diatribe by saying, "This guy's as lucky as he is stupid."

Outside the courthouse, journalists swamped the triumphant district attorney for any sound bite, and they were not disappointed. Foulston couldn't hide her glee over the sentence and the defendant's obvious misery in court.

"This is like a going-away party for Dennis Rader," she announced to the reporters and cameras. "We should pop some Coke cans."

When asked where she hoped Rader would eventually wind up in prison, she flashed a coy smile and did not say he should be placed in solitary so that his life wouldn't be in danger.

"I'd vote for general population," she replied.

Judge Waller's courtroom had emptied and most everyone involved in the hearing had either slipped away quietly or come out onto the cement plaza in front of the courthouse, where all the media tents and interview equipment were set up. TV personalities were straightening their clothes or patting down their hair, preparing to go on camera live. As the DA and her public defender counterparts, Steve Osburn and Sarah McKinnon, made the rounds with reporters, other people lingered outside in the feverish sunlight, not wanting to leave just yet, not quite ready for the event to be over. A small pack of journalists surrounded Wichita police chief Norman Williams, who was dressed in his official brown uniform and said, "It's a bittersweet day." That was close to the feeling in the air around the courthouse, because it was a day of victory for law enforcement, but a victory that had come so late, and now it was ending, and all the excitement and fear and prayers and hopes that had swirled around the WPD and City Hall for so many years were going to go away and fade into the past.

By dusk, the media tents were coming down in the plaza and reporters were scattering to other cities for new assignments. Main Street was nearly empty, the town was quiet, and the burning afternoon sun had become a perfectly huge orange circle in the milky sky over Wichita. You could look right into it without hurting your eyes.

EPILOGUE

Early the next morning, wearing a red jumpsuit and shackles on his wrists and ankles, Rader was transported to the El Dorado Correctional Facility, where he would begin his life sentences by spending twenty-three hours a day alone. Not even Pastor Clark would come to visit him in the near future as he underwent a series of medical and psychiatric tests. His cell was eighty square feet with a concrete slab for a bunk, and his companions now were a chair, a sink, a toilet, some metal shelving, and a plastic trash can. His wardrobe was a brown jumpsuit and blue slip-on shoes, and the five hours a week he was not in the cell would be spent in a caged outdoor pen, where he still wore restraints. Judge Waller had accepted the district attorney's recommendations, and if he had his way, Rader would never be allowed to draw in prison or read anything about himself. Representative Todd Tiahrt of Kansas, who'd played a significant role in getting more funding for the BTK investigation in mid-2004, was about to come forward and introduce a bill in Congress that would keep veterans serving life sentences, such as Dennis Rader, from being buried in military cemeteries. If Tiahrt had *his* way, America would isolate the murderer from other honorably discharged soldiers even in death.

On the ride to the maximum-security prison that Friday morning, the car radio was on and Rader felt more need to express himself, offering a steady flow of talk to the driver and the officers guarding him. He spoke about the weather and how healthy and green the Kansas countryside looked for the middle of August. Sometimes in late summer, droughts came and the entire landscape was parched a variety of beige colors, but not this year. When a news station started broadcasting clips of the victims' comments at the previous day's hearing, he stopped talking and listened intently to their words. Then he began crying once more, turning his face away from the other passengers. The men who were traveling with him glanced out the windows or down at the floor, and for a while everyone rode in silence, except for the sound of the radio.

When the report ended and Rader's voice had regained its strength, he said that he hoped going to prison for the rest of his life might prevent someone else from becoming a serial killer.

Church was letting out following the second service and worshippers were slowly making their way across the parking lot toward their cars, shaking hands and nodding with friendly gestures because everyone at Christ Lutheran knew everyone else. Tim Clark emerged from the front door in his wheelchair, next to his big black dog. Heat waves bounced off the asphalt in the spaces between the vehicles, and a soft breeze rattled the branches overhead, the tall pines rustling and restless, whispering their constant desire for change. The wind was always blowing out here north of Wichita, but the people had become so used to it that they rarely stopped to hear the subtlety of its rhythm or felt its gentle touch or imagined the secrets it was concealing. They sat on the tree limbs like a flock of small birds, always ready to be spooked by the breeze and to take flight for all to see.

The minister walked outside with a smile and some laughter for the congregation, two of the many gifts he'd given them over the past six months. After returning from his visit with the exorcist in Minnesota, he'd come to a conclusion about Dennis Rader, something he'd resisted doing since the arrest. He didn't speak easily or openly about his adventure north, but said enough to show that his long journey in his pickup truck had brought him some resolution. His voice was a little different now, as if he'd grown weary from everything he'd learned about Rader and seen in the courtroom. Only his faith remained undisturbed.

"In Minnesota," he said, "I learned more than I expected to. I

talked with a psychiatrist who's done a lot of work in demon afflic-
tion and with a Lutheran pastor who's done missionary work in the
third world. We spoke about demonic possession, and it's my opinion that it's safe to say that a demonic force controlled Dennis. I don't
know if an exorcism would help him or not because you cannot force
this on someone. It has to happen voluntarily."

In another part of Wichita on another day, Dr. Howard Brodsky
sat in his cluttered office and said, "What happened to Rader as a boy
is in some ways less important than his interpretation of it. His interpretation is 'Mom spanked me as a child and I got aroused so that
makes me strange. I saw pictures of women in bondage so I have to
tie up women. I have these sexual fantasies so I have to act them out
with real torture and real murder.' He made no attempt to change any
of this or to pray over it to help himself—not once do we hear about
that. Well, guess what? We all have fantasies. We all think weird
things. We all have antisocial impulses and demons, but it's what we
do with them that matters. Having demons doesn't make Rader
unique. It just makes him a human being."

In time everyone filtered out of the church and got into their cars
and drove away to their Sunday dinners or summer afternoons. The
parking lot was empty, except for stray pinecones, and the only things
left were the whispers in the trees and the songs of the birds and a
hot wind moving through the fields of rural Kansas, altering everything it reached. For a moment or two, the air turned quite still and
one could only wonder what other secrets were sitting on limbs everywhere, just waiting to be revealed.

ACKNOWLEDGMENTS

Nonfiction books are about the art of the possible, and many people and things had to come together to make this one happen as it did. The process began in the spring of 2005 with a quirky incident in my small Kansas hometown. Because my young son, Eric, wanted to go to the gym and play basketball, I ran into someone who knew someone on the BTK task force. Five minutes later, I was on the phone talking to this Wichita investigator, who encouraged me to write about the case, which came as a surprise. He wasn't looking for publicity, but felt that much about this story had not yet been told. Twenty-four hours after that, I'd done sit-down interviews with the investigator and Pastor Michael Clark. Both men laid the groundwork for my interest in pursuing this project and contributed generously to the book. In the next two days, my agent, Reid Boates, followed his instincts and contacted Lisa Drew at Scribner, who expressed interest in the subject. Once my son had insisted on showing off his jump shot to some local boys, all the pieces suddenly fell into place.

I owe a special thanks to Nick Dawson and his family for giving me the right tip at the right time. I'm deeply grateful to my parents, Mary and Bill Singular; my aunt, Ruth Singular; and my sister, Nancy Singular, for their endless hospitality and keeping the fires burning through some long and cold winter nights. Joycee Kennedy and Dr. Howard Brodsky were most incisive in interpreting the BTK saga through the lens of their professional expertise, and the reporting of the *Wichita Eagle* made up the first draft of anything that would later be written about this case. About halfway through the book, I spent two weeks at the UCross Foundation in northern Wyoming. Led by Sharon Dynak, the foundation's artists-in-residence program provided an excellent atmosphere for creative thinking and work.

Lisa Drew and her assistant Samantha Martin were terrifically helpful in every phase of this project. I've never seen more efficient or effective people anywhere, and their responsiveness in moving this manuscript forward was critically important. Lisa's confidence in the book has been a great gift. Georgia Cole, of the Sedgwick County district attorney's office, was instrumental in providing photos for the book.

The biggest thanks are reserved for my wife, Joyce, who encouraged me to jump into this river and then offered both hands as the water got faster and deeper. She was involved in virtually every aspect of putting the story together: research, editing, photo selection, inputting chunks of information, interviews, digging through documents for more facts, creative ideas and rewriting, title suggestion, and word improvement. For fifteen years, we've had a wonderful writing partnership, and doing this book together only made it better.

ABOUT THE AUTHOR

Stephen Singular has authored or coauthored seventeen books, including two *New York Times* bestsellers and a *Los Angeles Times* bestseller. Formerly a staff writer for *The Denver Post,* he has also written for major publications including *Rolling Stone, The New York Times Magazine, New York* magazine, and *Psychology Today.* He lives in Denver, Colorado.